Blessed Assurance

Blessed Assurance

Beliefs, Actions, and the Experience
of Salvation in a Carolina Baptist Church

M. Jean Heriot

The University of Tennessee Press / Knoxville

Library of Congress Cataloging in Publication Data

Heriot, M. Jean, 1954–
    Blessed assurance: beliefs, actions, and the experience of salvation in a
Carolina Baptist church / M. Jean Heriot. —1st ed.
            p.   cm.
    Includes bibliographical references and index.
    ISBN 0–87049–850–9 (cloth: alk. paper)
    1. Baptists—South Carolina—Membership. 2. Southern Baptist
Convention—Membership.   3. Salvation—Case studies.   4. Assurance
(Theology)—Case studies.   5. Conversion—Case studies.   I. Title.
BX6462.4.S6H47   1994
286'.1757—dc20   94-6089
                                                               CIP

Dedicated to the people
of Cypress Pond Baptist Church,
who made my life richer

Contents

Tables

Preface

This book is about the cultural theme of salvation, as expressed among the members of one Southern Baptist Convention church congregation in South Carolina, a congregation I call Cypress Pond. Members of this congregation knew from the moment I met them that I was a cultural anthropologist pursuing a doctorate at the University of California, Los Angeles. They also knew that I had promised to give their church, their county, and all church members pseudonyms. I have kept that promise in this work and have given my sources in the county pseudonyms as well.

Church members used to joke with me, asking if I was writing down this comment or that piece of gossip for my book. They may be surprised, not to know that I was recording their stories, but rather at the degree and kinds of analysis I have undertaken here. I wish to emphasize to those readers, and others, that this work is a deeply felt personal, as well as academic, attempt to understand how the cultural system of salvation works in this milieu. The paradoxes of belief I point out here are the same ones that churchgoers puzzle over in their own lives. Since I grew up in a similar religious context, I believe that my questions go straight to the heart of their beliefs about salvation. Though the answers I give here may not be the ones anticipated by members of the Cypress Pond congregation, I have found in researching and teaching the anthropology of religion that nothing excites the mind and the soul more than the sincere quest for an understanding of the divine.

Acknowledgments

To all those who participated in the creation of this work, I give whole-hearted thanks. The warm reception and cooperation given me by members of Cypress Pond made the months of research a true learning experience. Since I have given members pseudonyms, I cannot thank them here by name. Yet each person I came to know retains a special place in my thoughts.

Over the years many colleagues have provided guidance as I sought to understand the nature of culture, anthropology, language, and religion. I thank Brenda Farnell, Alejandro Frigerio, Lewis Langness, Paul Kroskrity, and Philip Newman for their continuing encouragement. I, of course, bear complete responsibility for the final version of this book.

In 1983, I was one of a small group of graduate students who formed what we termed a "study group." Over the years this group became a major source of personal and academic support for its members. For ten years now, we have read and criticized each other's works, and, despite geographical separation, we remain close. To the members of this group—Dana Baldwin, Betsy Hall, Kathy Hayes, Dixie King, and Kathy Mann—I express deep thanks for this ongoing exchange of thought and friendship. Of the many "Beethoven House" roommates I had in graduate school, I acknowledge especially the friendship of Lenore Cohen, Reinhard Honert, Lee Kane, Gwen Rosengren, and David Witherspoon.

As a gypsy scholar, I have moved to three states over the past four years. My latest stop has brought yet another personal transformation. Of those friends who make a difference in the very experience of life itself, I want to acknowledge Joan Kaspin. Finally, I would like to thank the members of my family for the drive and initiative they have given me. From them I gained the courage to complete this project.

Introduction:
Questioning Belief

But in the Bible only one definition is attempted of the word faith. And it is in our text today, Hebrews 11, verses one and two: "Now faith is the substance of things not seen. For by it the elders obtained a good report." The author defines faith as the very foundation and conviction for Christian living. The message for us today is that we must build upon faith. We must build our lives upon faith in the Lord Jesus Christ. . . . Faith is not only hope, but listen, it is the conviction of things not seen. He [the author of Hebrews] said that faith is the evidence of proof of an eventful order of spiritual reality. Proof of an eventful order of spiritual reality.

—Terrance Nichols, Morning Worship Service,
Cypress Pond Baptist Church, December 8, 1985

At a Women's Missionary Meeting at Cypress Pond Church, Shirley, in her seventies, told how she had prayed that her daughter, Belinda, would become a member of the church. Belinda had been attending revival worship service meetings with her family all week. She had kept asking her mother about how she could make a decision for Christ. Shirley talked with her as best she could but told Belinda that whatever decision she made, it would be her own. She told her daughter, "If I could push you into heaven, I would, but I can't."

On the last day of the revival, Shirley came home from Sunday morning services afraid that Belinda would not go forward to the altar that night to declare that she had been saved by Christ, or "born again." Shirley prayed on her knees in her bedroom, pouring her heart out to God. Then she went to sleep. She dreamed that a string of girls went to the altar, with Belinda the last in the line. She told no one of her dream.

That night, Belinda was the first to go forward, followed by a number of other girls. Shirley thanked the Lord that Belinda had made a decision for Christ, she had been saved.

Members of evangelical Christian churches hear sermons and accounts such as these from the moment they enter the church community, often as children brought to services by their parents.[1] They learn the importance of the dominant cultural theme of salvation, defined by believers as a personal encounter with Jesus Christ in which the individual acknowledges her or his personal sins and asks for forgiveness through the "saving grace of Christ." Having made the decision for Christ, individuals like Belinda receive assurances that, because they are saved, they will go to heaven and not hell upon death. They also learn means by which to assess who has been saved, who has faith, and who does not.

The evangelical perspective can be sketched in as few words as these. But giving meaning to these words can take a believer's whole lifetime and can constitute a researcher's agenda stretching to infinity. Furthermore, while the world view of the "saved, born again" Protestant permeates much of American society, the underlying logic of that world view, the cultural contexts in which it is found, and its influence on the lives of individuals all are too easily overdramatized or misunderstood. Take, for instance, fictional portraits of such charlatan ministers as Elmer Gantry. These show persons of no real faith deliberately misleading those to whom they preach. The much-publicized trial and conviction of Jim Bakker, who used church funds for personal gain, lends credence to the view that at least some evangelical ministers preach falsely (Harris 1991). As a news item, the subject of much ridicule, Oral Roberts's threat that supporters must contribute millions of dollars or God would call him home (that is, he would die) has few rivals (Black 1987:43). By implication, supporters may seem to be dupes, stupid and deluded by promises of blessings, health, wealth, and admittance to heaven after death. But such cases do not represent the majority of "born-again" Christians. Many of these—like members of the church that I, as a cultural anthropologist, studied for fourteen months—deplore the antics of such mass media preachers and instead live lives based on a centuries-old tradition of faith in salvation through Christ.

I record here the viewpoints of the members of this one church,

Cypress Pond Baptist Church, a Southern Baptist Convention (SBC) church in South Carolina. In contrast to sensationalistic media portraits, this account examines how a religious world view is established, maintained, lived, and changed among a relatively small group of people. While generalizations based on one case study must be carefully undertaken, this church is representative of one of the main strands of American Protestantism.[2] This book focuses on the cultural theme of salvation, framed by these Southern Baptists in terms of two crucial questions asked of every individual: "Are you saved?" and "How do you know if you are saved?" These questions are explored from several perspectives: that of the believer who already has found a personal answer, that of the "seeker" looking for answers, and that of a social science observer, myself.

Members of Cypress Pond Baptist Church provided the ethnographic material upon which this account rests. Despite some initial doubts about the study, most members were warm and welcoming from the beginning. At first they gave brief glimpses into their world of salvation; later, many told of their ongoing personal Christian triumphs and struggles. For many, acquiring and maintaining faith remained difficult. Like Belinda, they wanted to know how to be saved. Once saved, they wanted to exert a positive influence on the salvation of others, especially their own kin. Like Belinda's mother, Shirley, they tried to convey in words and deeds their saved status. Not only did they have to make a decision for salvation and live as saved, but, in addition, many somehow had to learn to live with doubt. Members knew that the experience of salvation rarely was like that of Paul on the road to Damascus—a blinding light and the voice of God communicating directly with the sinner.[3] How, then, could one be assured of salvation? There were many answers to this question, perhaps none of them truly satisfactory to those who struggled for an absolute, personal knowledge of the transcendent.

At Cypress Pond, few could escape deep-seated doubts, though equally few were willing to express them openly. Yet, one night Sim, a deacon in his sixties, had the courage to ask whether he was really saved. Sim had been a loyal churchgoer all his life; he had been baptized as saved in a creek near Cypress Pond when he was fourteen. In a small group meeting composed primarily of women and men in their fifties and sixties, he instigated a discussion.

Sim said that he thought he was a good Christian, that he was saved. But there were times when it occurred to him that he was doubtful about it, he was not sure. He felt there ought to be a place other than heaven or hell for those who were more middle-of-the-road. "It just doesn't seem right," he said, "for all those to be burning [going to hell], especially since the Bible says that few are chosen."

Taking up this theme, several others in the group expressed the opinion that it was possible to be mistaken about one's status as saved. They noted that many, especially those who showed up once a quarter to attend church, were only deluding themselves, thinking they were saved.

Sim mentioned that some pastors would get a person to "go up" (that is, answer an "invitational call," declaring publicly that he or she was saved) by scaring them about hell. He recalled a former pastor who apparently had been mistaken about his own salvation. That pastor answered the invitation to declare salvation at another church's revival meeting during the time that he was preaching at Cypress Pond. This, Sim stated, showed how hard it was to tell who was saved.

John, another deacon, agreed with Sim that "few are chosen."

Eunice took up the idea that some respond out of fear. Her idea of hell was not burning eternally, but rather separation from God. She felt that those who went up because they were afraid of hell were not really saved. They had just made a "public declaration."

Victoria noted that these were good questions but argued that one should not dwell on them: "You have to take a lot on faith. There's no way that man can know everything. If you have these questions, then you should pray about them."

John, the Training Union leader, closed the discussion, asking Sim to lead the group in prayer. Afterwards, on the way to the sanctuary, Michelle commented to me that the questions Sim had raised were good ones, ones that she had thought about. Sim, she said, was "a good man."

The doubts acknowledged in this discussion, its focus on how to know who is saved, its stress on prayer, and Michelle's evaluation that Sim was "a good man"—all these provide glimpses into the underlying logic of this belief system. Subsequent chapters explore these dimensions of salvation, as expressed among the pastors and members of Cypress Pond. As we look at the various methods members used to assess salvation, we shall see that their assessments were not absolute, but fluid, changing as their lives change. The contexts in which these assessments emerged varied as well, contributing to an overall world view in which salvation dominated. From these discussions, we shall see how these committed Southern Baptists created and maintained an orientation toward living which made their identities as "saved" paramount in their lives.[4]

The Cultural Setting of
Cypress Pond Baptist Church

As background to understanding the problem of salvation in this cultural context, visualize Cypress Pond in your mind's eye. The church buildings stand in pastoral splendor on the coastal plain of South Carolina. The surrounding countryside shimmers with that deep forest green of pine and hardwood trees, interspersed with rolling grassland or crops. This agrarian scene is a product of adequate rainfall, a temperate climate, and the labor of generations of farmers. Walking around the church building, one takes in a panoramic view that includes sloping pastures directly in front, a thinly forested region behind, a cemetery to the right, and a sawmill to the left.

Looking at this scene, one newly arrived pastor asked, "But where are the people?" Members directed his gaze to the few homes observable from the church itself; they were distant and difficult to spot behind the trees. No stores were visible, and only one paved road fronted the church. All other roads in direct proximity to the church were dirt and disappeared into the surrounding forest.

In such a setting, the church grounds and buildings might have seemed incongruous, especially to a visitor from outside the South. The two church buildings were large and impressive, with brick veneers. Above one rose a steeple topped by a small cross symbolically marking that building as the sanctuary. Next to the sanctuary was the "educational building," housing classrooms, a meeting room, and a kitchen. Amid the pastures facing the church nestled a softball field, complete with lights for night games, spectator stands, and a concession building. Members of Cypress Pond took pride in such material evidence of their success.

Yet these modern facilities did not stand on a main road. Their rural location lay six miles from Southville, the nearest town of five thousand, and forty-five miles from the nearest movie theater. Most of the members lived within a four-mile radius of the church. Average attendance at Sunday worship services was 125, and almost all of the four hundred resident members were kin to others in the church. Those who attended Cypress Pond did so, they said, in part because their families had belonged here for generations. Local kinship networks remained complex and intertwined.

On Sunday mornings, a few churchgoers started arriving as early as 9:30, as deacons and the pastor assembled for a prayer service before Sunday school began. The parking lot began to fill, as members gathered for the ten o'clock Sunday school services. Still more people arrived shortly before eleven, for the main worship service. As members assembled, many talked with each other outside on the grounds or quietly inside the sanctuary. Families usually sat together in extended family groupings on pews informally designated as theirs through the force of tradition. Four generations of related churchgoers might spill into a second pew, with mothers holding babies and grandparents watching older children. When the service began, the chatting died down as prayers were given, hymns were sung, and a sermon was preached by the pastor.

Afterwards, members filed outside the church, greeting and visiting with each other and catching up on local news. They shook hands with the pastor at the door; he knew each person by name and greeted everyone with comments reflecting his personal knowledge of that individual's family. Depending on their afternoon agenda, some families left the grounds immediately, while others stayed to talk. The children formed play groups and ran across the churchyard as their parents chatted. By 12:30, approximately one-half hour after the service ended, the churchyard was deserted once more.

Much of the social and family life of this community centered around the church; many activities were organized, and arrangements were made both formally and informally, before, during, or after regularly scheduled church services. For example, after a Sunday morning service in July, three first cousins and the wife of the pastor, all mothers of children under twelve, called me to join them. While watching a softball game that week, they had decided to organize a trip to a nearby lake for the following Saturday. Arrangements were being made after church to include others. Parents and children not present that Sunday would have to be notified, and different members volunteered to call.

Or take for example a Sunday morning discussion the following spring. After a service, members of the Nichols family made final arrangements for the picnic they had scheduled in honor of Marie Nichols's eightieth birthday. Family members had to decide who would ride with whom and who would pick up food from their respective homes. Some out-of-town relatives had driven to Southville that morning in order to attend services at Cypress Pond, their former church, before going to the picnic. These visitors were greeted warmly by members. Family news was exchanged. Scenes such as this one occurred throughout the year, as members arranged projects, small family gatherings, or large family reunions.

This vignette introduces a relatively small, tightly knit, kin-bound, rural Baptist congregation. Demographic and kinship factors significantly influenced the boundaries within which the cultural system of these churchgoers operated. Chapters 3 and 4 situate Cypress Pond more fully in its historical and demographic contexts, showing how family settlement patterns, larger economic trends, and the early establishment of Baptist churches in the county contributed to the religious and kinship patterns present at the time of the study.

The Anthropologist at Work

Whenever I talk about my research, someone invariably asks, "How were you accepted during your fieldwork?" This question pertains both to the methodology of ethnographic research and, more subtly, to my own religious background and beliefs. Many social scientists readily address the first question and avoid the second, saying that the social scientist can or should remain detached in the research that he or she undertakes. I shall answer both questions, however, starting with my own beliefs (or, rather, my doubts), since they constituted the driving force behind my research.

Growing up on a farm in South Carolina, I went with my parents each Sunday to a nearby small town to attend services at the United Methodist Church. From an early age, conforming outwardly and rebelling inwardly, I asked questions which occasionally brought my teachers consternation. Some of these question were epistemological in nature. Where did the devil come from? How could Jesus live a good life without sinning? What does salvation mean? How can one receive assurance that one is saved? Other questions I asked, about the problem of evil and the nature of suffering, every religious tradition must attempt to answer (Geertz 1973:100). Why do bad things happen to people? How can a good, omnipotent God allow persons to suffer and die? Continuing to question, I nevertheless formally joined the church at age eleven. At the time, I knew emphatically that I had not had an experience of religious revelation and, furthermore, given my observations of behavior, I was certain that I was not the only one to profess and live "as if."

Of all the routes towards understanding, I chose an intellectual one, undertaking years of graduate study in anthropology at the University of California, Los Angeles; doing this ethnographic fieldwork with Southern Baptists; and writing about the experience in my dissertation and in this book. In retrospect, however, I feel that I have come full circle— to my own form of religious meaning, a mystical one having little to do with "born-again" Christianity as it is commonly practiced. Mysticism, however, is religious in nature and provides a viewpoint much more sympathetic to religious beliefs than a purely intellectual attempt to "understand." So it happens that I now concur with the implied criticism of the Reverend John Manning, pastor at Cypress Pond during the last eight months of my fieldwork, who sought to turn the congregation against my research with the following joke, spoken from the pulpit one Sunday morning.

He told of a researcher who took a flea off a dog, pulled out a notebook, and set up an experiment. The researcher removed the flea from a box and asked it to jump. It did. He wrote in his book that the flea jumped when he heard the command to jump. He removed one set of legs, told the flea to jump, and it did. A second set of legs was removed; the flea still jumped. Once the third and last set of legs was removed, the flea no longer jumped as commanded. The researcher concluded that the flea did not hear the command to jump. This "experiment," Manning asserted, showed the futility of all attempts to study religion scientifically. He stated further that he did not know what anyone could gain from such study.

That problem continues to haunt all social scientists who have chosen to study religion. While I now believe that Manning was right, that intellectual, "scientific" answers are only partial ones, this book takes a perspective that is largely intellectual. I strive to understand how people translate beliefs about the transcendent into "something" that, however imperfect, can be measured concretely. In this sense, all attempts at understanding the transcendent must go beyond the profession of inner belief to the social world in which such beliefs are communicated. That is, the sublime somehow must become accessible through the mundane practices of daily living, and it is this process which can be documented by the observer, by the anthropologist at work. For Southern Baptists, a person's status as a saved believer often hinges on outwardly measurable behaviors, such as whether an individual does or does not curse, commit adultery, drink alcohol, or watch R-rated movies. I have taken these members' own approaches to belief and used them to formulate a theoretical approach to the study of religious belief which uses observable action(s), including verbal attestations of faith, as criteria of beliefs. My focus throughout the book is on this process—how Southern Baptists monitor and evaluate beliefs in actual social contexts—rather than on the nebulous and essentially unmeasurable quality of religious experience itself.[5]

Since I wanted to document people's religious beliefs about salvation as they were expressed in actual social contexts, I limited the scope of the research project to one church congregation. As a methodological strategy frequently employed in anthropology (Pelto and Pelto 1978:129), situating the research within a small community circumvented many problems involved in defining group boundaries. Thus, the homogeneity of the Southville community surrounding the church congregation made assessing who identified with Cypress Pond a matter of historical tradition and local adherence.

Having selected the Cypress Pond congregation from initial interviews with pastors and site visits to rural SBC churches made in April 1985, I moved to the community of Southville in Salkehatchie County in early May 1985.[6] From that moment on, I plunged into church life with a zeal that soon identified me with the "faithful." Because I went to church "every time the church doors opened," I was viewed as "committed." From my previous experiences in rural Protestant communities, I knew that this label would be applied and that constant role management would be required if I were not to be drawn completely into the life of the congregation. For example, while I was willing to work in the church occasionally (such as teach a class when a teacher was ill), I would not take any specific job (such as agreeing to teach a class every Sunday). Walking this thin line between participant and observer, I constantly evaluated my own performance, trying to determine where it was appropriate to be a full participant and where to be the observer.

One of the problems I had in role management concerned answering the evangelical question of whether I myself was saved. One culturally acceptable strategy I utilized was to point to my own religious affiliation with the United Methodist Church—a "suitable" religious background to members of Cypress Pond. Because the Methodist Church requires its members to be baptized and to be saved, that affiliation apparently satisfied Baptist requirements.[7] It also helped that I had close relatives in a community about a hundred miles from Salkehatchie County. That was distant enough not to affect the research, yet it established the essential fact that I was a native "southerner." Having told church members of my background and having explained the nature of the research project, I made a relatively smooth entry into the community.

Even though my cultural background helped me gain acceptance, my training and my questions about evangelical Christianity made the fieldwork difficult. I knew what roles were expected of me and how to seem to be part of the community, even when my underlying feelings sometimes remained rebellious. As a single woman, I baked lemon pies, kept my mouth shut at business meetings (women in this church were unsure of their right to speak and to vote in such meetings), and helped in traditional female roles. I think that often I was seen as both faithful (because I came to church so much) and anomalous (in that I was unmarried and a scholar).

In addition to attending all regularly scheduled church meetings, I attended church basketball games, went on church trips and picnics, attended church parties, and played church softball—until I failed to catch the ball that broke my nose. In short, I became involved in all the church's religious and social functions. Shortly after each event, I wrote fieldnotes describing those events. Occasionally I took notes on site, but that practice was intrusive and always drew attention to my observer role. I found that collecting naturalistic data in my own culture required that I truly be seen as a participant.

After being in the community for about eight months, a change occurred in the level of my acceptance within the community. Finally I became privy to more of the insider "gossip." This gossip network revealed a new layer of information about how people in this small community evaluated each other's beliefs. The night I found myself eating delicious homemade cake, drinking coffee, and listening to members demolish the reputations of pastors who had served during the last thirty years marked a turning point in the research.

During the last four months of fieldwork, I visited members at home and collected genealogical and religious information through semistructured interviews. To gain knowledge of the larger religious community, I attended ecumenical functions held during the fieldwork period, visited in other churches in the Salkehatchie area, and interviewed pastors of all the major Protestant religious groups found in the community.

Because I was interested in how religious knowledge was communicated, I asked the pastor to tape the worship services for me. Although, for various reasons, not every service was taped, fifty-three worship services were taped on audiocassettes. While Cypress Pond had only one full-time pastor at any given time, different pastors often spoke on special occasions or filled in when a pastor was away. A total of eleven speakers gave the main message during worship services in the fourteen months of research. Of these, nine speakers were recorded on tape.

Specifics concerning data analysis are presented in later chapters. Like many others who have used qualitative methods over an extended period, I collected more data than it was possible to analyze in the course of preparing this book. I always approached the task of interpretation with rigorous attention to what actually had been said and done in social contexts, insofar as I was able to reconstruct events. For this reason, I have focused heavily on the sermon data, since much of it was recorded on audiocassettes.

Throughout the work, the direction of analysis was guided by my interest in the central cultural theme of southern Protestantism: salvation. My intention was, and is, to portray the means by which the members of Cypress Pond both made sense of, and lived lives influenced by, this cultural tradition, irrespective of whether or not they actually "believed." To understand how the system worked, the reader must experience, through my account if not directly, what it means to live in a small, bounded community. Such communities are places where almost every individual action can be surveyed by others and evaluated as morally good or bad. It is in this social context that much of the Southern Baptist stress on being "born again," and the apprehensions and uncertainties about one's status as saved, take on significance. Here I am not speaking solely in cognitive terms, for the belief system is powerful in the sense that Geertz conveys when he says that religious beliefs, as *symbols*, "establish powerful and long-lasting moods and motivations in men [humans] by formulating conceptions of a general order of existence and clothing these conceptions with such an aura of factuality that the moods and motivations seem uniquely realistic" (1973:90).

Salvation is so powerful a religious belief system that, in Susan Harding's terms, once one encounters a strong spokesperson for the belief system and begins to listen, then the membrane between belief and disbelief becomes permeable (1987). The Cypress Pond congregation had experienced many such encounters through the years. Whatever their personal opinions, members could not easily escape the influence of the commanding and compelling vision of salvation.

Chapter 1 introduces the cultural theme of salvation as an evangelical belief system and, using perspectives from the sociology of knowledge and culture theory, considers how one can "know" about salvation. Grasping the theoretical import of chapter 1 is essential for understanding both the strengths and the limitations of this work, but it is not essential for understanding the book's ethnographic content. Though it is customary to delineate the content of each chapter at the close of the introduction, for theoretical reasons I have chosen to delay this discussion until the end of chapter 1.

1

The Cultural Theme of Salvation

It is a hot night in July; the air-conditioning in the church emits waves of chilling air. The Reverend Ted Squires preaches an "old-fashioned, hell-fire-and-damnation" sermon entitled "What Is Sin?" At the close of his sermon, he issues an "invitation" asking listeners to respond to the need for personal salvation:

> The question tonight, have you realized the awfulness of sin in your life? Have you realized what it is? And what it has done to you? Have you realized it to the point that the Holy Spirit has convicted you of sin in your life? And you've confessed it? And you know Christ is your lord and savior? If not, tonight during this service, we encourage you to accept Christ, to confess your sins, and to have them covered in the blood of the lamb. (Evening Worship Service, July 14, 1985)

Beth Nichols, twenty years of age, and Rachel Donnon, a teenager, rise from their seats on the very last pew in the church. Both walk forward toward the front of the church, as the young child who has been sitting with them, stands, too, swinging back and forth at the end of the pew, watching intently. Tears stream down Rachel's face as she stands in the aisle, waiting while her friend Beth talks quietly with the pastor, her arm over his shoulder. During the time it takes for each young woman to speak with the pastor, the entire congregation and choir is also standing, singing four verses of this church's most popular "hymn of invitation," "Just As I Am":

Just as I am, with-out one plea, But that Thy blood was shed for me,
And that Thou bidd'st me come to Thee, O Lamb of God, I come! I come!
. . .
Just as I am, poor, wretched, blind; Sight, riches, healing of the mind,
Yea, all I need in Thee to find, O Lamb of God, I come! I come.
(Elliott and Bradbury, in Sims 1956)

The two return to their pew, and the pastor asks John Thames, a deacon, to give the benediction. The organ postlude is played as the congregation turns to leave the seats.

For me this was an unusual night. In two and a half months of fieldwork, it was the first time that I had seen someone respond to one of the "invitational calls" for salvation. Yet I gathered from the pastor's silence about the two respondents and from the congregation's cheerful demeanor that nothing really untoward had happened. Both young women, I knew, already had been baptized as saved. Why, then, did they walk down the aisles? Why the tears? Why had the pastor constantly preached about salvation during the previous months, closing each sermon with an invitation that "someone" be moved, that "someone" come forward? And why did the two young women respond to this particular sermon, on this particular night?

As we shall see in subsequent chapters, the worship service itself is, to use Geertz's (1973) terms, a model of and for life outside the church. By "models of and for," he means that cultural patterns "give meaning, i.e., objective conceptual form, to social and psychological reality both by shaping themselves to it [model of] and by shaping it to themselves [model for]" (1973:93). Thus the worship service, as a ritual, both encapsulates church members' world views and provides them with a blueprint for living outside the church doors.

The essentials of this world view and the guidelines it gives for living are discussed in this chapter. The key to understanding both the salvation rituals themselves and their models for living is contained in the following view of the relationship between language, belief, and action. For Southern Baptists, as for many evangelicals, to hear the "word of God" means that the listener encounters a spokesperson for the message of salvation (Harding 1987; Borker 1974). Once the message is heard, they believe, the message is automatically internalized. Once it is internalized, the hearer must act. He or she must make a decision for or against the truth of the message. According to this belief system, a person cannot hear the words of salvation and be indifferent. Belief, then, entails action: to believe means to act. To reject the message is to deny its truth and to continue to live in sin, a path that ultimately will lead to eternal damnation in hell. To accept the message is to recognize its truth and to commit oneself to that truth, a decision that ultimately will lead to eternal life in heaven. Once an individual is committed, other features of the belief system allow members to measure the strength of that person's commitment to action. Of course the system is more complex and, in practice, extremely problematic, but on the surface its message is clear: to hear the word requires action. Beth and Rachel heard the "word" as preached by their pastor, and as they walked the aisles in response, their actions could be observed by those present.

Why is it so crucial that one be able to visualize, to "see," the responses? The logic of this belief system, like that of all belief systems, both establishes the system and makes it difficult to question its central beliefs.[1] While salvation is of *utmost concern* in this particular belief system, the attainment of salvation is *never certain*. This paradox of Protestant belief Weber (1958) made the cornerstone of his analysis of the Protestant ethic. According to Weber, since Calvinism established a framework in which, from the beginning of all time, some souls were preordained for salvation and some for damnation, individuals on this earth never could know directly whether they were among the elect, predestined for heaven. To allay their fears, though not to obtain a certain knowledge, believers attempted to live morally upright, ascetic lives on earth, to show their probable status among the elect. Weber termed this path to salvation as "inner-worldly asceticism" (1958; elaborated in Weber 1963). While some other Baptist denominations still believe in Calvin's doctrine of predestination (Peacock and Tyson 1989), the SBC position is usually considered to be that of modified Calvinism, "with an emphasis on conversion, by faith" (Yance 1978:16). Through an emotional, concrete experience of salvation obtained at the crisis point when the individual accepts Christ, assurance of salvation is gained.[2] In practice, however, the words and ritual reenactments of the SBC churches seem to convey the opposite message: the assurance of salvation is tenuous indeed, requiring constant validation through actions, lest the initial experience itself be proved spurious. Thus, the emphasis on overt markers of salvation, required to "prove" their internal believing state, continues to echo Calvinistic beliefs.

This chapter situates Cypress Pond Baptist Church in the larger context of evangelical religion, portrays both the Cypress Pond consensus concerning beliefs about salvation and the church members' emphasis on actions which manifest salvation, and links this view of language, belief, and action with larger theoretical concerns in anthropology. Even though members of Cypress Pond did not always agree on the exact means by which salvation could be attained or measured, they did agree on the major parameters within which this belief system ideally should function. Variation, an integral part of any belief system, cannot be assessed without first delineating the larger framework: that is the task at hand here.

Conservatives, Fundamentalists, and Evangelicals

Within the religious and cultural setting of the United States, Cypress Pond can be viewed as an evangelical religious denomination. Even though SBC church members seldom use the term "evangelical" to describe their denomination (Garrett 1983), most social scientists do not hesitate to categorize the SBC under this rubric (Hill 1981:101; Hunter 1982:370). Given its size (approximately fifteen million members, according to the *Yearbook of American and Canadian Churches 1990*), the SBC cannot be dismissed as "unimportant," although frequently, and mistakenly, its membership is identified with the South alone or solely with conservative or even fundamentalist beliefs. The identification with white southerners means that, as a group, SBC members often are viewed as racist, classist, sexist, and fundamentally at odds with mainstream American culture (Rosenberg 1989). The association with fundamentalism often casts the SBC as a foe of modernity, battling against the Enlightenment ideals of secular humanism (Harding 1993). Like most stereotypes, these contain kernels of truth, but in fact the picture is much more complex.[3]

Clarifying the nature of such stereotypes is beyond the scope of this particular inquiry, though it is important to note that they exist. Rather, the focus of this investigation is the nature of the SBC's evangelical beliefs. Following Roof and McKinney (1987), I use the descriptive term "Conservative Protestants" to situate the SBC within the wider context of American religion. Conservative Protestants share "a traditional religious and cultural outlook" which consists of evangelical beliefs in

> the necessity of a conversion experience, the authority of the Bible, and the importance of a moral life freed especially from such barroom vices as drinking, dancing, and card playing. These latter have receded in emphasis, but religious conservatives continue to stress the importance of a strong personal and moral life. (Roof and McKinney 1987:91)

Roof and McKinney find that Conservative Protestants, because of their commitment to this belief system, are the religious group most resistant to modern American trends toward greater individualism. These evangelicals have elicited and maintained a high degree of institutional loyalty among their followers (Roof and McKinney 1987:100). This loyalty apparently was one factor which enabled the SBC to weather tremendous internal disputes within the past decade.

Roof and McKinney claim that Conservative Protestants were able to maintain this high degree of internal cohesion in part because they withdrew from public interest and public politics after the Scopes trial of the 1920s (1987:79–80). Since the 1960s, moderate and liberal Protestant churches have faced a widespread loss of membership while, at the same time, evangelical churches maintained and even increased their memberships. Today evangelicals, while remaining opposed to the "vices" of modernity, increasingly are entering the public arena and seeking to redefine American values and religious beliefs.

In their struggle to have a larger voice in American society, SBC evangelicals frequently have been labeled fundamentalists by outsiders. However, from a social science perspective, this designation is problematic for several reasons. According to Ammerman, both fundamentalists and evangelicals share "a conservative theology that affirms the divinity of Jesus, the reality of his resurrection and miracles, and the sure destiny of human beings in either heaven or hell. They believe that salvation is the result of a personal faith in Jesus that starts with the experience of being born again" (1987:4). The two groups differ, however, in how they identify themselves and in how they cope with the demands of the larger world. Although both respond to the pressures of modernity, they do so in different ways. Fundamentalists generally are found, Ammerman argues, in the city and suburb, where they have daily contact with groups representing alternative world views. To preserve their world view, they establish rigid boundaries between themselves and the diversity they encounter. In contrast, evangelicals are more accommodating to the modern world and enforce fewer and less rigid boundaries between themselves and others. Finally, Ammerman notes that there are a number of localized, traditional communities (many of them in the rural South and many members of the SBC) whose members, in their everyday lives, remain isolated from religious diversity. Consequently, they preserve their Protestant evangelical beliefs without having to defend them daily. By these criteria, the latter group score high on evangelical scales though they are not yet fundamentalist (Ammerman 1987:8).

Beginning in 1979 and throughout the 1980s, the SBC was embroiled in internal disputes which pitted a conservative Fundamentalist faction against a more progressive Moderate faction (Ammerman 1990 and 1993). A large portion of the SBC membership did not really understand the conflict because they were "traditionalists." Not yet Fundamentalists, these evangelicals, with dumbfounded consternation, watched their leaders fight for power. The Fundamentalist faction won control of the SBC, some Moderates stayed within the convention, and others left to form a separate Southern Baptist Alliance (Ammerman 1990:271). As a result, some members of the SBC can be considered fundamentalists, others are evangelicals, and still others represent a traditionalist world view that shares evangelical beliefs without yet having to live their beliefs in a pluralistic world (see also Heriot 1993).

Members of Cypress Pond were representative of this latter traditionalist group. Chapter 2 delineates their community life, showing how these southerners had managed to maintain their belief system with few outside challenges. As traditionalists, their evangelical religious ideology was framed within the overarching theme of salvation.

The SBC and Southern Protestantism

As a historian of religion, Hill (1966) convincingly argues that Baptist and Methodist beliefs about personal salvation came to dominate southern Protestantism in general and that the Southern Baptists, in particular, focus on this theme more than any other group. According to Hill, the central characteristics of southern religion stem from revivalism and fundamentalism. They are revivalistic because they stress the "memorable, usually emotional, moment of entrance into the Christian life." He goes on to note that "[t]he remainder of one's life" is often seen as "an appendix to the fact of entrance—or at least so much is made of the initial experience that hearers are likely to conclude that this is so" (Hill 1966:25). They are fundamentalist in the sense that they believe that the Bible is the only source of authority for humankind's salvation. They have made the biblical injunction to save souls the cornerstone of their belief system. Hill notes that their emphasis on revivalism is also a type of fundamentalism though not "classical fundamentalism," because its stress on the "Great Commission" to save souls (see Matthew 28: 18–20) outweighs all other considerations (1966:26; see also Yance 1978).[4]

For southern Protestants, the central goal of life is not establishing a community of believers here on earth or living life to show one's status among the elect. Rather, the emphasis has shifted dramatically, to an individualistic concern: personal salvation (Hill 1966:58–59). Mathews characterizes the emotional dimension of this experience as follows:

> The Christian life is essentially a personal relationship with God in Christ, established through the direct action of the Holy Spirit, an action which elicits in the believer a profoundly emotional conversion experience. This existential crisis, the New Birth as Evangelicals called it, ushers the convert into a life of holiness characterized by religious devotion, moral discipline, and missionary zeal. (Mathews 1977:xvi)

Southern Baptists, the denomination which stresses this form of salvation more than any other group, fuse personal and historical time dimensions by emphasizing the moment of salvation for each and every individual as the most important decider of one's fate for all eternity (see also Borker 1974). The message itself is linked in an intimate way to words and to the actions of one aspect of the Trinity, the Holy Spirit; therefore, the actual speaking and hearing of the biblical message of salvation changes the world.

The Holy Spirit facilitates "decisions for Christ" by preparing the "hearts and minds" of individuals. As a consubstantial manifestation of God, the Holy Spirit is invoked both to prepare individuals to hear God's message of salvation and to move them to action with respect to accepting the personal truth of this message. An intellectual knowledge of the truth of the gospel is not enough; one also must accept the message as somehow encompassing the entire "soul" of the individual. Accepting salvation entails receiving the gift of the Holy Spirit. That is, the Holy Spirit now dwells within the individual, and, to the extent that one listens to its guidance, it can direct the individual to live in harmony with God. Rejecting the Holy Spirit's work eventually can make individuals so "hardened" that they never repent of their sins. In every "decision for Christ," the process operates on two levels: the action of God through the Holy Spirit, who spiritually prepares the individual; and the individual's wholehearted act of will in an acceptance encompassing intellect, emotion, and personality.

Borker's (1974) summary of the core messages she found within three evangelical denominations in Scotland (one of them Baptist) is similar to the core messages about salvation expressed at Cypress Pond. The Scottish core messages she describes are based on three central themes about the relationship of God and humans: "sin which necessitates the gospel, the cross which provides the solution to that need, and grace or love which is the agent or motive behind it [salvation]" (1974:27). The function of worship services is to provide an opportunity for the "word of God" to be spoken aloud, to be heard, and thus to allow the Holy Spirit to influence individual decisions for salvation. Borker (1974), Harding (1987), and Hill (1966), when writing about the evangelical belief system, note that speaking and hearing are thought to be the primary means of communicating about belief. When examined from the point of view of religious behavior, southern Protestant worship services are designed to have people "decide and act" about salvation— that is, to achieve this emotional turning point, to be converted (Hill 1966:96).

This explicit plea to be "born again" both presupposes and demands a response. As Hill notes, "Assurance of salvation was the pivotal issue in religion. If one did not know he had got religion in terms of an epistemology based on an emotional awareness—he did not possess it" (1966:86). Since that personal emotional knowing is fraught with uncertainty, not least because of the impossibility of sustaining a heightened emotional awareness through time, pastors and members alike address the uncertainty by offering sets of criteria whereby the individual can judge her or his salvation. Members are asked to "measure" themselves against an institutional catalog of right actions—actions that lead to the status of committed Christian—and wrong actions, or "sins," that can indicate that an individual's status as saved is questionable.

Theoretical Implications of This World View

Throughout my fieldwork, my goal was to delineate the folk epistemology underlying these SBC beliefs about the necessity for salvation. The preceding sections have sketched the framework within which Southern Baptists establish the parameters of an emotional epistemology which equates hearing the word of God with the necessity for action. In effect, their epistemology posits the following relationship between belief and reality. Language is used to convey the true message of God, or the Southern Baptist version of "ultimate reality." Ultimate reality in this life is manifested by the individual in a dispositional state which shows, by overt verbal and behavioral actions, two things: first, that one has access to the Holy Spirit's guidance and so is living in accord with the biblically-based directives of God the Father and Jesus the Savior; and, second, that ultimate reality is not merely "believed," it is "known through personal experience." "Faith" is the mechanism by which one lives as if that spiritual reality or knowledge was present in daily life. Thus, in the sermon excerpt cited on the first page of the introduction to this book, Nichols claims that "faith is the evidence of proof of an eventful order of spiritual reality."

To delineate how the Southern Baptists distinguish between true knowledge and false knowledge in this epistemological system is extremely difficult for a number of reasons having to do with the stress these Baptists place on an inner emotional epistemology and on overt morality. In the larger theoretical context, this epistemological system is difficult to portray because each postulate within the religious system has its counterpart in the vast literature in Western philosophy concerning the distinctions between belief and knowledge, and much of this literature is at odds with the folk system.

How can one distinguish between belief and knowledge? Western philosophy has been preoccupied with answering this question for generations, and little philosophical agreement exists (Hallen and Sodipo 1986). At the same time, an ordinary person using the English language, in which much is made of the distinction between belief and knowledge, employs the two terms as if there were relatively little doubt about their meanings. In fact, the distinction between the two terms is so taken for granted that they are presumed to be translatable into any language, and anthropologists typically apply them uncritically in portraying other cultural systems. As a result, anthropologists seem to assume that *knowledge* systems have to do with truth and empirical evidence and constitute a sort of rough-and-ready "science." Thus "traditional" or "primitive" members of a culture at times may reason based on fallacious assumptions, but they nevertheless use logical, analytical principles thought to be identical with, or at least similar to, those employed in the West (Hollis and Lukes 1982). *Belief* systems, on the other hand, are thought to be secondary, inferior ways of knowing about the world; here the "irrational" and the "nonempirical" are consigned into such categories as religion, magic, superstition, and even common sense (Geertz 1973 and 1983; Skorupski 1976).

Among those anthropologists who question these distinctions between belief and knowledge are Mary Black (1974) and Needham (1972). Black argues that anthropologists tend to use collective belief and collective knowledge as interchangeable terms. This usage is problematic because no sufficient comparative basis for a distinction between the two exists in anthropological accounts. Needham (1972) asks how it is that anthropologists have come to distinguish cross-culturally something that they label "belief" and to which they consign religious activities and symbols. As philosophers Hallen and Sodipo (1986) note, Needham addresses this question by collapsing the ordinary usage of the term *belief* with philosophical usage and proceeds to examine belief as a concept indicating either a psychological state of mind (a distinctive type of mental "act that can be introspected by the person who experiences it" [Hallen and Sodipo 1986:51]) or a dispositional state (in the sense of a latent tendency which is manifested in behavior and is not a distinctive state of mind [Hallen and Sodipo 1986:51]). Looking for an empirical basis on which to pin the concept *belief*, Needham argues that there is *no* empirical basis for the term *belief* except that people make statements about their beliefs (1972:6). He claims that, even in the English language, anthropologists and philosophers do not know how "to determine exactly what exactly are the grounds for our own concept of belief," making it impossible to find a correspondence with terms in other languages. Needham concludes that it would be best not to use the term at all when talking about other cultural systems and languages (1972:185).

Such a radical position leaves the anthropologist with no place to stand in trying to describe the difference between belief and knowledge. If the anthropologist must have an empirical basis for assuming a dispositional or psychological state, and if, as Needham argues, there are no natural signals (such as a facial expression) denoting a universal human emotional experience of belief (as there are natural signals, he asserts, for such emotional experiences as pain), then we cannot examine belief (1972:100–101). Nor, of course, could we examine many other aspects of culture which anthropologists routinely claim to have examined: for example, meaning systems of most types not directly tied to empirical measurement. Needham does note that anthropologists gain access to people's "interior states" through verbal statements (1972:15) and that they can report on "the received ideas to which people subscribe" (1972:2). He, however, finds this insufficient for establishing empirical criteria for belief even among English-speaking people.

Hallen and Sodipo (1986) have challenged Needham's conclusion with cross-cultural research done among the Yoruba in Africa, and I too find this position challenged by the folk epistemology of Southern Baptists. Needham is quite correct, however, in saying that we do not have the basis for a cross-cultural comparison of beliefs. The search for ways to "know" about our own cultural basis of knowledge/belief, and about alternative knowledge/belief systems, has led anthropologists and philosophers into "tangled webs" dense indeed, as they have tried to pinpoint a basis upon which people can be said to believe or to know anything.

When Sim asks how can he have assurance of salvation, how can he know if he will go to heaven when he dies, the answers he is given by his fellow churchgoers are drawn from a repertoire based on their particular cultural tradition. Similarly, when the Azande want to know which witch is making them sick, they draw on their own cultural tradition for answers (Evans-Pritchard 1976). Since the answers given in each case are drawn from a particular cultural tradition, the means by which to examine the nature of belief and knowledge depend on the sociocultural knowledge systems of the members. Examining the foundations of such different sociocultural knowledge systems leads the inquirer immediately to the theoretical perspectives found in the sociology of knowledge.

The Relativist Perspective on Belief

The most basic theoretical debate in the sociology of knowledge concerns whether there exists a universal method for studying "reality," a methodology of "science"; or whether "science" itself is only one among many ways of knowing (Hollis and Lukes 1982; Katz 1989; Morkzycki 1983; Wilson 1970). The latter relativist position leaves open the question of religious knowledge as a valid means of "knowing," while the former usually relegates religious knowledge to the realm of the irrational and the mistaken (that is, "belief"). Rather than attempt to lead the reader through this vast literature,[5] I shall simply assert that, of the two, I find the relativist position a more apt basis from which to examine the claims of religion, because it is open to the examination of alternative reality constructions without necessarily judging them invalid. "Science," in contrast, while purporting to be "objective" and value free, is neither; its strongest adherents rightly view religion as hostile to the scientific perspective.[6] According to the relativists, "science" itself is a socially constructed form of knowledge which, *a priori*, has no greater right than other cultural systems to be taken as the model methodology for finding truth. However, this philosophical position directly contradicts the political and social constructions of "science" in much of popular culture and certainly in the academic community (Reynolds 1991). In fact, in the American academic community, the methodology of science and its attendant mythology have prevailed to such an extent that religion is rarely studied or taught in the classroom. As Sollod recently pointed out (1992:A60), this form of ethnocentrism perpetuates the tendency not only to judge *any* religious belief system as an invalid way of knowing but also to treat religion itself as a "taboo and mysterious subject."

If the relativist position were granted (and it is by no means the standard position, recent social science claims to the contrary[7] notwithstanding), then the researcher could examine the criteria used by the members of Cypress Pond to create a social reality in which religious knowledge was taken as a reflection of an ultimate reality, *even if* the researcher questions the nature of that ultimate reality itself. That is, members of Cypress Pond sometimes acted as if that reality were self-evident, and at other times they acted as if it were not. To what criteria and what standards did they appeal in the creation of that reality, in the questioning of that reality, and in the transmission of that reality from one generation to the next? When Beth and Rachel walked down the aisles of the church, answering an altar call for salvation, when both were already known as saved members, what did that mean for them and those who watched? When the Reverend John Manning asserted that, on Judgment Day, the saved would receive "crowns" with "jewels" in them showing the amount of service they had given the Lord, we can ask what this statement meant to members. Did they speak of these crowns metaphorically, or did they have some "literal" vision of a jeweled crown placed upon their heads? When the Reverend Ted Squires spoke of cursing as a sin that might keep other individuals from realizing the true message of salvation, how did church members interpret this injunction not to curse, and how did they evaluate people who do curse? These examples relate actions to the manifestation of belief and, as such, allow the researcher to ask questions about action as a criterion of belief/knowledge in the church members' folk epistemology. It is possible for outsiders to come to understand the meaning of the system, the degrees of questioning and variability allowed, the monitoring invoked, and the methods of reasoning utilized, without necessarily "believing" the "truth" of the system. According to a relativist position, "believers" may not necessarily be "right," but to judge them as "wrong" is to invoke a set of *moral* principles and not an absolute standard of, or even a methodology for determining, "truth."

While the preceding questions have to do with understanding the church members' world view,[8] usually anthropologists also attempt to determine functional and causal reasons underlying any particular belief system. For example, among the vast number of actions that Southern Baptists could have chosen as indicators of salvation, why did this particular group choose, for example, to evaluate morality as an indicator of the truth of the state of believing, instead of, as the Pentecostal Holiness groups do, such practices as speaking in tongues while possessed by the Holy Spirit (Bourguignon 1991; Peacock 1988)? Or, to take the questioning even further, why be preoccupied at all with the question of how to know? Why not just take as a given the reality of the spirit world, as the Afro-Brazilian religion of Candomblé apparently does (Wafer 1991), and focus instead on the various manifestations of that reality?

None of these questions have easy answers. Even (or perhaps *especially*) a relativist position that attempts to document a cultural system is fraught with problems of translation—how do we know if any portrait even approximates that which it purports to portray? Thus, in every interpretation, we must consider problems of reductionism, selectivity, bias, and subjectivity. Translation posits the existence of someone competent in both "languages" who can shift from one to the other, as I claim to be able to do in going back and forth between the SBC world view and academic interpretations. It is often presumed, however, that an attempt to answer questions of function or causality presupposes an "objective" observer or an "objective" perspective that goes beyond translation. The observer stands outside the given system and compares it with others, looking for *explanations* that have varying degrees of generality and utility. Taking a radical relativist position would preclude the possibility of such an outsider position (because everything must be tied to social context and to abstract anything would be to negate its meaning). It would also, by definition, preclude the translation of any cultural system into another's terms; yet, anthropologists routinely do make such translations. Thus, by default, they assume that an outsider perspective is possible and that translations are in principle possible.

The idea that outsider perspectives can exist often is taken as presupposing a "scientific" perspective, but alternative approaches for making comparisons also exist, more compatible with a relativist position. Chief among these alternatives are symbolic anthropology approaches which take interpretation as their explicit goal. Lett summarizes the questions symbolic anthropologists ask in this manner:

> First, what is the significance of meaning for the operation of human identity, and second, what is the significance of meaning for the operation of human social systems? (In this context, the term *meaning* refers to shared patterns of interpretation and perspective embodied in symbols, by means of which people develop and communicate their knowledge about and attitudes toward life.) (1987:110)

While Lett reserves judgment on the extent to which symbolic anthropologists achieve their goals, he notes that there is a sense in which these anthropologists do search for outsider perspectives on the universals of human nature.

The main problem with the choice of symbolic anthropology as an alternative to science lies in the perceived incompatibility between its relativistic and its universalistic assumptions. To illustrate this dilemma, let us once more consider the Southern Baptist stress on personal salvation. If Michelle tells me that she believes that Sim, the sixty-five-year-old deacon who openly doubts his salvation, is a "good man," she also tells me by inference that she believes that he is saved. From a relativist perspective, the anthropologist trying to understand Sim, Michelle, and the meanings encoded in their verbal and behavioral actions must place the statements and behaviors in their social context. This social meaning the outsider probably can grasp, but what of the claim, which Michelle and Sim would make, that the outsider cannot understand the meaning without experiencing it? If the relativist agrees with that *a priori* claim to privileged knowledge, then the point of incommensurability has been reached, and no further translation is possible (unless

the anthropologist converts). The universalist claims of symbolic anthropology flatly deny this incommensurability, because the symbolic
anthropologist assumes that, since humans interact and communicate
their beliefs in a social world, the anthropologist can come to understand what Sim and Michelle claim from the point of view of a social
being. The anthropologist may not be saved, but she or he can know
how salvation is constructed socially. Furthermore, she or he can, just
as Weber did a century ago, compare alternative soteriologies.

The perceived incompatibility between relativism and universalism
is the methodological conundrum of a symbolic anthropology that assumes that one can know the "other," but only *partially*. This compromise makes the specification of a methodology for knowing others problematic, because the researcher is never sure where the line is being
drawn between a physical "twitch" of the eye and a "wink" that car-
ries meaning (Geertz 1973:6–10). Thus, when Evans-Pritchard, himself
a recent convert to Catholicism, writes that he must leave interpretation of the inner state of Nuer religion to theologians, he poses the problem of knowing the meaning of Nuer sacrifices in this fashion:

> To the mind sickness caused by sin is the sin and in the mind it is wiped
> out by the sacrificial act. We seem indeed to be watching a play or to be lis-
> tening to someone's account of what he has dreamt. Perhaps when we have
> this illusion we are beginning to understand, for the significance of the
> objects, actions, and events lies not in themselves but in what they mean
> to those who experience them as participants or assistants. If we regard
> only what happens in sacrifice before the eyes it may seem to be a succes-
> sion of senseless, and even cruel and repulsive, acts, but when we reflect
> on their meaning we perceive that they are a dramatic representation of a
> spiritual experience. What this experience is the anthropologist cannot for
> certain say. Experiences of this kind are not easily communicated even
> when people are ready to communicate them and have a sophisticated
> vocabulary in which to do so. Though prayer and sacrifice are exterior
> states, Nuer religion is ultimately an interior state (1956:322).

Evans-Pritchard's point of view echoes the claim of the Southern Baptists that an outsider cannot "know an internal believing state." A dis-

tinction is made between social knowledge and the "inner" believing state which makes the latter inaccessible to the anthropologist.

In terms of a methodology for assessing internal states, the line drawn by Evans-Pritchard is exactly the same line drawn by members of Cypress Pond. They, too, recognized that it was difficult to assess an internal state. But they did it anyway. Examining how they did it reveals a parallel between the methodology of symbolic anthropology, which assumes that meaning is socially constructed, and the folk epistemology manifested at Cypress Pond. Here I am simply claiming that, when members of Cypress Pond wanted to make sense of their cultural system, which distinguished between internal believing states and the external manifestation of those internal states, then they relied on inference, just as social scientists do. They had to do so, because individuals may believe or not believe and yet act "as if" they do believe. Conversely, while an individual might believe and act "as if" they did *not* believe, Southern Baptists would note the discrepancy and reject the individual's claim to privileged knowledge about salvation. Thus, they are constantly making inferences about internal believing states in social interaction.

In that sense, the distinction between internal and external becomes blurred and instead becomes a social construction. As a social construction related to truth or falsity, the focus on an internal believing state, I find, reifies the Cartesian dualism between mind (where one really "knows" the truth of the religious experience) and body (the agent that manifests the internal state) while at the same time it attempts to transcend that dualism by preaching a monitoring of the self which, when (or if) fully incorporated into the self, makes the goals of the self identical to the goals of the community. Of course, no social system ever fully succeeds at making automatons of its members; nevertheless, the social system found at Cypress Pond overtly emphasized constant monitoring as "proof of an eventful order of spiritual reality."

Criteria of Belief/Knowledge

The criteria by which Cypress Pond Baptists measured their own and others' internal believing states—criteria which made "belief/knowledge" accessible—are considered throughout this work. The church members used language and rituals to convey the meanings of their system, just as members of all social systems do. They further codified the English-language distinctions between belief, knowledge, and action into an evaluative system which allowed them to use manifest commitment to the belief system, expressed through verbal and behavioral actions, as the criterion of the internal believing state. While Needham rejected "action" and "spiritual commitment" as criteria of belief,[9] Southern Baptists have managed to fuse the two in such a fashion that they live "as if" belief in salvation were accessible to the social actor. Needham rejected "action" because he claimed it did not necessarily reflect the inner motives of the actor. These Southern Baptists were aware of this "truism" and yet utilized external "action," despite the problems its use entailed. I believe that they had settled on verbal and behavioral actions as criteria because these actions were the only means by which humans can infer a dispositional or psychological state of being; and that, further, these Southern Baptists invoked both dispositional and psychological states when they wanted to "know" if they truly "believed" (see chapters 4 and 5).

In examining the criterion of "spiritual commitment," Needham selects for inquiry a Jesuit account of belief (Clark, cited in Needham 1972:86). According to this Jesuit, Clark, belief "is a mode of existence, of personal existence, and not primarily a set of propositions held to be true, though the latter point to and safeguard the former" (Clark, cited in Needham 1972:86). Needham discusses this claim as both an act of will and an act of commitment. That is, one uses one's will to commit to the truth of the belief system, and then one commits to live by its precepts. Thus, "the spiritual commitment in question, which is superadded to the assent, has total consequences, to the extent that the purported act of belief entails a special mode of personal existence" (Needham 1972:87). Proceeding to show that he cannot distinguish this kind of commitment from other kinds of commitment (for example, to a marriage) and that there appears to be nothing on which to pin a definite "believing" state of mind, Needham leaves the use of these kinds of criteria to the theologians. However, at least among religious groups speaking the English language, the use of *belief* as an emic term implies a complex set of meanings.[10] The "meanings" given the term *belief* in the social system of Cypress Pond, the "meanings" given the ways to "measure" the act of will invoked in making a statement of belief, and the "meaning" given to a range of subsequent behaviors closely scrutinized to "see" if the verbal attestations of belief do indicate a dispositional state of "spiritual commitment"—all these are subject to social science scrutiny in a system that invokes belief as an emic category and makes its manifestation proof of a cosmological reality.

In proposing both verbal and behavioral actions as criteria of belief, I do not maintain that actions necessarily denote actual belief, but rather that actions always have been the only means by which an outside observer can come to *infer* belief. Nor do I maintain that all beliefs are accessible through the action criterion, since some tacit beliefs may never be stated or acted upon. Though the presence "in" a person of a "belief" will always be imputed rather than categorically proved, cultural systems such as the one found at Cypress Pond function with members constantly evaluating their own status as believers and evaluating the beliefs of others in various social contexts. Members primarily use the criterion of action in assessing who apparently believes. They usually do not assess the truth of claims made by the religion itself through a monitoring of actions, for, at the group level, these are taken as given, as a criterion of membership. But when it comes to knowing who belongs to the group, actual self-assessments and the assessment of others always invoke action criteria. In so doing, church members constantly return to commitment as an overt criterion of religious belief.

Commitment, for Southern Baptists, translates into certain objective actions such as church attendance and a willingness to live one's life by the *moral* standards established within the church community. Questions about "true" religious belief are addressed tangentially, only when members attempt to decide whether or not their inner states and outward behavior sufficiently conform to the declared goals and states advocated within the religious group. For example, speaking of whether one truly loved the Lord, one Cypress Pond church member said, "If you love, you give, whether it's time, effort, or money. And if you don't love, you begrudge it." This statement makes a direct connection between an internal feeling state, love, and the external expression of that feeling state in action; that is, giving time, effort, and money. These public actions can be measured directly or indirectly by those within the community, as tokens of individuals' inner states.

Goodenough says of belief systems generally that often people may not "really" believe and only act "as if." He notes:

> But what is important for coordinated social interaction and mutual understanding is not necessarily a common personal commitment to the truth of a particular set of propositions—although such a common commitment may be essential for cooperation in some kinds of endeavor—but a knowledge by all parties of the propositions on which actions are predicated and a common acceptance of these propositions as a basis for action. Whenever we cite propositions in justifications for our acts, we are treating them as if they were true, regardless of our private convictions (1981:73).

As noted above, members of the Cypress Pond congregation were well aware that it was possible to declare religious belief publicly and act "as if." Consequently, they spent much time and effort attempting to decide whether belief was "true" or whether it was "faked." A member of the congregation made these distinctions:

> Many in Cypress Pond Baptist Church who think they are saved ["born again"] may be surprised. If they think being a member of the church and going under the baptismal waters is all it takes, and that they can then continue on in their old ways, I'm afraid they may be greatly surprised [upon death, to find that they were not saved and have gone to hell].

Certain behaviors are considered necessary in the "saved"—for instance, to profess belief, be baptized, and come to church. However, "something" more should also be expressed. How to measure religious states involves a complex code and interpretation of behavior, subjects we shall explore fully.

While many social scientists have chosen to place into different orders of analysis the verbal and behavioral components of expressed knowledge, I treat both verbal and behavioral components as equally valid expressions of belief. Holy and Stuchlik, in their extensive treatment of this methodological point, argue that the anthropological literature contains many references to the problem of explaining the discrepancy between "what people say they do (have done, will do) and what the anthropologist observes as their activities" (1983:12). The assumption that there should be a "necessary or nonproblematic congruence between what people say and what they do" is invalid (1983:13). Rather, verbal statements are actions of a certain sort, which may or may not be congruent with other behaviors.

Language, Belief, and Action

Paying careful attention to the nuances of expressed beliefs in their social contexts and to the stated evaluations of action, I formulated a multilayered picture of the religious belief system of the congregation. Often, when researchers present an analysis of the religious beliefs of a particular community or religious faith, their ethnographic accounts undergo such reductionistic processes that variation and contextual subtleties are lost. To counter this reductionism, in much of my data collection and analyses I adopted an approach based on the ethnography of communication. Hymes, who established this field in linguistic anthropology, argues that all aspects of language usage require description and analysis (1965). In particular, the ethnography of communication focuses on language use in social context, as the primary means by which humans can attempt to integrate language and society (Eastman 1990). Bauman (1974), Crystal (1976), Dorgan (1987), Gossen (1976), Sherzer (1983), and Titon (1988) have described religious language usage, primarily as it pertains to religious rituals. In my work, language usage and the actions that accompany it are the data from which we may begin to understand how pastors and members try to construct a certain agreed-upon public concensus about their religious beliefs and how that public consensus is undermined by the variation occurring in different contexts. For instance, while religious sermons present to believers what local leaders consider the most salient aspects of belief, pastors do not always present the same story. Nor do the religious actions taken in response to the pastor's words always present identical expressions and evaluations of belief.

Conrad notes that when researchers study the participation, involvement, and commitment of members of religious organizations they usually treat the communicative process as a "black box, the contents of which largely are assumed to be either incapable of being examined systematically or of minimal theoretical interest" (1988:346). To go beyond the "black box," he asked six Southern Baptist congregations to send him audiotapes of their business meetings. He analyzed these for the communicative processes involved in decision making and self-identity with the church. But, as he admits, since he did not know the pastors or the members involved, the actual social context and the antecedents which defined these interactions were not documented (1988:359). My research, however, examines religious communications as they occur in social contexts. Ritual and nonritual contexts are defined and examined throughout this book and illustrate how religious beliefs are translated into action.

The meaning that participants attribute to their actions helps explain why they claim to believe and why their beliefs are maintained over time. Their statements of belief, as actions, enact the belief system for the participants, create the context for new interpretations of belief, and transmit the belief system to those in the process of being socialized into belief system itself. Berger and Luckmann state that the subjective reality of an individual is "always dependent upon specific plausibility structures, that is, the specific social base and social processes required for its maintenance" (1966:154). From this point of view, an individual's subjective reality is dependent on the social contexts in which he is born (primary socialization) or with which he chooses to identify. A person can move from one world view to another, but the commitment to endorse the structure either consciously or unconsciously must be there. Thus, religious communities maintain plausibility structures that individuals encounter either because they were socialized into them or because they choose to identify with them.

Berger (1969) also argues that the key source of power still available to religion in the modern world is the language of persuasion. Commitment to an institution means hearing the language of persuasion and coming to adopt it as one's own. For Berger and Luckmann, commitment not only involves self-identity with the institution; it also entails active involvement and discourse, or the self-identity will become "subjectively empty of living" (1966:155).

The meaning that participants attribute to their beliefs, again, can only be studied through inference. In this book, then, belief and knowledge are examined first as emic constructs which equate the experience of religious belief with the actual religious knowledge of ultimate reality. Since such an equation was closely scrutinized by members of the Cypress Pond cultural system itself, researching that world view actually yielded a folk epistemology of belief and knowledge. We shall see that belief and knowledge were equated at Cypress Pond, both in the context of religious discussions and in the manifestation of salvation in daily life. Strongly rejecting a rationalism based on intellect alone, these believers said that an "intellectual knowledge" of the "word of God" was insufficient. One had to have an "emotional knowledge" that transcended thought alone and united the believer with religious reality in such a way that he or she "lived it." Because Cypress Pond church members posited and monitored "belief/knowledge" in their social interactions, they offered a pragmatic means of transcending the problem of distinguishing between belief and knowledge. At one level, the differences between the two terms became irrelevant; at another level, because these believers lived in a social world, the methods they adopted for "knowing" (emotional experiences and spiritual commitment shown through morality) created a set of dilemmas about belief and knowledge that epitomize the problems of Western thought itself. That is, the search for an emotional knowledge of a spiritual reality and an absolute assurance that the experience was valid seems to me to parallel the scientific-rationalist quest for an absolute sense datum point to "prove" that reality exists as one has defined it. I return to this comparison in more detail in chapters 4 and 8.

Assessing Beliefs about Salvation through Actions

I spent much of my time at Cypress Pond attempting to understand these questions about "belief" in terms of the cultural theme of salvation. It is true that much of what I found was determined *in part* by my own biases and questions. However, the demands of fieldwork and my personal integrity required that I constantly look beyond my own motivations to observe the behaviors of, and the words spoken by, the people of this community. Though I cannot claim that the subjective reality I experienced, or that members of Cypress Pond apparently experienced, actually corresponds to some empirically founded reality, nevertheless I found strong evidence demonstrating both the cultural centrality of salvation and the ways in which action is used to assess belief.

Before analyzing that evidence, I present, in the next two chapters, ethnographic portraits of the Cypress Pond community of believers. Chapter 2 discusses the relationships among family, place, and church in this rural southern setting, showing how the community was constrained by legacies of its past and by its current patterns of economic subsistence. Chapter 3 provides a detailed account of the specific demographic characteristics of this church congregation, its routine activities, and its formal and informal social structure. Knowledge of these cultural contexts is essential in coming to understand how church members translated beliefs into actions which they could assess on a daily basis.

The communication of religious knowledge in worship services forms an important source of data about beliefs. Beliefs concerning salvation colored virtually all pastoral sermons. All eleven pastors who spoke at Cypress Pond constantly stressed the need for every individual to be "born again," for that very invocation is part of their role as evangelical leaders. To cite only one example, Mac Jackson, a visiting pastor, preached these words on being "born again":

> Jesus says, "I'm telling you the truth, that no one can enter the kingdom of God unless he is born again." This is ever on the mind of God, on the mind of Jesus, and should be upon our minds. No one can enter the kingdom of God unless he is born again. . . . How often Jesus said, the kingdom of heaven, the kingdom of God, is at hand, and what did he say? Repent and enter. . . . And entrance into God's kingdom is by way of spiritual experience, by way of rebirth. It is the only way to enter. Yes, we are born first of all of the flesh, we are born out of water, though Jesus said, we

also must be born of the spirit, born of God, born by the power of God, as God would bring into our lives as we have faith in his Son, Jesus Christ, faith in God and all of the provisions that God has made. We would be born by the power of God. Yes, we are born one time physically, but we need, all of us, you and I, those who are lost in the world, need to be born again, born of God through faith in Christ. (Morning Worship Service, July 28, 1985)

Chapters 4 and 5 analyze the logic and basic beliefs of evangelical Christianity as these were presented in the sermon messages given at Cypress Pond. As a speech genre, sermons are verbal performances which provide evidence of beliefs on many different levels. At the level of content, I show which beliefs apparently were undisputed at Cypress Pond and which beliefs showed variation. Sermons also can be linked to overt criteria of belief, because Cypress Pond pastors purposefully used sermons during worship services to motivate actions. These calls to action usually were linked to standards by which the pastors and members can measure salvation. Chapter 4 examines the rhetorical styles of sermons designed to motivate the religious experience of salvation, while chapter 5 looks at sermons designed to motivate individual commitment to the belief system.

Chapter 6 examines the most culturally salient of the outwardly observable congregational responses to the sermons: the "altar call for salvation." As the central focus of almost every Cypress Pond worship service, traditional altar calls asked persons present who were not already saved to make a declaration that they had been saved. Since the declaration was public—the respondent was required to walk down the church's center aisle to the front and speak to the pastor—it certainly fit the criteria of overt action. In addition, pastors had begun to change the traditional format of the altar call, adding to it other manifest behaviors designed to show commitment to the church. Discussing the old and new forms of altar calls given by pastors and the members' responses, I show how this belief system creatively used action to assess belief.

The stress on the church worship services does not, however, tell us how churchgoers tried to live their beliefs. Chapter 7 focuses on the lives of individual believers. Using Turner's distinction between the impulse self and the institutional self (1976:991–92), I examine salvation as a conversion process in which the individual attempts to adhere to the high standards of the Christian faith. I portray the lives of three women who were striving to live as "true believers." Once more we return to the theme of assessment, as it preoccupied these believers. They asked me, they asked themselves, they asked their pastors: "How do I know if I am saved? How can I assess my own salvation and that of others?"

Chapter 8, the conclusion, discusses the wider implications of this perspective on belief and delineates how actions as criteria of belief made it possible for Cypress Pond members to assess their own and others' salvation experiences. Throughout the work, I ground a pragmatic approach to the epistemological status of belief in the context of social action. To understand belief, we look not to theologians, but rather to the leaders and the members of Cypress Pond.

2

Place, Church, and Family: Contextual Boundaries of Belief

In my memories of Cypress Pond, family, place, and church often seem blurred. I suspect that the shading of these concepts, one into the other, also happened often for the southerners among whom I walked. Their Christian identities were bound up with so many other aspects of their lives that sometimes it seemed as if the textures and rhythms of daily existence were variations on the hymns they sang. "Blest be the tie that binds" sings of the Christian love uniting Christians here and beyond the grave. "Faith of our fathers! Living still" reminds them that their religion is not new but is a direct heritage from their past. "Just as I am, and waiting not, . . . I come! I come!" directs the gaze inward, evoking incessant calls to faith and to action.[1]

Life there had many such reminders of the past, of family, of images that remained only in memory; yet, when evoked afresh, they took on new life and meaning. The past was not another country; it lived, breathed, sang.[2] The accuracy of the memories, often problematic from the outside observer's point of view, might not even be addressed by the insider. Since what we remember is filtered through our own life experiences, through cultural conventions, through self-will and desire, we should not be surprised to find that cultural institutions deliberately celebrate the past and, in so doing, evoke meanings in the present.[3] Before we turn to an analysis of Cypress Pond's cultural and historical milieu, journey with me to a ritual enactment of the past: a family reunion.

It was August in the South. The sun-baked daytime seemed to stretch into an unbearable forever. I had made arrangements to return to Cypress Pond for a weekend visit some two months after completing my year's fieldwork.

When I arrived at Michelle's house on Friday afternoon, bedraggled from the heat, she greeted me happily. A gregarious, charming woman in her early fifties, she had always been friendly. She had six daughters of her own, all but the youngest of whom were married. Her relationships with her daughters were characterized by an underlying tension that occasionally manifested itself in flaring tempers. From her perspective, I might well have fit into a fictive kin relationship, as another "daughter," albeit a temporary one. Adding fuel to the fires of already strained relationships, Michelle sometimes praised my behavior at the expense of whichever daughter she happened to be in conflict with at the time.

Expecting to be the sole guest in her household, I was surprised to find her home full of visiting kin. Two of Michelle's mother's sisters, Isobel and Susie, and Susie's husband, Johnny, had driven down from North Carolina earlier in the day. Michelle explained that she had not told me that a family reunion was scheduled for this weekend, rightly suspecting that I would have refused to add to her household at such a time. Initially disconcerted, I found myself delighted to have the opportunity to watch at first hand all the preparations, to listen to the remembrances, and to see how family was defined in this group of kin.

Early Saturday morning, the women prepared food to take to the family reunion being held for all the descendants of John Nettles, Michelle's maternal grandfather (ambilineal kinship reckoning). We cooked ham, peas from Michelle's father's garden, macaroni, pound cake, and biscuits. After packaging the food, everyone else drove to a nearby community center for the event. I was dispatched to pick up Michelle's father, Lance, also a resident member of Cypress Pond. A widower of seventy-four, Lance was well respected for his faith in Christ. He did, in my opinion, live his beliefs. He always had about him an air of quiet dignity and a steady assurance of faith. He had told me that his belief had been sorely tried by his wife's death a few years ago; yet I never saw him discomposed. Though he had only a fourth-grade education, he read the Bible intently, both puzzling over the nature of salvation and taking delight in the words themselves. A wonderful orator, Lance knew whole passages by heart, often including them in public prayers.

People he did not even know, as well as those he did, often asked him to pray for them.

Upon our arrival at the community center, formerly a country schoolhouse, people standing outside started to tease Lance about me, saying that he had a rather young girlfriend. Introductions were made as I surveyed my surroundings. I had driven by this place before but had never stopped to examine it closely. Built in the style of older, small rural schools, the building was brick veneer. Boxy, with floors set well above ground level, it had a decrepit look: a few windows were boarded up, the painted trim was cracked and peeling, even the yard looked dusty and a little scuffed. Set almost on the edge of a tiny village settlement, Hattiesville, a ballfield and the Hattiesville Southern Baptist Church broke the vista of plowed fields and the distant deep green of a row of trees.

Leaving Lance with the men outside, I climbed the high steps and gained entrance to two large rooms. On the right was what once must have been the cafeteria. Long tables had been set up here, and women were arranging rows of food for the upcoming midday feast. The room was decorated with streamers, balloons, paper bells, and a banner reading "Welcome to the Annual Nettles Family Reunion." To the left was the old auditorium. The wooden floor stretched toward a raised stage with faded purple curtains still hanging. Rows of folding chairs faced the stage.

Between fifty and sixty people attended that day. Called from the greetings, hugs, and food display by the organizer, Elsie, we all entered the auditorium for a short program. She prayed, spoke of a recent death in the family, read a poem dedicated to the memory of those who had died, and presented a series of gifts to fellow organizers and to the oldest living family member. When we returned to the cafeteria, Lance was asked to bless the meal. With practiced ease, he thanked God for his goodness and petitioned for safe return journeys for all those who had driven to the reunion.

Over dinner, people generally appeared to sit in groups of close kin, with mingling occurring afterward. For instance, at one table I noticed a large family whom I knew from Cypress Pond. Wallace, the father, had started to attend church again, bringing with him his new wife Betsy, her daughter, and his three children by a former marriage.

Betsy had been raised Methodist. After her marriage, she decided to become Baptist, and she and her daughter recently had been baptized by immersion at Cypress Pond to signify their salvation. Now Betsy was noticeably pregnant, carrying a fifth child to add to a household where the oldest was probably no more than ten.

Looking around the room and talking with those about me clarified once more the significance of class differences in America and the markers by which assessments of class are made. Before undertaking fieldwork, I had not personally experienced the very real boundaries between working-class and middle-class families in America. My background had been primarily in the middle class, while most of those who turned up at the reunion, like those who attended Cypress Pond, were of the working class. Markers of this status could be seen in their clothing. Few were dressed in the latest styles. Many women wore flowered, double-knit polyester tops; some men wore faded jeans and work shirts; a few women had on more stylish light cotton sweaters with pants. Listening to conversations, I heard expressions that researchers place as part of American working-class dialect. For example, many said "he done," "them is," and "ain't."[4] Finally, since I was introduced in my anthropologist role, it was fairly easy to ascertain who also had been to college. Of those I talked with only two, a young couple from out of town, had any higher education.

After eating, people visited with one another, catching up on family news. Most people commented on the attendance at this family reunion, which was much lower than the hundred-plus who had come for the past two years. While many blamed the recent funeral of a local family member—a man in his seventies who had been buried the day before—others expressed the opinion that one funeral was not sufficient to explain the difference. I heard many negative evaluations of local folks who could have come but did not. While acceptable excuses for absence include such things as illness, bereavement, or job requirements, some were absent simply because they did not want to come, perhaps because they were mad at one or more members of their family. In fact, one of Michelle's own daughters who lives in the area did not appear and had no acceptable reason for not turning up, much to her mother's chagrin. Being present at such events seems to signal both family solidarity and a willingness to visibly embody family solidarity. When local persons, especially, fail to appear, the image of togetherness is marred.

At about 3:30 P.M., the exodus began with slow farewells. I left with Michelle's family, only to find that the celebration of kinship was not over. A more private reaffirmation of family ties followed later, around 5:00 P.M. Michelle and her aunts decided to visit the places where the aunts and Michelle's mother had been raised. On our journey, we traversed farm-to-market roads and turned off onto old, infrequently traveled dirt roads. This was not a casual afternoon drive, undertaken to fill idle time. It was a deliberate journey into the past, into definitions of place and family. As Michelle drove, she and her aunts Isobel and Susie, both in their seventies, looked for places which had had special meaning for them. We began this pilgrimage at the site of an old mill, no longer in existence. Isobel and Susie recalled walking past that mill on their way to school. On cold winter days, they would stop midway and sit, warming each other's feet under the skirts of their dresses.

Michelle then took us to an abandoned, overgrown cemetery hidden in the woods. Near this cemetery, Michelle used to come with her mother to picnic. Michelle's mother, Mary, frequently had mentioned the good memories she held of this place. It was here that Lance, her future husband, had proposed to her, and here she had spent the first few months of her married life, in a house no longer standing.

As we left this spot, Isobel and Susie began to direct Michelle as they hunted for the place they had been raised. They pointed us down more dirt roads until these, too, petered out. We kept going. Eventually Susie recognized the place where her home had stood years ago, the places where her uncles and aunts once had lived, the hill she used to walk up following her brother. As they stood in this overgrown field, now devoid of buildings and surrounded by woods, they told stories of their youth: which parents had beaten their children, who had married whom, and how they had picked cotton. The time must have been the 1920s, a time long before electricity, phones, and "horseless carriages" were common in their world. Even Michelle, a member of a younger generation, on a different occasion recalled riding home from church in the back of a wagon, looking up at the stars.

This was not my first such pilgrimage with members of Cypress Pond Baptist Church, nor my first family reunion. Sunday afternoons were favorite times for similar excursions. I was often taken along as a fresh face, listening to stories of the good old times, seeing or imagining the places, hearing tales of the past and the dead. But this particular experience struck me strongly, as I stood in that houseless, deserted field, trying to imagine it crowded with sharecroppers' homes, children, mules, well-used roads, and fields of cotton. It seemed as though Isobel, Susie, and Michelle were engaged in reconstructing their ties to kin, to place, and to church.

Moments of discernment, like those I experienced surveying a place that offered no obvious clues to its teeming human past, happen often in fieldwork. Anthropologists then search past experiences for clues to illuminate the cultural patterns underlying the insight. They seek other instances to substantiate what is, at first glance, undocumented (Agar 1980, 1986). Working backward, I shall try to tease apart the fusion I felt between family, place, and church, showing the factors which help to create this world view. To understand the multiple facets of Cypress Pond members, it was necessary to look at many sources: historical records, church history, community dynamics, and accounts given by members themselves. This background knowledge made available a "past" from which to interpret the contemporary structure and activities of Cypress Pond.

Before beginning, however, let me add descriptive weight to this portrait by sketching more of the community's features. Cypress Pond Baptist Church, at the time of my study, was one of twenty-two Southern Baptist Convention churches in Salkehatchie County. Located six miles from the county seat of Southville,[5] it seemed to be completely rural. There was no small village or population center nearby. Yet an informal designation existed for this region of Salkehatchie County: "Jingletown." The name was the subject of much speculation and joking. No one seemed to know for sure what the source of the name was, where its boundaries were to be found, or even if the name denoted a positive sense of belonging or a derogatory evaluation of its inhabitants. The term Jingletown nevertheless provided a handy label for its rural population. It apparently encompassed residents living within a four-mile radius around the church. Cypress Pond members claimed that the term derived from the homestead of one of its founding congregational members, but the term applied to all residents of the area, irrespective of church membership. While there was not even a cluster of stores amid the fields and forests to identify Jingletown's location, the area apparently included Cypress Pond and six other rural churches: two black Baptist churches, two additional SBC churches, a Pentecostal Holiness church, and a church simply called the "Christian Church."

Sometimes visiting pastors would get lost in Jingletown as they attempted to find Cypress Pond. They would drive the unmarked paved roads, trying to find the correct church among these rivals. When told of the misadventure, members would describe Jingletown as an almost mythical place known only to locals. People would laugh aloud at the impossibility of describing its actual dimensions. I once asked a couple, members of the church, to situate its boundaries for me. They could not agree on the boundaries and kept asking each other whether this place or that should be included. The resulting debate, held over a local map, may have clarified Jingletown in their minds. I left still mystified about the specifics but with my prior tacit understanding reinforced.

While most of the members of Cypress Pond were born in the Jingletown area, some few lived in small villages such as Hattiesville (located about three miles from the church buildings) or in Southville. Since Southville was the largest local town, members would drive there to shop for groceries, to take care of county business, to pick up videotapes for their VCRs, and to dine. Southville, a rather sleepy town, had two "centers." The town hall and older businesses were located around a circular drive which, in turn, surrounded a well-kept grass park, complete with a fountain. To the north, a "strip" of highway held the ubiquitous fast-food chain restaurants and newer shops. Much excitement was generated during the fieldwork period by new arrivals to the "strip": a large chain discount store, Wal-Mart, and two fast-food restaurants, McDonald's and Pizza Hut. Residents greeted these with such enthusiasm that soon I found I had only to go to Wal-Mart to strike up conversations with church members "out on the town." Friday and Saturday nights brought droves of teenagers to McDonald's. Having no theater or other places of entertainment nearby, they forsook parking around the town circle for this newer, "trendier" location.

The countryside of Jingletown, the rural church of Cypress Pond, the small-town atmosphere of Southville—these were the geographical boundaries of daily life for most Cypress Pond members. A few expanded their horizons by driving forty-five miles to the larger community of Bigtown to work, take in the movies, or shop. In tone and quality of life, however, Salkehatchie County as a whole exhibited a quintessentially southern atmosphere of quiet, slow sleepiness, increasingly interrupted by the frantic energy of modern consumerism.

Social boundaries also existed in Salkehatchie County, and they, too, reflected the juxtaposition of old to new. Perhaps the most striking social feature was the continued ethnic segregation of African Americans and whites. For historical and demographic reasons, these two groups constituted almost all the ethnic diversity in Salkehatchie County.[6] Because Cypress Pond SBC members were all white, they were part of the dominant ethnic group. While the civil rights movement had brought many changes in education, use of facilities, elected officials, and some job opportunities, the color barrier still existed in the religious traditions.[7] All the SBC churches in this county had exclusively white memberships (*Salkehatchie Baptist Association Report* 1985). Ecumenical programs occasionally included both African Americans and whites, but these were the exception rather than the rule.[8]

Segregation brings with it a host of boundaries and rules for any interethnic communications which do occur. While all Cypress Pond members interacted with African Americans on occasion, and some did so daily in the context of business relationships, I never saw an African American at any Cypress Pond function or an African-American guest in their homes. The one countywide ecumenical event in which African Americans had a nominal role (a revival held in 1985) elicited minimal Cypress Pond participation and support. Most Cypress Pond members backed up such behavioral cues with statements in favor of continued ethnic segregation. Pastors further reinforced the boundaries in sermons, affirming that African Americans belonged in their own churches. While members seem concerned to maintain the status quo, the actions they take are not militant. When the Ku Klux Klan burned crosses at the home of a racially mixed couple elsewhere in the county, and when the Klan held a march around the town circle, members condemned these activities.[9]

Salkehatchie County has a class structure similar to that found in other regions of the American South—a structure reflected in church affiliation. Caplow and his colleagues succinctly state the usual trend when they say, "It is well documented that among American Protestants the well educated and the well-to-do are overrepresented in certain denominations, especially the Episcopalians and the Presbyterians, and underrepresented among the Baptists and the Pentecostal-Evangelicals" (1983:125). In this region of the South, Protestant variation constitutes almost all of the religious variation. Salkehatchie County, at the time of this study, had fewer than two hundred Catholics in a population pool of twenty thousand (Quinn 1982). With no resident parish priest, these Catholics had low visibility and little apparent impact on community activities. By contrast, there were at least seventy-seven Protestant churches, including Episcopalians, Methodists, Pentecostal Holiness, Church of God, and even a few recent Amish immigrants.[10] These churches could be grouped roughly into categories reflecting the county's class divisions. Local church "status" reputations coincided with class divisions, while the locations and exteriors of the buildings themselves offered many clues to each church's place within the hierarchy.

Southville's elites were composed of wealthy whites (many of whom were descendants of plantation owners) who interacted at the local country club, funded the Southville museum and historical society, helped elect powerful representatives to the state legislature, and generally attended the Episcopal Church. At other points along the class continuum stood middle-class agricultural landowners, schoolteachers, and businesspeople who attended the Presbyterian Church and the United Methodist Church. When discussing the Baptists, however, caution must be exercised in describing a "typical" pattern. The members attracted to the twenty-odd SBC churches and at least thirteen more independent Baptist churches in Salkehatchie County varied significantly. The various Baptist churches gained informal reputations through gossip networks.[11] For example, First Southville Baptist Church, in the folk accounts, drew "elite" or middle-class Baptists. Churches such as Cypress Pond were considered middle-of-the-road, and attendees tended to belong to the middle working class or the upper working class.[12] Lower still on the economic scale were other country SBC churches with smaller numbers and correspondingly smaller budgets. Finally, the Pentecostal-

Evangelical churches were ranked on a par with the smaller SBC Churches, drawing most of their membership from the lower working class. Thus, the resident membership of Cypress Pond was ranked toward the lower end of the county class structure, but by no means at the "bottom."

Aware of the differences between themselves and African Americans, between themselves and their richer and poorer neighbors, Cypress Pond members knew something of the boundaries of their world, both geographically and socially. But, like most of us, they chose not to think of themselves as representatives of categories. Nor did they seek to understand the origins of their current status in the historical processes that formed their world. Members of Cypress Pond lived lives influenced by the past, but they tended only to refer to it on a personal, familial level. Their main concern was the present, and memories seemed to stop with life events recounted by the elderly. When I interviewed two of the oldest residents of Salkehatchie, a 95-year-old Cypress Pond man and a 105-year-old deacon of an African-American Baptist Church, I found a dearth of historical information about the conditions that formed the county and a curious silence about relationships between African Americans and whites. This pattern was repeated in other interviews and in gossip sessions. Specific facts bound to larger historical processes were not reported. Even the fact that Sherman had burned Southville on his famous march through South Carolina in 1865 was mentioned only in passing and only in direct response to my probes. Instead, the recalled memories, such as those of Michelle and her aunts, tied family to place. Members usually spoke of common interests they deemed important—that is, family of origin, status at birth, and church affiliation.

This selectivity in memory parallels that found by other researchers in the South. Criticizing southern churches for ignoring social issues, many researchers blame southern racial segregation and tension for the continued silence (Eighmy 1972; Greenhouse 1986; Hill 1966; and Ellen Rosenberg 1989). The reasoning seems to be that, if the obvious causes of segregation are never mentioned, then no one has to be held accountable for the past, and no one has to take action to change the future. While the characterization rings true, and while I certainly found it verified at Cypress Pond, from the insider's point of view these questions of social responsibility were rarely raised. To the extent that church members dealt with reform at all, they displaced responsibility to the cosmic level and asserted that salvation was the answer to all problems (Heriot 1993). Lifting their voices in song, telling their tales of events bound to concrete place, these southerners affirmed a grounded, static, timeless world where the "right" patterns of their Christian past became the now.

Place

"I've been here twenty years, raised two children in the church, and I'm still an outsider because I wasn't born here."

More than one member of Cypress Pond made such a statement. "Outsiders" generally were persons who had married someone local and moved to the area. "Local" in this context meant born and raised in the community. Even as little as fifteen miles could mark a person as forever a stranger, as alien to this place. Affinal (marriage) kinship ties never were sufficient to make one a "true" resident. Consanguinal (blood) ties were necessary for complete belonging.

In a rural southern community, such views of resident membership are not unusual. I had encountered them in all the small communities where I had lived. Even at funerals of persons in their eighties, in situating and evaluating a life, someone invariably would remark on residence patterns as well as kinship connections. Where a person grew up formed part of her or his identity for life.

In the wider context, using the tie to a particular, circumscribed place as a crucial marker of identity can be effective only if there is little movement from place to place, at least during formative years. Such was the case at Cypress Pond. To document this pattern, I looked beyond the statements of local members and researched historical records. In archival documents found in the Salkehatchie County Library and in the University of South Carolina's Caroliniana Library (repository of many state historical texts), I found evidence for Cypress Pond family ties to place. The overall county settlement pattern was characterized by an initial in-migration of two groups: a relatively homogeneous group of white settlers who came to Salkehatchie in the late 1700s and early 1800s and African Americans forcibly brought to work as slaves on cotton plantations in the early 1800s.[13] Most residents of modern Salkehatchie could trace their ancestral heritage back to these early settlers. Yet these same inhabitants also had many kin who had left the area over the years and formed the pool from which family reunion "returnees" were drawn. This leaving, or outmigration, had been a feature of Salkehatchie generation after generation, from the early 1800s until the 1950s.

Over the years, most people left Salkehatchie County for economic reasons. Dependent on agriculture for most of its history, Salkehatchie suffered greatly in the aftermath of the Civil War. Sharecropping on tenant farms replaced the plantation system as the major means of livelihood. A large wave of outmigration began shortly after the Civil War and continued through the 1870s. Another exodus occurred as African Americans left in record numbers in the 1920s, 1930s, and 1940s (Kovacik and Winberry 1987:123–24).

The situation changed in the 1950s. Forming a large part of current discourse about "history" and helping to shape the community today, industries began to move into the Salkehatchie area. Part of a general upswing in the state's economy, these industries brought with them increased prosperity. Within driving distance for residents at the time of the study were the Federal Plant (a government project developed partially on Salkehatchie County land), a waste processing center, two textile mills, and an optical plant. As these employers became increasingly important sources of income, work patterns changed. With continued depressions in the farm economy, many persons shifted from agricultural work to factory employment (*Salkehatchie County Newspaper* and Salkehatchie County Library Pamphlet File). Reflecting the increased industrial prosperity, the population of Salkehatchie County grew slightly between 1870 and 1980, although its population in 1985 was less than it had been in 1930 (U.S. Department of Commerce, Bureau of the Census 1930 and 1980). Nevertheless, the years of outmigration had taken their toll, and in 1980 Salkehatchie remained a sparsely populated county, with less than forty persons per square mile (U.S. Department of Commerce, Bureau of the Census 1980).

Those who stayed in the county joined a long line of stayers: people whose connections to place had generational depth and a historical weight that was taken for granted. Those who left also joined a long line of leavers. Each generation had had its share of outmigrants. When these outmigrants left, they forsook these rooted cultural contexts by varying degrees. If the distance they went was only twenty-five miles or so, then a person might visit her or his former home frequently and could attend all the family reunions and church Homecomings. But if the move was to the city or to another state, then returning "home" was more problematic and might only be undertaken for special occasions like family reunions.

Another kind of leave-taking well might have been forthcoming. With industrialization replacing agrarian modes of subsistence, it seemed possible that Cypress Pond residents' outlook on life and their place within the cultural milieu might shift. For the moment, however, because of the rural nature of their home lives and the low population density, members still identified with their agrarian heritage. Pastors preaching at Cypress Pond made frequent references to farming lifestyles. Church members referred to themselves as country people. They grew vegetables, did home preserving and canning, and assessed the weather with an eye to its effects on crops. Place, for them, grounded their lives both in concrete reality and in shared cultural images that interlocked the stayers and the leavers under the umbrella of a common rural world view.

Church

"Our family has always been Baptist."

This statement, made frequently at Cypress Pond, accurately reflected the religious affiliations of the original settlers, the ancestors of today's members. While Cypress Pond Baptist Church was not founded until 1874, its membership was drawn from two older, well-established Baptist churches: Turkey Creek, founded in 1826 or 1835, depending on the account chosen, and Calvary, founded in 1832 (*Salkehatchie County Newspaper* and *Salkehatchie Baptist Association History* 1867). Both these churches were offshoots of the Salkehatchie Baptist Church, which was founded in 1802 from one of the oldest churches in the county: Green Pine Baptist Church, first constituted in 1780 (*Salkehatchie Baptist Association History* 1867).

Cypress Pond thus had ties to the oldest churches in the county. Members' stories about the foundation of Cypress Pond itself offered two contradictory tales. One, the version printed in the official church history, states that Cypress Pond was established to accommodate large numbers of people who were driving in carriages or walking to either Calvary or Green Branch Baptist Church, both about seven or eight miles from Cypress Pond. The land chosen for Cypress Pond was said to be equidistant from these two churches. Maps bore out this claim, as did the kinship bonds among members of all three churches. Many from each church attended the others' revivals and annual Homecoming celebrations.[14] In offering the second story of the church's origin, Cypress Pond's oldest living member, "Uncle" Willie Jones, said that the church site was established by his maternal and paternal grandfathers. Cypress Pond was, he noted, equidistant from the homesteads of these original founders of Cypress Pond. Whatever the rationale, the congregation began meeting in the years shortly after the Civil War.

It was difficult to determine the exact nature of denominational affiliations during the initial settlement period of 1740 to 1780. However, all the earliest recorded churches in the county were Baptist and dated from 1780 when the first Baptist church was founded in Salkehatchie County.[15] Nine Baptist churches were constituted in the county before 1840 (*Salkehatchie Baptist Association History* 1867). After the Baptists, other Protestant denominations arrived, with the Methodists, Presbyterians, and Episcopalians building churches during the 1840s. The Catholics had established a parish in the county during the 1830s, but their numbers remained small (*Salkehatchie County Newspaper*).

At the time of the study, the county was still overwhelmingly Baptist. In the 1980 report *Churches and Church Membership* (Quinn 1982), approximately 70 percent of persons in Salkehatchie County who reported a religious affiliation were SBC members. Since the survey excluded most African-American churches, this figure represented a high percentage of the total white population, approximately 70 percent.[16] Interviews with African-American pastors indicated that most African Americans in the county also were members of Baptist denominations, though not the SBC.

In light of these demographic and historical features, it is clear that, when Cypress Pond members said, "Our family has always been Baptist," they accurately referred to over two centuries of Baptist dominance in their community. Even when forced to consider denominational variability, they did so in the context of Protestantism. Only on rare occasions in their day-to-day lives were they confronted with persons not having at least superficial knowledge of Protestant Christianity.

Families

"We're all kin."

We have seen that many members of Cypress Pond accurately referred to a perceived commonality of Baptist ancestry. Further, they asserted that they were "all kin to each other." In this statement, too, they were accurate, referring to overlapping kinship bonds which linked not only the Cypress Pond membership but also the memberships of most of the local white Baptist churches.

To trace these ties, I conducted structured genealogical interviews with congregational members.[17] Once again, memories seemed limited to the living or the recently dead. Many in their seventies could not remember their own grandparents' names or dates pertinent to these ancestors. Even though this may not seem unusual, what struck me was the paucity of written family records. Some members actually visited cemeteries to obtain dates of birth and death for me. Fortunately for my purposes, county courthouse records had been researched by a member of Southville's elite. He had compiled a countywide genealogy that was privately printed in the 1960s. Using this source in conjunction with the interview data, I traced ancestors of many of today's members of Cypress Pond back to the founding of the county in the late 1700s and early 1800s. Among the early settlers were the John Sims family, who settled in Salkehatchie prior to 1830; the Lawrence Green family, who settled there about 1830; several Thames brothers, who were established by the time of the 1850 census; and the Wayne Eckhart family, who arrived around 1785. Even though tracing the genealogical ties of church members proved complicated, I established that most church members were indeed related through consanguinal or affinal ties with others in the church.

I soon discovered, however, that knowing that everyone was related to everyone else was only a beginning point. As Bryant (1981) discusses at length in *We're All Kin*, such statements do not tell the whole story. The pool of potential kin was much larger than the entire list of those on the church rolls—451 names at Cypress Pond alone. How did members decide which kin were closest to them in the church or in the larger community? Or, as Alice Kasakoff once observed to me, southern kin groups appear to function as a pool from which the southerner draws friends (Kasakoff, personal communication). Both these researchers refer to the element of choice involved in deciding with which kin one will ally oneself.

This puzzle manifested itself in concrete terms when I first asked the pastor to name the central families found at Cypress Pond. At that time the Reverend Mr. Squires had been living in the community for seven years. He gave the family names as follows: Green, Davidson, Thames, and Jones. Initially, his characterization presented difficulties for me: I was introduced to numerous people with quite different last names. It was only as the fieldwork progressed and as I interviewed members about their genealogical ties that I came to regard his characterization as accurate.

At Cypress Pond, kinship appeared to influence church affiliation in the following manner. Members chose among their bilateral kindred the persons with whom they would affiliate. These choices might differentially emphasize either the mother's or the father's kin. Choices reflected the actual cultural practices of the "native" actors, rather than absolute rules for determining kindred (Keesing 1975:123). One blatant clue to the reckoning of kinship came early in my fieldwork as I watched a church softball game. Samantha Green Richardson, a married woman in her thirties with two children, was talking with her cousin. She made an exaggerated, joking, yet intensely serious statement: "I was a Green when I was born, and I'll be a Green when I get to heaven." This assertion clearly showed Samantha's feelings about her kinship alliances. These alliances were borne out by her associations. She attended Cypress Pond, the church to which her Green ancestors have belonged for generations. She brought her children with her, and they attended regularly. Not so her husband, who was a Richardson. His kinship ties were affinal, having married into the church, and he attended sporadically. At times when I visited in her home, Samantha was surrounded by friends who were also Green kin. She lived on Green land and took her children to play where she played as a child. Sometimes she came early to church and walked alone through the cemetery, looking at the graves of her kin. In effect, she had chosen to remain allied to her father's kinship network and was bringing up her family in the context of those associations in both home and church surroundings.

Others traced their ties in the church through similar paths. Even though an initial examination of the Nichols brothers appeared to indicate a strong emphasis on the male line, this was not the whole story. Three of the four sons of Marie and Elmer Nichols still attended Cypress Pond. These three sons took active roles here, two of the sons having served as deacons. They brought their wives and young children with them, and all their children were baptized at Cypress Pond (though some of the children, when grown, did not remain members there). Despite these patrilineal leanings, the Nichols brothers trace their kinship ties to the church through their mother, who was a Thames. When she was younger (she was in her eighties in 1985), she had exercised a strong hold on her family, insisting that her grown, married children come to her home each Sunday for huge family dinners. At these dinners the doings of family, church, and community were discussed with relish and sometimes, according to one daughter-in-law, with a tinge of malice.

Another example of family membership comes from a woman who married into the Davidson family. In this instance, her maiden name was Green, and she had grown up in Cypress Pond. So had her husband. Consequently they could claim affiliation with Cypress Pond on both sides. Nevertheless, Joan had distanced herself from many of her Green kin by the time she was sixty. Her parents were dead, and though her siblings lived in the area, they did not attend Cypress Pond on a regular basis. Her husband's family attended in large numbers. All of her immediate neighbors and her best friend also were Davidsons. When asked about her kinship ties to other Greens in the church, she claimed that they were "distant" kin, when, in fact, according to the county courthouse records, they were not so distant. It appeared that, over time, she had identified more and more with her husband's kin network.

As I have noted, I do not claim to know all the "rules" by which the choices of alliance are made. Though the "natives" spoke of their kinship ties as natural and as predetermined by blood, they were not fixed in any absolute sense. There are many persons to whom one can claim kinship in such a community. Boundaries of those who can be classified as kin exist: members usually spoke of kin as related through some ties of "blood" or common ancestry (see Schneider 1980). But, among kin, numerous individual decisions are made about which persons in fact are to be counted among one's close kin. The most prominent strategy seen at Cypress Pond for choosing who would be considered close kin rested upon intensity of social interactions. For example, Samantha Green Richardson spent much time in church and in other social settings with a first cousin, Pat, whom she identified as "like a sister." Her "real" sister did not attend Cypress Pond; in fact, she lived about fifty miles away, making close contact more difficult. Samantha had ingeniously transformed her relationship with her cousin into one of sisterhood. Another strategy, illustrated in this discussion, was to identify one's close family ties in terms of the potential family affiliations found within the church itself. Those at Cypress Pond constantly made decisions about how to represent the nature of their kinship ties and how they traced their ties to the church fellowship.

These decisions about kinship were not God-given or even culturally given. They represented actual options. On occasion, persons living in the area and attending Cypress Pond might decide to break their membership ties. Reasons used to justify and rationalize changes usually related to either quarrels with the current pastor or with other members of the church (often kin). Since, by definition, they could not sever their ties of kinship, dissenters might simply stop attending any services. They might also invoke kinship ties in other local churches and switch their membership. Since kin groups usually were quite large, almost everyone had kin who belonged to competing churches. For example, ties with Calvary Baptist Church were especially strong, and several current members of Cypress Pond previously had been members at Calvary.[18]

Seating patterns on Sunday mornings also indicated kinship patterns. Early in my fieldwork, I inadvertently discovered something about seating patterns when I simply sat down in an empty pew. A few minutes later, I looked up and noticed a somewhat distraught woman who stood staring at me as though she could not believe her eyes. Her perusal puzzled me, since there were plenty of empty pews surrounding me, but eventually I learned that I had violated an unwritten rule. This pew informally "belonged" to her family. Though there were no plaques or markers to specify family names for pews, traditional seating patterns were known to regular churchgoers.[19] These seating patterns usually reflected extended kin groupings. Grandparents or great-grandparents sat with their married children, grandchildren, and sometimes great-grandchildren. For instance, one grandfather sat on the third pew from the front, with as many of his eight grown children and their children as happened to attend. One of his daughters, now in her thirties, referred to this custom with tolerance and humor, as she discussed how her father continued to watch the behavior of his children and grandchildren in church, to be sure that it met his approval. Not all members sat on designated pews, since some shifted around and some sat with friends rather than close kin. Nevertheless, the church seating arrangements, viewed with a knowledge of kinship connections, constituted a type of social map based on kin.

The Larger Picture

Throughout this discussion of Cypress Pond, we have encountered a recurrent theme: individuals choose to identify themselves as Baptist through kinship bonds. Since believers formed part of a larger kinship network, the entire church organization was affected by the kinship alliances of its members. These alliances extended beyond the local congregation to encompass much of the white community surrounding the church. Being Baptist was more than a statement of doctrinal belief; it was also a statement about family, kinship ties, place, and history.

Beginning with my concrete experience of fusion between place, church, and family, this chapter has traced that fusion to underlying historical and demographic realities. Other studies of American kinship in the South also have noted a close relationship between these factors. Bryant, in her work on Appalachian kinship, specifically relates the proliferation of churches to the tendency for a family group to form its own church (1981:92–93). She sees family reunions and church homecomings as evidence of the link between church and family. In Appalachia, homecomings, which usually are held annually, center around cemeteries associated with each church. Families return to the church and its associated cemetery to celebrate their common heritage. Bryant suggests that these homecomings or family reunions symbolize the close kinship that should exist between members of the family of God.

Of course, this closeness cannot be maintained because of outmigration and because of "the frailty of human beings and the imperfections of the world" (1981:120).

Neville, in *Kinship and Pilgrimage*, argues that a cultural complex of family reunions, church homecomings, and denominational conference centers offer southerners who have left their home communities a chance to return and to renew their ties with the Protestant community of believers from which they came. In addition, she analyzes these events as cultural texts which created meaning for those who left the tightly knit communities of Europe for the American South and for each subsequent resettlement and move farther west. Taking the perspective of the "leavers" rather than the "stayers," Neville argues that the texts enacted at southern family reunions and church homecomings unite, however briefly, the American cultural themes of individualism with corporatism, with *communitas*. To return to the family fold for a brief reunion is, she believes, an inversion of the medieval Catholic pilgrimage to holy places. Southern Protestants make pilgrimages to their places of family origin and derive from their pilgrimage a meaningful tie to a sacred community of believers that also happens to encompass their kin ties.

My analysis differs from Neville's in that the focus has been on the world view of those left behind in each generation's outmigration. For the most part, residents of Cypress Pond had not experienced the displacement or severing of ties to place, even though each generation had undergone disruption when members who were kin left. For "stayers," like Michelle, deep roots of belonging reached back into a common past that was taken for granted—a past that was represented physically in places like the fields across which Michelle, her aunts, and I walked; and actualized through narratives that shaped shared meaning in subtle and almost intangible ways. The aunts, Isobel and Susie, were outmigrants, engaged in evoking *communitas* when they spoke of their past lives and their experience of the bonds between place and family.

Both Neville's and Bryant's analyses focus on the unification of family and religion. The "real" meanings of events stem from their affirmation of the community, the family of God, as a family here on earth. This chapter has looked not so much at researchers' interpreted "meanings" of family reunions or of family or of community, but rather at the fusion of these markers with self-identity, and at the historical and cultural reasons for that fusion. Let us make the contrast with researchers' inferences more explicit. Members did not talk about family reunions as reunions of the family of God. Nor did they consciously or overtly tease apart the fusion to show how it became their world view. For them, it simply *was* their reality.

When researchers infer that these various representations of the family on earth are equivalent to symbolic statements about the family of God, they make a Durkheimian symbolic leap from the concrete group to the sacred moral community. While I do not dispute this link, I am suggesting that family, place, and church mean more here than the reification of the family on earth with the family of God. Meanings come from the feelings evoked, the ethos experienced, on a day-to-day basis. These meanings may not be articulated, may not even be thought about consciously, because they are so much a part of self-identity. To separate notions of family, place, and church from each other or to equate them solely with this larger truth would, in a sense, diminish their meaning. In fact, if members took an analytical point of view, they might well raise the question of why this world view exists. Doing so, in all likelihood, would lead them to explore the reasons why this world view remains both so all-important and so far from their conscious awareness.

So we return again to the provincial nature of these SBC members' lives. The very truths and realities created in their interactions define, just as all cultural traditions do, the boundaries of their world, and the limits beyond which the foundations of knowledge would be questioned. Thus, it is necessary to separate meanings here, because seeing what family, place, and religion mean from an analytical standpoint does not translate into the interactional level of meaning where culture is created and sustained.

3

Cypress Pond Demographics, Activities, and Social Structure

In the previous chapter, I argued that the ethos of family, place, and Baptist affiliation creates a bounded and rooted sense of identity for church members. But not all church members are alike. Some come to church frequently and center their lives around church activities. Others come infrequently or not at all. As in any social organization, some members lead, others follow, and still others actively dissent from the main position, whatever it is. Such variation constitutes an inherent part of any cultural system. This chapter presents demographic and ethnographic information to show how Cypress Pond is organized, the activities available to members, and the range of variation in the membership and in participation in church affairs. Even though each Southern Baptist Convention congregation has local autonomy and local authority in how it chooses to organize, in practice most SBC churches have organizational structures similar to those described here. Individual variation thus occurs within a highly developed bureaucratic context.[1]

We begin by examining church attendance, since whether or not one attended church had a significant bearing on participation in the local church community. Bear in mind, however, that in this context church attendance was more an indicator of faithfulness than an absolute gauge of involvement. Since family ties cut across church attendance patterns, and since the community itself traditionally was demarcated by these same kin ties, it was possible for a local resident to know most of what happens at Cypress Pond without setting foot on its grounds.

Cypress Pond Demographics

Attendance

After religious affiliation, church attendance was the second most important aspect in assessing a person's religious status. This emphasis on attendance can be found in historical documents concerning Baptist memberships. In the earliest minutes of church meetings at Cypress Pond, references are made to members who were derelict in attending church services. For example, in 1891, the clerk was instructed "to 'write off' the names of absentees and give them to a Committee that would be appointed to cite them to attendance" (*Cypress Pond Church History*). This monitoring of fellow churchgoers' behaviors has continued. Although Cypress Pond no longer formally cited those who did not attend, members informally noted who came and who did not. They also sporadically organized a "Visitation Committee" which drew up a list of Cypress Pond members who were not attending and potential "prospects" for evangelical recruitment. Representatives from the committee then drove to the homes of these individuals and told those who were not attending that they should be coming to church. Such visits might also involve explicit censuring of other behaviors and verbal accusations that a particular individual was not truly saved.[2]

Given the importance assigned to church attendance, I too monitored attendance patterns and used information from key informants to determine which members did not come to church regularly. After classifying members by attendance, I interviewed households of church attenders.[3] Those who never attended or who no longer resided in the area were excluded from household interviews, since my research interests lay with those who were currently attending.

In developing my classification, I began with the church rolls. While, according to Baptist tradition, this roll list should not include the names of unbaptized children, in fact the list given to me by Squires did include these. To the list he gave me, I added the names of infants born into the church and those baptized while I was in the field. I also included the names of those individuals who died during the fieldwork period. The final tally included 451 names. Of these, Squires told me that he thought about 100 names on the list referred to people who had once lived in the community but who had since moved away. Interviews with key informants indicated that only 33 of those listed actually lived outside the community. Potentially, then, 418 members could attend regularly if they chose to do so.

Of the three regularly scheduled weekly meetings, Sunday morning worship services drew the biggest crowd, numbering between 120 and 130. The Sunday evening worship service was poorly attended, with between 30 and 45 attending. Attendance at the Wednesday night prayer meeting also numbered between 30 and 45.

After attending services for ten months, I still found that I had not met everyone on the church rolls. I went down the roll list with key informants, asking about each name. From this information and from my own observations, I categorized the members of Cypress Pond into one of five groups based upon their attendance patterns: *core attenders, regular attenders, occasional attenders, nonattenders,* and *nonresidents.* In this classification I defined *core attenders* as members who attended all three weekly services on a regular basis throughout the duration of my fieldwork. This group would probably have looked quite different if Squires had not left Cypress Pond to serve another congregation in the middle of the fieldwork period. His departure exposed political factions in the church, affected attendance patterns, and provided a unique opportunity for observation. Some "three-meeting" attenders suddenly stopped coming. Other members began to come to all three meetings. By my definition, neither of these sets is included as core attenders; that is, I have characterized core attenders by their loyalty to the church community itself, rather than to a particular pastor. This core group was small; only twenty-five persons met the criteria.

The category of core attenders (those members who come faithfully to all three church services despite changes in pastors) also corresponds to a folk category of faithfulness. One joke circulating during my fieldwork captures the essence of this belief: "Those who come to church on Sunday morning love their pastor; those who come on Sunday evening love their church; those who come on Wednesday night love the Lord."

Four other groups were based on Sunday morning attendance. *Regular attenders* came frequently to services throughout the year but were not present for all services. *Occasional attenders* came just a few Sundays out of the entire year. The attendance of someone from the latter category was often noted by fellow churchgoers as "unusual." There were 154 regular attenders and 83 occasional attenders (34 percent and 18.4 percent of the total list, respectively).

Nonattenders lived in the area but never came to Cypress Pond. Some attended other churches but, for one reason or another, left their names on the rolls of Cypress Pond. Others never attended church at all, eliciting much censure from their churchgoing relatives. The nonattenders matched the regular attenders in number, 154 or 34 percent. Finally, as mentioned above, 33 persons (7.3 percent)—the *nonresidents*— had moved from the area and did not attend Cypress Pond.

Though the sanctuary could have been packed beyond its seating capacity every Sunday, my observations indicated that 41 percent of church members never came during the fourteen months I was in the field, and another 18 percent came rarely. Such absences, a phenomenon well known to congregations of all denominations, raises a deep, fundamental concern at Cypress Pond, for churchgoers worry not about unknown others, but about kin.

Education, Sex, Age, and Economic Distributions

In the process of collecting genealogical information, I also collected basic demographic information.[4] The educational level of the Cypress Pond congregation was high in one sense and low in another, when compared with the state's white population as a whole (U.S. Department of Commerce, Part 42, 1980:41–42). On the one hand, few members had completed college, and few had attended college or technical schools of any sort. Thus, there were no doctors, nurses, lawyers, or judges, and just a handful of teachers. On the other hand, a higher percentage of Cypress Pond adults had completed high school than the state average. Still, more than one-fourth of the congregation had not finished high school, and many of the older members had only a grade-school education.

Parents at Cypress Pond expressed discontent with the impact of state and federal laws governing the separation of church and state. They bemoaned the absence of prayer in the public schools. Many of these parents felt that the school system itself constituted one more corrupting influence, separating children from the church. These parents believed that only one world view should be taught in the school system, that of evangelical Christianity. At the same time, they did want their children to excel in the academic subjects taught in the classroom.

Among adults who attended Cypress Pond, the numbers of males and females were roughly equal. Though there were more older women than men, both sexes were represented equally in each age grade during Sunday morning worship services. However, young adults, both men and women aged twenty to twenty-nine, were significantly underrepresented among church attendees, numbering fewer than those in any other age group.

In attendance at Sunday evening services and on Wednesday nights, age discrepancies were apparent. Here there was a bimodal distribution. The "youth," aged three to seventeen, came as did those aged fifty and older. Very few in the middle age range attended; parents in their thirties and forties routinely dropped their children off at church and picked them up afterwards. Squires remarked on this demographic pattern, stating that attendance was good among the "youth" and "older folks."

In the recent past, a significant shift had occurred with respect to the economic status of church members. Though Cypress Pond stood on a country farm-to-market road, surrounded by fields and forest, members of Cypress Pond no longer were able to support themselves by farming. During my fieldwork, the last full-time farmer was forced to take a job at one of the local manufacturing plants to make ends meet. He and several others were working full-time at industrial jobs while continuing to farm part-time. Despite this shift, members continued to identify themselves as part of an agrarian community. Pastors preaching at Cypress Pond made frequent references to the lives of farmers and to the farming lifestyle.

However, 44 percent of the church's adults (males and females, excluding those who have retired) worked for one of five local plants. These five employers all had come to the area after 1950, constituting the major sources of economic growth for the region. The other sources of employment for church members were local stores, government agencies such as schools and state offices, and, for a privileged few, their own small businesses. Only 14 percent of the women of working age stayed at home. Of these, half supplemented their family income by caring for the children of other working women.

This shift in employment to the industrial sector had brought with it an increased prosperity. Some church members with combined family incomes of approximately $50,000 in 1985 were able to afford pleasure boats, vacation homes, and new homes. Others, especially the older generation, had difficulty making ends meet on Social Security (as low as $5,000 a year). Several church members had either applied for federal aid or had received federal aid in the form of food stamps. Thus, Cypress Pond members' income varied widely. Members in 1985 supported a church budget of $78,000, maintaining a $5,000 savings account. This budget appeared to be sufficient to meet the needs of this congregation, including paying the salary of a full-time pastor ($16,000). Indeed, no financial difficulties of any sort were faced by this church congregation during the course of my fieldwork, though there was some discussion of potential difficulties if contributions were not increased.

In summary, the congregation of Cypress Pond attended Sunday morning worship services with more regularity than any other weekly service. Though not everyone who could came to church frequently, there were no major financial or personnel difficulties in maintaining this viable organization. Congregation members saw potential problems for the church in the economic sector and in recent "secularization" of the schools.

Activities

Church activities were the central social outlets for many members. In addition to the three regularly scheduled weekly meetings—Sunday morning services, Sunday evening services, and Wednesday night prayer meetings—the church had other regularly scheduled events. Depending on their age and sex, members could choose from monthly meetings for the "youth" and for senior citizens; monthly Women's Missionary Meetings; and, for men, monthly meetings of the Brotherhood. Within the church context, members marked significant life events and celebrated an annual cycle of church, national, and local holidays. Many of these might be attended by both church members and visiting family and friends. Depending on the event, attendance might swell beyond the capacity of the church to seat all who came. Church activities such as recreational sports and parties, considered to be most "social" in nature, might draw some members who seldom attended the worship services.

Throughout the year, various ceremonies marked significant life events for individuals. Baptism, weddings, and funerals were scheduled as need arose. During worship services, special rituals recurred each year to celebrate various stages in the life cycle. The life events celebrated at Cypress Pond during the main worship services were:

1. Baby Dedication Day: Recognized parents and their infants. Parents pledged to raise the child in the church.
2. Baptism by full immersion: Ritual marking an individual as saved. It usually occurred between the ages of eight and twelve.
3. Graduation: Marked graduation from high school or college.
4. Mother's Day: Recognized the role of motherhood. Often the oldest and youngest mothers present were specially recognized.
5. Father's Day: Recognized the role of fatherhood.
6. Men's Day: Honored men's roles in the church. A special breakfast for men only was cooked by women prior to the worship service.
7. Senior Citizen's Day: Honors senior citizens' roles in the church. A special dinner on the church grounds prepared by the younger members was served after the worship service.

The annual church calendar also celebrated Christian and national holidays. Other special events recurred during week-long periods of each year. The yearly calendar included:[5]

1. The Lord's Supper: A ritual celebration of the Last Supper of Christ, or communion. The Lord's Supper was held on the first Sunday of each quarter during the year (that is, the first Sunday of January, April, July, and October).
2. Easter: Celebrated with a special sunrise service, breakfast, and regular worship service.
3. Spring Revival Services: A week of special worship services held on Sundays and each night of the week (except Saturday night and some-

times Friday night). These services were designed to bring new members into the group and to revitalize the current members.

4. Vacation Church School (VCS) or Bible School: A week of activities designed for the church youth, aged 3–17. Bible classes were held at night each day of this week. Children also participated in craft activities and played softball for recreation. A hamburger cookout occurred on the last evening of VCS. Finally, during the subsequent Sunday evening worship service, the youth presented a program demonstrating what they had learned in VCS.

5. Independence Day: Celebrated in a day-long event on July 4, including softball games and a barbecue meal.

6. Fall Revival Services: Another week-long series of worship services. See Spring Revival Services above.

7. Harvest Day: A "Homecoming" worship service held each year in October, in which relatives, neighbors, and former members were invited to a special service and dinner on the church grounds.

8. Thanksgiving: Marked by the pastor in the sermons immediately prior to and after the national holiday had been celebrated in the home.

9. Christmas: Marked by holiday parties; a pageant enacting the nativity scene, given by the church children; and sermons immediately preceding and following Christmas Day.

Of these activities, Homecoming formed a special category of celebration. Once a year, neighbors and former church members were invited to attend services at Cypress Pond. Neville (1987) terms rituals of this type "rituals of renewal," since they bring former members back ritually to reaffirm a common origin with friends and kin. This service drew about 350 persons for the Sunday worship service and the barbecue held on the grounds afterwards. An invited guest speaker gave the Sunday morning message to a church so packed that chairs had to be brought in to supplement the pew seats. A party atmosphere pervaded as members visited with relatives who had driven from afar to attend.

Important social activities surrounded the athletic events sponsored by Cypress Pond during the summer and winter. Church softball filled the summer days for players from early May to July. Cypress Pond maintained three teams: a women's team, a men's team, and a children's team. These played as often as two or three times a week, with practices held once a week. After long, hot summer days, members could relax in the evenings as they watched the teams play for hours. Usually, the women's team played first, then the men's, on the same night. Mothers who played on teams would bring their children with them and stay to watch their husbands play. Grandparents came to be with their families and sometimes to watch. The children had their own opportunity to play ball on Saturday mornings. The softball season was followed by a church basketball league in the winter, though fewer members participated in this sport. A typical week's activities during church softball season was packed, as illustrated by this schedule for late May 1985:

Sunday

    Sunday school classes (10–11 A.M.)

    Morning worship service (11–12 A.M.)

    Choir practice (5:30–6:30 P.M.)

    Church training classes or Training Union (6:30–7:30 P.M.)

    Evening worship service (7:30–8:30 P.M.)

Monday

    Women's Missionary Meeting (7–9:30 P.M.)

    Women's softball game (6:30–8:30 P.M.)

    Men's softball game (8:30–10:30 P.M.)

Wednesday

    Prayer meeting service (7:30–8:30 P.M.)

Thursday

    Women's softball game (6:30–8:30 P.M.)

    Men's softball game (8:30–10:30 P.M.)

Friday

    Women's softball game (6:30–8:30 P.M.)

    Men's softball game (8:30–10:30 P.M.)

Saturday

    Children's softball game (10–12 A.M.).

Clearly, church activities at Cypress Pond occupied far more time than the three regularly scheduled services would suggest. Congregation members participated in an annual round of events marking traditional sacred and secular holidays, life cycle events, and these special activities: revivals, homecomings, Vacation Church School, and church athletics. Committed members might occasionally wistfully wish for a night at home.

Formal Social Structure

Since all Southern Baptist Convention (SBC) churches have autonomous standing within the convention, each individual congregation chooses to be affiliated with the SBC and can sever the ties at will. Church property and monies all remain under the control of the local congregation (Eighmy 1972; Hays and Steely 1963). This arrangement affects the local congregation in a number of ways.

Most importantly, the congregation sees itself as having control of its leadership. At the top of the local hierarchy stand the pastor, chosen by vote of the congregation, and six deacons, elected and ordained by the congregation. The nominating committee, also elected by the congregation, chooses additional church leaders who are also ratified by congregational vote. This organizational structure, typical in SBC churches, provides one link between disparate congregations and helps to create an overarching "Baptist" identity for the SBC.

The Pastor: Spiritual Leader of the Congregation

Baptist church members considered the pastor, who must be male, to be the spiritual head of the local church.[6] Pastors were thought to be called by God to their position, and this "call" set them apart from others. Among the tasks performed by the pastor at Cypress Pond were preaching at the two Sunday services and teaching Bible studies on Wednesday nights during the prayer meeting service. Pastors also conducted the ceremonies marking important events in the life cycle: they married couples, conducted funeral services, and baptized new members. Pastors were expected to visit the sick, comfort and counsel bereaved families, and constantly recruit new church members.

Because members perceived pastors as set apart by God, they expected pastors to adhere strictly to the moral code of the Ten Commandments. This code included injunctions against cursing, lying, cheating, stealing, and adultery (see Exodus 20). Not only were pastors required to live within these constraints, but also they were expected willingly to manifest certain behaviors emulating Christ. These included "selflessness" when called upon to visit the sick or comfort the bereaved at any time of day or night. Pastors received criticism if they did not attend assiduously to these duties. Another area of tension between pastors and their flock stemmed from the congregation's perception that pastors should not be concerned with material success. The congregation paid the pastor's salary, provided him with a home, paid for his transportation costs, and believed that these expenses constituted sufficient compensation for "a man of God." If the pastor had a family, they too were expected to show dedication to God through their behaviors. In everything they did, pastors and their families were expected to lead exemplary lives.

Pastors were called not only to the ministry, but also to the churches they served. In this system, pastors were not assigned churches by hierarchical administrators but instead waited on the "call of God" before accepting a position as pastor of any church. In practice, this meant that a congregation often was left without a pastor when its pastor decided to shift churches.

After a congregation lost its pastor, a "pulpit committee" or "search committee" was elected. These members, five in the case of Cypress Pond (three men, two women), visited other churches and talked with pastors, searching for a replacement. When a candidate was found, they prayed about whether he was the right person for the church to "call." The candidate too prayed, seeking to know if God had called him to this church. Once both the search committee and the candidate acknowledged receiving affirmative answers from God, the pastor preached a trial sermon to the congregation. The congregation then voted on whether or not to accept that pastor for their church. A congregation also could decide that its pastor should leave. Some churches gained reputations for being hard to please, asking pastors to leave every six months to a year. Among the reasons a pastor might be asked to leave were flagrant violations of the moral code, failure to meet the congregation's standards in preaching style or visitation, or simply that he did not "suit."

Since most pastors did not serve in their home communities, they had to please the local congregation and its leaders without being able to draw support from kinship ties. This left the pastor especially vulnerable to criticism. In actuality, pastors' behaviors frequently fell short of the perfection expected. During my time at Cypress Pond, there were two pastors. The first, Squires, had served the church for seven years before leaving to accept a call to another church. He had both supporters and detractors among the congregation. At the time I met him, he was in his fifties. A tall man with erect bearing, he reported being called to the ministry in his twenties. Following that call, he attended a Bible college for two years before pastoring his first church. This was his only training beyond high school. While members praised his preaching style, they frequently criticized his family. In the opinion of many, his wife wore jeans too much, did too little in the home and church, and sometimes failed to attend services. His son, they said, was "wild" and uncontrollable, drinking alcohol and staying out too late. These criticisms spilled over onto Squires, since he was supposed to control their wayward behaviors. He commented on these criticisms in his last, rather accusatory sermon to the church, noting that pastors and their families lived in a "fishbowl."

The second pastor, Manning, was an interim pastor; that is, he had retired from full-time ministry several years before and now was serving as a temporary, part-time pastor for churches searching for a full-time pastor. In contrast to Squires, Manning had extensive college and seminary training. His sermons, while traditional Bible-Belt Baptist in content, were frequently too sophisticated for his "flock." Many members complained that they could not follow him when he preached. As interim pastor, he did not live in the community, nor did he take an active role in local church affairs.

Despite the limitations on their authority, pastors at Cypress Pond did have considerable power to influence congregation members. Though they had to rely on persuasion and on their personal reputations as men of God, they had many opportunities to sway the congregation. They preached sermons in which they could air opinions and, depending on their skill, subtly alter opinion. They conducted Bible classes in which they could actively "educate" the congregation. A pastor who was a good speaker and had a spotless reputation had tremendous personal clout.

Deacons: Ordained Congregational Leaders

As leadership ultimately was in the hands of the congregation, the six deacons, in a sense, held more power than pastors at Cypress Pond. Pastors came and went, but deacons were part of the local community and remained part of it when a pastor left. According to the by-laws of this congregation, the deacons were elected and ordained by the congregation, served three-year terms as unpaid leaders, and had to be male. A deacon had to step down at the end of his term and take a year off before he was eligible for reelection. Each year two deacons stepped down and two new ones were chosen. Even though the pool of ordained deacons at Cypress Pond was more numerous than the six positions available, many deacons frequently served multiple terms.

Because deacons were elected from the local congregation and because the congregation was kin-based, those men elected as deacons tended to have multiple kinship ties within the church, drawing their support from these ties. Of course, the behavior of individual men was considered in the selection of deacons. Those elected deacons during the fieldwork period were observed to be regular churchgoers. They exhibited concern for the church and took an active role in church affairs. The personal lives of deacons were scrutinized closely by the congregation, and deacons were expected to abide by the moral code of the community.

Deacons met in closed sessions with the pastor to make decisions about the ongoing operation of the church. These decisions generally were relayed to the congregation, and no important decisions could be made without a vote of the congregation. Other duties of the deacons involved public and private prayer and public service during worship services. For example, they collected monetary offerings to the church by passing plates to the congregation during worship services. Deacons also were responsible for conducting portions of an important church ritual, the Lord's Supper (Communion service), given four times a year at Cypress Pond.

Additional Church Leaders

Other church offices entailed decision-making authority. While, technically, the occupants of these offices were elected, recruitment for any such position usually was more like a draft. Typically only one name was proposed per position, and all were ratified in one vote of the congregation. The only time members selected from one of several candidates was when vacancies occurred for the paid positions of church secretary and church custodian. Then members voted by secret ballot for one of the candidates available for the job.

Each year a nominating committee of six individuals was proposed by the previous year's nominating committee. The nominating committee generally worked long hours in filling all the positions available. Each year the committee formally presented its recommendations to the congregation, which then voted on the choices. For example, the list the group submitted for the church year running from October 1, 1985, through September 30, 1986, contained a total of 195 names (some members filled more than one position). Listed were different committees (e.g., youth committee, bus committee, flower committee, benevolence committee); teaching positions (for all the various classes on Sunday morning, Sunday evening, and Wednesday night); and positions such as church hostess and music director. The committee had checked with persons nominated to make sure that those they chose would agree to take on the responsibility. Sometimes it was difficult to find persons willing to accept a job. For example, the committee had asked at least two people to teach the Sunday morning women's class, aged twenty-five to thirty-four, before finding a third person who agreed to take the class.

Among those leaders frequently asked to meet with the pastor to discuss church affairs were the following: director of the Sunday school,[7] director of the Training Union, music director, church treasurer, director of the Women's Missionary Union, and Brotherhood director. These positions were representative of the typical bureaucratic structure of SBC churches. Each of these persons, except for the treasurer, oversaw major portions of the church's ongoing social activities.

The Sunday school director reported on Sunday school meetings and made sure that the classes ran smoothly. Sunday school met for an hour every Sunday morning before the main worship service began. Members came to classes for training in Bible study. In Baptist churches, these classes traditionally had been graded by age and sex. At Cypress Pond, boys and girls attended classes together until age twelve, at which time they were segregated by sex. Teenagers of high-school age and young, single adults returned to mixed classes. At Cypress Pond, adults aged twenty-five to thirty-four could attend sex-segregated classes, or they could choose to attend a "Couples' Class." After this age, all classes were once again divided by sex and age grades.

The Training Union director oversaw the classes held on Sunday night prior to the evening worship service. For adults, this training concentrated on learning about the various mission programs of the church and about how to reach potential converts. For younger children, the classes were a time to learn more about missions and about the Bible, in conjunction with play activities and singing.

The music director had responsibility for the choir, organist, and pianist. The number of choir members ranged from five or six for Sunday night services to about fifteen for Sunday mornings. The music director conducted choir practice and trained the singers in the "special music" sung solely by the choir during worship services. She generally chose these special songs and might sometimes assist the pastor in choosing congregational hymns as well.

The Women's Missionary Union (WMU) director was responsible for coordinating the Women's Missionary Meetings in which Baptist missionary activities were discussed. These meetings were age-graded and were open only to adult females. Traditionally, southern women met once a month in "missionary society" gatherings. These might be held either in a home or at church and involved a prepared program about missionary activities, followed by socializing as members ate either a home-cooked meal or dessert together. There were three such groups meeting monthly at Cypress Pond. They ranged in size from a group of about five women to one with an average attendance of twelve.

The Brotherhood meetings were the male equivalent of the WMU. At Cypress Pond, these meetings took place once a month during Wednesday night services and did not involve communal eating. Not being male, I did not attend these activities.

From the standpoint of formal social organization, the church bureaucracy was tied directly to the local congregation. All positions had to be ratified by the congregation, and all positions were subject to recall. There were many opportunities for service in the local congregation, as teachers or leaders of the many classes or groups which met on a regular basis. Directors of programs had decision-making power, as did deacons and the pastor. Such a system worked well when group consensus was high. When discord developed, the potential for disruption was great, since the ultimate locus of power was the individual voter. Baptists have tended to minimize this disruptive potential by focusing strongly on an ethic of "togetherness in the Lord" (Farnsley 1993; Greenhouse 1986; Heriot 1993).

Informal Social Structure

While control of the formal social structure resided in the patriarchal power invested in the pastor and deacons, an informal basis of power underlay the formal structure and allowed women more input than the preceding section would indicate. One gained status informally in the same way one gained power as an elected church leader—that is, through frequent church attendance and willingness to help. As long as members knew nothing detrimental about an individual's character (e.g., that he or she drank alcohol, cursed, or "fooled around"), then church service provided a way to ensure that her or his opinions would be taken into account.

Many women gained prestige in this fashion. While women, especially mothers in their late twenties and early thirties, expressed discontent that their views were not heard, in fact they had some input into church decisions. However, they could wield influence only in roles traditionally defined as appropriate for women. For example, those women who were members of the core group often were consulted about church affairs. Several of the women in this core group were wives of deacons, but others had gained prestige in their own right. Though women did not feel that they had the right to make motions at church business meetings, they would talk about their concerns during the meetings. One telling interaction occurred in a business meeting a month before a scheduled church Homecoming.

Each year Cypress Pond members provided a dinner for this once-a-year event. Members of the local congregation, neighbors visiting from other churches, and former members were invited to the celebration. Held on Sunday morning, attendance generally swelled to over 350 persons. Providing food for that many people was no small task. Since the women were expected to do the cooking—which would involve days of preparation, getting up early on Sunday morning to finish preparing the food, and serving it at the event—many did not look forward to the work. The discussion that night revealed tension concerning gender-role expectations and shifting power relations.

Squires, the pastor, introduced the subject of the Homecoming preparations, saying that the deacons had agreed that they preferred to have a picnic lunch afterwards. John Thames, one of the deacons, however, inquired, "Didn't we half-promise the ladies we'd do a barbecue this year?"

Sara Eckhart said adamantly, "Yes, you did."

The women present went on to say that preparing the food was quite time-consuming and that their husbands did not help.

Squires acknowledged that it was hard to enjoy yourself at such an affair if you had been up since five A.M. cooking. He teased Edna Davidson, saying, "Doesn't your husband help you?"

She replied, "Well, at least I can get him to peel potatoes."

Another one of the deacons present, Sim Davidson, requested that the women bring apple pie for dessert. Sara crisply said, "Bring it yourself if you want to be sure it's there!"

After this lighthearted but serious joking between the members of the two sexes present, a motion was made by John Clark and seconded by Sim Davidson that the church pay to have the barbecue provided by a male member of the church who operated a barbecue restaurant. The men then began making arrangements to help with the barbecue, maintaining a traditional division of labor based on sex. The sexual division of labor in the church was fairly rigid. Women managed all aspects of cooking (except barbecuing), arranging for parties, dinners on the church grounds, and food to be taken to sick and bereaved families. Thus, when a young, single male who had newly joined the church baked and brought a lemon custard pie to a social event, everyone commented on his pie and teased him unmercifully.

Women also were in charge of both the secretarial and custodial duties. They sent out newsletters, swept, and kept the buildings in order. In contrast, men managed the money decisions of the church and did most of the public speaking.

Since women had most of the primary childcare responsibilities, they had a large say in the choice of church literature for teaching children. They usually taught the children's Sunday and Wednesday Bible classes. Women organized the Easter Egg hunts, the Christmas program given by the children, the week-long Bible training program for children during the summer, and innumerable tasks of this type. In these traditional women's roles, women freely made decisions and took charge. But it was clear from discussions of their role in the business decisions of the church that they knew their power was a *limited* power.

Conclusion

This voluntary church organization, operated by the congregation, depended on the goodwill of its constituents to maintain its weekly activities. While about 60 percent of its membership never came to church, or came only rarely, the other 40 percent sustained an active, viable church. Financially sound, with activities scheduled throughout the week and backed by a core group that continued to support the church despite pastoral vicissitudes, Cypress Pond stood as a symbol of the evangelical tradition made manifest in the community.

4

Preaching Salvation

Blessed assurance, Jesus is mine! Oh, what a foretaste of glory divine!
Heir of salvation, purchase of God, Born of his Spirit, wash'd in His blood.
This is my story, this is my song, Praising my Saviour all the day long;
This is my story, this is my song, Praising my Saviour all the day long.
—Crosby and Knapp, in Sims (1956)

"Blessed Assurance, Jesus is mine!" Thus begins the song from which the title of this work is drawn. So evocative of the evangelical themes discussed throughout this book, it was my favorite hymn when I was teenager attending the United Methodist Church. The words of the entire hymn are more optimistic than either the usual hymns or the typical messages of salvation spoken in southern Protestant churches. The hymn's emphasis on the achievement of salvation celebrates the joy that ideally accompanies such assurance.

But in the introduction to this book and in chapter 1, we saw that others do not accept that this joy, this assurance, on the part of believers is authentic simply because the believer says so. Rather, the song would seem to embody an illusory aim. This chapter shows that sermons at Cypress Pond conveyed, in subtle and not-so-subtle ways, a different message: rather than celebrating salvation, they often implied that the believer's salvation experience might be spurious.

The worship service itself, in which sermons routinely are delivered, is of central importance in southern Protestantism, because believers generally expect the moment of salvation to occur and to be affirmed in this ritual context. According to Hill, "evangelism of this type considers the church important precisely because it is the place where life's greatest event [conversion] occurs. Moreover, it is regarded as the primary sphere for one's living out his service to God" (1966:82).

The focus of the Christian's world in such a cultural system is the church institution. There is almost no sense in which these Christians think of their "work" outside the church as a vocation. Rather, their primary concern in the world outside the church is the saving of souls (Hill 1966:82). This separation of two domains, sacred church from secular world, was epitomized in Cypress Pond by members who worked for a company making weapons of war, apparently without seeing any contradiction between such a pursuit and Christ's commandment that individuals should "turn the other cheek" in conflicts.[1] For many devout Southern Baptists at Cypress Pond, this emphasis on the church institution as the context in which Christian life was experienced translated into a view that church attendance was mandatory. To support the local church was to uphold salvation itself.

Pastors, as leaders of the local church and as primary spokespersons for the belief system during the worship service, had, in sermons, a vested source of power, since it was their task to foster belief through the practice of this powerful genre. Here pastors could, and in fact were expected to, influence or persuade their audience to hold certain beliefs and to take certain actions. Pastors used their rhetorical skills to motivate their congregations, first, in the sacred context of the worship service, and second, in the secular world. Since this belief system demanded of its adherents "proof" of salvation through actions, pastors had to persuade their congregations that they knew the path to salvation, knew how to evaluate who was saved, and knew how the saved manifested salvation. More important, they also had to persuade the congregation that their church was a viable spiritual institution, a place where God spoke to the saved and the saved responded. Though pastors were overtly powerful because of their command of the sermon genre, this system paradoxically required that pastors seem to abdicate that power by humbly asserting that they were mere spokespersons among the fellowship of saved believers.

Though this chapter emphasizes the verbal art of sermons, the reader should keep in mind that sermons constitute only one portion of the worship service and that the "invitational calls" for salvation that generally follow sermons are the major means by which the audience can respond to emotional pleas made during the sermons themselves. These two segments of the service, analyzed in separate chapters of this book, in reality constitute a whole linking the verbal expression of belief with certain behavioral markers that can be measured during the worship service itself. For example, during revival services, pastors and their audiences keep track of how many people have made public professions that they are now "born again." Beyond the traditional focus on the moment of salvation, pastors at Cypress Pond had added a new dimension to the invitational calls during the worship service, by asking members to commit publicly to certain Christian practices. Chapter 6 examines these changes in congregational responses, but their very addition to the worship service supports my arguments about the relationships among language, belief, and action in this cultural system. That is, to hear is to invoke the necessity of a decision about belief, and to believe is to act as a believer.

To show *how* sermons use language to motivate the audience to take action, I draw on theoretical insights from the ethnography of communication. Pioneered by Dell Hymes in the early 1960s, this field examines the "meaning of language in human life" (1972:41). As Duranti summarizes it:

> The ethnography of speaking (henceforth ES) studies language use as displayed in the daily life of particular speech communities. Its method is ethnography, supplemented by techniques developed in other areas of study such as developmental pragmatics, conversational analysis, poetics, and history. Its theoretical contributions are centered around the study of *situated discourse*, that is, linguistic performance as the locus of the relationship between language and the socio-cultural order. (1988:210)

Over the years, the ethnography of communication has developed a clear focus on the patterns of variation which exist in daily language use, both across and within cultural systems (Duranti 1988:210–11). In pioneering the study of language variation, the ethnography of communication has allowed researchers to go beyond simplistic renditions of social systems as monoliths "causing" actors to follow "set" cultural patterns, to reveal instead the processes whereby variation is introduced into a system by the actors themselves. When such variation is introduced, the possibility exists for the creation of new forums for the expression and evaluation of cultural knowledge or belief. Such a process has been occurring at Cypress Pond in the context of changes in the invitational calls.

Pastors' sermons are considered here as verbal art, as linguistic performances that involve both performer (the pastor) and audience (the congregation) in a heightened and emotionally charged atmosphere (Bauman 1977). According to Bauman, "performance as a mode of spoken verbal communication consists in the assumption of responsibility to an audience for a display of communicative competence" (1977:11). Such a perspective assumes that the performer knows that he is accountable to his audience, while the audience, in turn, has standards for evaluating the performance. Because performances create an atmosphere of "heightened awareness of the act of expression" (1977:11), the sermon as a performance serves as an especially intense means of communicating belief. What a pastor says and does from the pulpit transmits powerful images and models to his audience. Verbal actions, as portrayed through verbal art, form one means by which to convey and assess religious beliefs. And, as was discussed in chapter 1, verbal actions in the evangelical tradition also are construed as the prime means by which the "word of God" can influence the hearer both to believe and to act.[2]

When examining how language is used in social context, Hymes argues, researchers should attempt, among other things, to separate the purposes or "ends in view" held by the participants in any given speech event from "the ends as outcomes" or the conventionally recognized purpose of the speaking (1972:62).[3] That is, he suggests that what speakers and hearers agree on as the normative aspect of any particular act of speaking may not necessarily be the same goals as those held during the actual speaking event. Because sermons delivered at Cypress Pond were constructed by pastors to serve different rhetorical functions, it was possible to look for both normative interpretations and possible variation in their actual usage.

Using these distinctions, this chapter considers the historically agreed-upon functions of the sermon genre and variation in the first of the two major rhetorical goals pastors attempt to achieve with their sermons: to bring salvation to the unbeliever. The criterion of belief sought here is an emotional or psychological state of being. The second major rhetorical goal, eliciting commitment to Christianity, is considered in chapter 5. "Commitment" sermons stress actions as criteria of belief. How these same two goals can be manipulated further is shown in chapter 6, which illustrates variation on the part of pastors and members in interpreting the ends, or outcomes, of sermons. Variation thus exists at the pastoral level, and to some extent at the congregational level, on the questions of how one internalizes beliefs and how one makes those beliefs consistent with the overarching theme of salvation.

The Sermon as a Genre of Preaching

Sermons at Cypress Pond represented actual performances of one particular genre of speaking (Hymes 1972:65). According to Hymes, genres have formal characteristics which are identifiable and traditionally recognizable by members of the speech community. Hymes, however, analytically separates the term *genre* from the speech event in which the genre may usually be thought to occur (Hymes 1972:65). That is, while members of Cypress Pond might classify the act of preaching from the pulpit during worship services as a "sermon," this does not mean that the sermon genre might not be invoked in other contexts (for example, when children at play give "sermons," as was reported to me by at least one person at Cypress Pond). Duranti also cautions the ethnographer against making the equation "'one genre: one event' (or, 'one genre type: one event type')" (1983:1). Within a given genre, a range of variation in performance can occur, depending on the social context in which the genre is performed, who the speaker is, and the audience to which the genre is presented (Duranti 1983:1).

Following Duranti, I use the term *speech genre* to mean "a recognized (by its users) unit of discourse with some well-defined features such as sequential organization (viz. which part should come before what), constraints (and expectations) on (some of) its content and form, and socially defined appropriate contexts of use" (1983:20). The term *genre* without the qualifier refers to the traditionally recognizable formal features generally associated with that particular form of speaking. Thus, *speech genre* denotes the sermon as identified and performed at Cypress Pond, while *genre* refers to the historically recognized formal features associated with preaching sermons in general.

Based on its formal characteristics, Samarin (1973) classifies the Protestant sermon as one example of the genre *preaching*. As a genre, preaching also is found in other world religions, such as Islam, Buddhism, and Hinduism, in which the preacher's spoken word is manipulated as an "artifact that his clients recognize as an effective instrument for coping with life's problems" (1973:243). In the case of Protestants, the various forms of preaching stem from the Reformation critique, or "protest," against Catholic liturgical forms of worship (Maltz 1985:118). Maltz asserts that, of the various Protestant reform movements, the one most critical of Catholic liturgical forms of worship was the Reformed-Presbyterian complex, which established

> the basic paradigm of Christian worship that came to dominate most variants of Protestantism in both Great Britain and America. In an important sense, "Calvin set the pattern of worship, though not always of doctrine, for Baptists, Congregationalists, Methodists, and Disciples, and of course Presbyterians, in the entire English-speaking worlds" (Jones 1954:128). This basic Protestant paradigm placed primary emphasis on the role of the minister as a preacher of God's word, maintaining a relatively passive but somewhat variable verbal role for members of the congregation. (Maltz 1985:119)

Within Protestant preaching today, broad differences in genre have been noted between those spontaneous sermons preached in many African-American churches (Davis 1985; Gumperz 1982:188–89; Bruce Rosenberg 1970) and in southern Appalachian churches (Bryant 1981:102–3; Dorgan 1987; Titon 1988), and the more formal preaching styles relying on some form of written text. Some Protestant groups such as the Quakers dispense with the sermon altogether, in part as a "protest" against the typical Protestant worship service (Bauman 1974; Maltz 1985). However, at Cypress Pond, these SBC Baptists appeared to be direct heirs of the Reformation, in that their general form of worship followed what Maltz termed the "basic paradigm of Christian worship." The pastor preached, the congregation listened.

The Setting of Cypress Pond Sermons

At Cypress Pond, sermons were recognized by the congregation as special linguistic phenomena, traditionally given only during worship services. Members of the church spoke of pastors' "preaching" and evaluated the performance of pastors based, in part, on their command of this speech genre. Pastors had two regularly scheduled services each week at which they usually were expected to preach. Of the two, Sunday morning services invariably were held. Sunday evening services sometimes were canceled on special days, such as local high-school graduation or Easter. Both of these worship services generally lasted about an hour, with the sermon occupying about half the time. The third type of worship service, the revival, called for a special emphasis on evangelism and occurred only over week-long periods in the spring and fall.

The audience for these services varied. Between 120 and 130 persons usually were present for Sunday morning worship services. Attendance dropped to between 30 and 45 persons for the evening services; many who attended this service were faithful churchgoers. Revival attendance also varied, from about 40 to over 100.

Pastors prepared a sermon during the week before a service, generally announcing the sermon title in the "bulletin," a printed order of worship distributed prior to each service. The order of worship served as a guide to the sequence of events. Given below is a typical order of worship for a Sunday morning worship service, though it would also describe the sequence of events at a Sunday evening or revival worship service.

Organ prelude (played by the organist)
Call to worship (sung by the choir)
Invocation (given by the pastor)
Choral response (to the invocation, a prayer sung by the choir)
Sunday school report (given by the Sunday school director)
Announcements (given by the pastor)
Hymn (sung by the congregation)
Moments with children (a mini-sermon given only during the morning
    worship service by the pastor to children present)

Prayer (given either by the pastor or a congregation member at the pastor's request)

Hymn (sung by the congregation)

Missionary moments (given only during morning services and read by a member of the choir, generally asking for money for special missionary programs)

Offertory prayer (given by one of the deacons at the pastor's request)

Worship with tithes and offerings (deacons collected money offerings as they passed "plates" down the pews to congregation members)

Special music (sung by the choir)

Reading of scriptures (given by the pastor)

Message (sermon given by the pastor)

Invitational hymn (sung by the congregation)

Benediction (given by the pastor or by a member at the pastor's request)

Organ postlude (played by the organist).

While services generally lasted about an hour, the Sunday morning worship service often exceeded the scheduled hour by five to fifteen minutes. Evening worship services usually ran on schedule, since the church paid for broadcast time on the local radio station. Revival services generally lasted about ninety minutes. In these, pastors preached longer sermons, sometimes extending their speaking for almost an hour. Sermons usually began halfway through the service, immediately after the choir's "special music." These "special" church hymns were chosen by the choir director to fit the theme of a particular sermon. As the "special" ended, the pastor moved from a seat on the raised platform in the front of the church sanctuary to stand behind a large oak pulpit. This visual signal, in this order of worship, indicated that the sermon portion of the service was about to begin.

During the sermon portion, the pastor had complete control, within a given range of expected behaviors. The congregation knew that he would preach a sermon; he knew that the attention of the congregation should now be focused on him and that some of his hearers (those who listened) would evaluate that performance. Since the local congregation had established a set order of worship, they knew when the pastor would preach. Lawless (1988), who studied Pentecostal women pastors, found that she had to rely on scripture readings to establish when the sermon began. Since Pentecostals actively eschewed a set order of worship, Lawless discovered the basic order which underlay the worship service only by repeated observation (Lawless 1980). In contrast, once the pastor of Cypress Pond moved to the pulpit after the "special music" had been sung, everyone in the audience knew exactly what he would do—that is, he would begin to preach.

Characteristic Format of the Sermon Speech Genre

The pastor had a range of options as he entered the performance mode of preaching. Two basic parts had to be performed: he had to read a selected text from the Bible, nearly always in the King James translation; and he had to deliver verbal commentary on the meaning of the text for today's believers. A pastor also might choose to add one or more of these optional parts: introductory remarks, which might include something he had forgotten to mention in the announcements; prayers, either before or after the scripture reading; a prayer at the close of the sermon; or invitational calls asking persons moved by the service to come forward to the front of the church. Some pastors characteristically included one or more of these optional parts; others, for example, rarely prayed during the sermon. Invitational calls had become such a fixed part of the sermon speech genre at Cypress Pond that they could be omitted only under unusual circumstances; they were included in all but six sermons.[4] Their patterning and format are considered in chapter 6.

At Cypress Pond, pastors depended, at least partially, on written notes as they preached. Their use of the sermon speech genre thus derived from a prepared text mode, rather than from a style directed at ongoing audience participation in the sermon. Indeed, during the sermon itself, the only spontaneous audience participation that ever occurred was an occasional sporadic "amen." Such a comment was voiced so infrequently that it always denoted an unusual degree of approval or interest.

In addition to recognizing the sermon genre by its placement in the order of worship and by its content, pastors and members alike recognize the sermon as a verbal performance by the manner in which it is framed, or set apart, linguistically. Speaking of framing, Bauman notes:

> All framing, then, including performance, is accomplished through the
> employment of culturally conventionalized metacommunication. In em-
> pirical terms, this means that each speech community will make use of a
> structured set of distinctive communicative means from among its re-
> sources in culturally conventionalized and culture-specific ways to key
> the performance frame, such that all communication that takes place
> within that frame is to be understood as performance within that commu-
> nity. (1977:16)

Among the communicative means that Bauman lists which may key
performance are: "special codes; figurative language; parallelism; special paralinguistic features; special formulae; appeal to tradition; disclaimer of performance" (1977:16).

At Cypress Pond, pastors frequently used *all* these features in their
performances, according to the norms of the community and of the institutions where the pastors received training. Special codes, which users often labeled as "old-fashioned" or archaic, have been demonstrated cross-
culturally as a feature of verbal art (Bauman 1977:17). For this congregation,
using the King James Version in the scripture readings represented a
special archaic code. While a few members carried modern English
translations of the Bible (such as the Living Bible or the New International Version), pastors still relied on the King James Version for the
pulpit. Members clearly expected them to do so. The few times that a
pastor used another translation always entailed elaborate justifications
for the choice.[5] While pastors, in their actual preaching and prayers,
generally avoided the use of the archaic "Thou," "Thee," "hath," and
similar forms characteristic of the King James Bible, many members of
the congregation adopted these archaic forms in their own prayers.

Pastors also used figurative language, parallelism, and special paralinguistic features to mark their performances. With figurative language,
they creatively related the scriptural text to some application useful for
their congregation. For example, in the sermon text presented in appendix A ("What Is Sin?"), Squires links the biblical account of King
David's adultery with Bathsheba to the sins of his congregation. He
speaks of how David began to think about disobeying God, and then,
"little by little," David began to disobey. He tells his congregation,

"That's the way sin is, and when sin, when that doubt comes into our minds, it always leads to disobedience. First the thought, then the deed."

Parallelism frequently was used to build the sermon to a climax, as a pastor pled with members to respond to the invitational call. For example, in a sermon describing the judgment day at the end of time, Manning included this parallel structure near the end of the sermon:

> Now you look at the judge as you see him sitting there.
> You look at him carefully.
> And you say that can't be Jesus.
> Look at the fire coming from his eyes.
> Look at the sword coming out of his mouth.
> Look (at) that can't be the Lord.
> (Evening Worship Service, March 6, 1986)[6]

Such parallelism, in conjunction with special paralinguistic features such as prosody and pitch, serve as defining features of what may be described as the affective component of the sermons. Pastors varied their tones and the loudness of their voices in a rhythmical pattern to enhance the emotional impact of their words. I identify this pattern informally as a "Southern Baptist rhetorical style" because it appeared to be universally shared among the eleven pastors I heard at Cypress Pond, and among other Southern Baptists I have heard elsewhere. Mastery of the pattern varied, however. Though these paralinguistic components of sermons beg for in-depth analysis, some glimpse of its powerful use can be captured in the following passage spoken by the Reverend Mr. Deere, a visiting pastor. To show prosody, this excerpt has been transcribed using techniques from conversational analysis:[7]

> [Speaking of Jesus' death and resurrection]
> (I) (I) I like to meditate on that,
> You know, I don't know how much we can love angels.
> You can stand there and be frightened to death of them,
> And stand in awe of them,
> And obey them,
> And bow before them, and all of that.
> But just actually to love an angel,

I don't know how much love you can,

You can find in your heart for an angel.

But when you think about Jesus,

One like us, that

Flesh and ˳blood

One like us ˳(that)

A man of SORROW as he stood by open graves and wept,

He wept.

He b:ore? our :infirmities, beloved.

:One? like? us, see.

He died for our sin.

He :arose from the dead on our part,

And now we can say, ":O DEATH WHERE? IS THY STING." [1 Cor. 15:55]

We can stand by the grave and,

Before Jesus that was final, that was final,

But now we can stand there and say to death,

"O DEATH? WHERE? IS THY STING?

O GRAVE? WHERE? IS THY VICTORY?" [1 Cor. 15:55]

It's not final,

It's not complete,

For # "[t]he sting of death is sin; and the strength of sin

    is the LAW.#

BUT THANKS BE UNTO GOD who giveth us the victory

Through our Lord Jesus Christ." [1 Cor. 15:56–57]

:All of it through Jesus ˳beloved.

The victory belongs ˳to ˳Jesus.

(Sermon by Matthew Deere, Morning Worship Service, June 9, 1985)

The "keying" accomplished through the use of special formulae and appeals to tradition in Southern Baptist sermons reflect their dependence on, and utilization of, the Bible. The biblical scripture references and pastors' emphases on the Bible as the word of God, upon which the church is founded, are key features of the genre as performed. Pastors consider the Bible to contain the word of God, and they use their reading of the Bible as the legitimate authority for belief.[8] Invoking the biblical tradition, paraphrasing the Bible, and quoting from the Bible throughout pastoral messages all function as metacommunicative framing of the genre itself. This usage of the Bible as a foundation for speaking is illustrated many times in the sermons analyzed, as pastors weave quotes from the Bible into their exegesis. When Deere spoke the passage just cited, which included several verses from 1 Corinthians, he recited these from memory, delivering them in a rhythmical fashion, with his voice rising to mark the biblical words as set apart. All pastors who spoke at Cypress Pond could quote the Bible from memory in this fashion. In fact, so could most of the congregation, including the children. (One of the functions of the Sunday school classes was to help children commit selected biblical passages to memory.)

Perhaps the most important characteristic that "keys" the sermon speech genre is the disclaimer of performance. Within the Southern Baptist belief system, the message of salvation is conveyed through the spoken word of God. This *is* the most important channel, or medium, of speech transmission (Hymes 1972:63) to persuade people to believe (Borker 1974). When pastors preach, they are thought to speak the word of God to their audience under the influence of the in-dwelling Holy Spirit. This in-dwelling Holy Spirit is thought both to guide the speaker in his choice of sermon topic and to speak through his human voice. A pastor can deny responsibility for his words, since "the artifact, the sermon, is not of his doing" (Samarin 1973:247). But, as Samarin insightfully observes, such abdication actually denotes artifice, because the preacher, despite his disclaimer, holds his authority through his ability to speak for God. At Cypress Pond, the congregation placed so much importance on the word of God as a primary symbol that they related accounts in which just one page of scripture, blowing in the wind and caught by an unbeliever, converted that individual through the power of the gospel message. Members placed special importance on the words of pastors, because the latter, in spite of their disclaimers, were required, by the very definition of their roles, to preach the word of God by reading the Bible and serving as channels through which the Holy Spirit would speak.[9]

Not all pastors gave explicit disclaimers of performance with every service that they preached, but the overt disclaimers, usually occurring in prayers before or after the sermon, were given frequently enough that their use seemed to be taken for granted.[10] Two examples are given here, one from a visiting pastor, the Reverend Jamie Truett, and one from Squires. In the following, notice how Truett begins his guest sermon with a request that the Lord speak through him:

> Our Heavenly Father, as we come now in this service today, enable us to set aside all that would prohibit the Lord Jesus Christ from speaking to us and through me. We thank you for this church, and we pray that you'll continue to bless them as they carry the message of Jesus Christ in this community and to the outermost parts of the world. Hear our prayer because we pray in Jesus' name, amen. (Jamie Truett, Morning Worship Service, December 22, 1985)

Similarly, Squires begins his sermon, "A Committed Christian," with this disclaimer:

> Two weeks ago, as we began to prepare the message that we brought last Sunday morning, the Lord gripped my heart about something as I looked at verse 10 [of 1 Corinthians 15]. And I'm gonna share with you today what he's laid upon my heart. And before I begin, I want to say that I'm saying today what I'm saying in love. (Ted Squires, Morning Worship Service, August 11, 1985)

Here the lines concerning responsibility for the sermon appear to be attributed to Squires's communication with God. In his reference to preparing the sermon, Squires speaks of a collective "we," implying direct access to God through the Holy Spirit. The words spoken are thought to come from, and be guided by, the Holy Spirit. It is no wonder, then, that the sermons were viewed by listeners as extremely important, in both their content and their functions of conversion and instruction. As we shall see, not all in the audience responded in ways that affirmed this "truth," but certainly all were familiar with the cultural code.

Within this milieu, pastors' command of the sermon genre reflected their claim to speak the message of God. They framed their performances by their use of the archaic scriptural code: the King James Version of the Bible, the repository of God's words. They constructed their sermons using figurative styles, parallelism, special formulae, appeals to tradition, and disclaimers of performance, all based on a combination of the biblical scriptural references and a belief that, when they assumed the pulpit, they did more than speak their own words; they spoke for God as well.

Audience Evaluations of the Sermon Genre

Congregation members constantly rated pastors on their skill, in preaching, in using the sermon genre. Members' evaluations took into account both the content of the sermon and the style of delivery. Their folk categories rated a pastor as "preacher" or "teacher." Both Borker (1974) and Samarin (1973) discuss the widespread use of this dichotomy in Protestant churches. Samarin notes that this distinction can be found at both the pastoral and the congregational levels. The terms denote different functions of sermons, but these functions are not clearly distinguished in practice (Samarin 1973:259). Similarly, Borker (1974) claims that both teaching and preaching are found in all evangelical sermons she studied. The distinction members make, she feels, rests upon the primary speaking style of the speaker. The difference is not so much in content but in affect. She states, "Preachers tend to use a much more dramatic and emotional speaking style than teachers, to make much greater use of voice modulation, gestures, etc. Teachers, on the other hand, tend to give more subdued and in some ways more overtly organized messages, as do teachers or lecturers anywhere" (1974:180).

At Cypress Pond, teachers and preachers appeared to be distinguished by the criteria outlined by Borker. Preachers were considered to have a dynamic style of delivery, modulating both pitch and loudness of voice frequently throughout the sermon to build dramatic effect. Teachers, by contrast, spoke with less variation in tone and tended more assiduously to instruct the congregation on points of belief. Squires, the pastor during my early fieldwork, was highly rated as a "preacher," while Manning, the second pastor, was thought of as a "teacher." Most congregation members preferred the "preaching" style because this style (an emotional delivery) made those in the congregation pay attention better and elicited more responses to invitational calls.

Those in the audience also evaluated the pastor's preaching on the basis of its visible results during the service. Since the Holy Spirit was supposed to speak through the pastor's words to the hearts of members of the congregation, its presence could be "seen" and "felt" if members of the audience responded to the invitational calls. When such responses were nonexistent or infrequent, the congregation might infer that the pastor had lost touch with the Holy Spirit. He, on the other hand, was even more likely to suppose that the congregation itself was at fault.

In fact, members had heard these requests for response so frequently that many seemed to have ceased listening. During the service, children, for example, drew pictures, sucked on candy, and slept. Teenagers glanced at their watches, sighed, and made unfavorable comments about the length of the sermon. Some adults, too, fell asleep (and might be pinched awake by their spouses). But a significant number present did listen intently, seeking to find personal meanings in the messages spoken from the pulpit, seeking the guidance of the Holy Spirit. These members cited their pastors' words and rhetorical arguments in other contexts, discussing them on the way home, over dinner, or even in heated disputes over doctrine.

When it came to any particular pastor's ability to speak on God's behalf or to judge whether any one sermon conveyed God's message, members did not doubt the gospel as contained in the Bible. But they did occasionally question whether the pastor spoke his own words or those of God. They did not entirely endure "a self-imposed impotence," as Samarin claims most Protestant audiences do (1973:246). As members of a congregationalist church, they frequently judged their pastor by his *words* and by his *life*, considering, if displeased, whether to exercise their right to dismiss him. While pastors claimed to be "called by God" and "inspired by God,"[11] and thus to hold unassailable positions of spiritual authority, in communities such as Cypress Pond, the pastor's daily actions came under congregational scrutiny, and his hold on authority was circumscribed by these appraisals.

Using Sermons to Motivate Action during the Worship Service

In evangelical churches, sermons persuade believers to action through the logic of their arguments, a traditional function of rhetoric. By design, they also trigger affective responses of one type or another (Samarin 1973:251; Borker 1974:313; Mathews 1977:124). Mathews, for example, says of evangelical religion, as practiced in the pre–Civil War South, that the purpose of preaching discourse was "either to trigger the emotional crisis which converted new disciples, or to remind mature Christians of their own experience of Grace. Out of this recurring celebration was to come the recurring commitment to the life of holiness and self-discipline" (1977:124).

Likewise, Samarin notes that, while affect is not generally considered one of the functions of preaching, it nevertheless forms an "essential component of evangelical preaching" (1973:251). Thus, both preacher and congregation take note not only of the content of the message but also of the emotional dimensions of the sermons and their intent to foster religious experience. In terms of Hymes's distinction between purposes as goals and as outcomes (1972), at Cypress Pond pastors often seemed to tailor the content and the rhetorical styles of their sermons to engage different persons in the audience and to trigger different types of affective responses.

During the fieldwork period, pastors preached a total of 111 sermons for which I have fieldnotes and/or audiotaped recordings. For various reasons, only 53 of these were taped. In my analyses I examined all the sermons to gain an overview of the types of sermons preached and affective responses evoked. First, I noted the title of the sermon, the scriptural references used, the main themes of the sermon, the preacher, the context of the sermon, and whether anyone had responded to the invitational call at the sermon's close. Second, I listened to all the taped sermons and read my fieldnotes from the sermons which were not taped. Third, all the audiotaped sermons by visiting pastors who spoke at Cypress Pond (eight, by seven different speakers)[12] were transcribed. Selected sermons by the two regular pastors at Cypress Pond, Squires and Manning, also were transcribed (a total of six). From this survey, I developed the following typology of sermons, based on overall content and function:

1. The individual's need for salvation
2. General guidelines for living the Christian life
3. Specific guidelines for Christian living
   a. Living one's life as a personal witness
   b. Taking salvation to the entire world

    c.   Members' roles, duties, and obligations within the local church (e.g., tithing)

4.   Teachings on themes, concepts, or symbols of the faith (e.g., sermons focusing on a concept such as Christian love or the nature of Christ).

This typology reflects the emphasis pastors placed on salvation. Three of the four categories directly concern some aspect of salvation and advocate some type of Christian action. The fourth category includes sermons about more abstract concepts in the belief system. These I call "teachings," since members generally cannot take overt action regarding these concepts except to develop their own doctrinal points of view. The typology corresponds closely to one developed by Hill, who felt that sermons emphasize conversion, commitment, or devotion to Christ (Hill 1966:81–83).[13]

Of the audiotaped sermons, I selected four to discuss with respect to their rhetorical styles and how they link belief with various actions. These four sermons emphasize the two major themes found in this SBC church: (1) the individual call for salvation, and (2) general guidelines for living the Christian life. The sermons selected provide examples of the range of different rhetorical styles employed by pastors. Exemplifying those sermons designed to motivate conversion, discussed in this chapter, is one of Manning's revival sermons that dwells on the need to be saved from sin. A second, much milder sermon by a visiting pastor, the Reverend Elliott Wayne, uses the biblical story of Nicodemus to insist that believers make a decision for Christ.

Of those sermons imploring the "born-again" Christian to become more committed, discussed in chapter 5, I selected another of Manning's sermons, one that lists seven criteria to use in judging whether an individual is living as the saved ought to live. Manning stresses the need to be as Christlike as possible, to strive for perfection. Squires's sermon, "A Committed Christian," holds up a similar set of standards but, in addition, discusses a folk category, the "backslider," yielding a more accurate picture of the range of behavioral judgments available in this community. Whenever a passage from a sermon is cited, the title of that sermon and the speaker are noted either in the text or in brackets. The complete texts of two selected sermons are presented in appendices A and B.

Motivating Salvation: The Fear of Hell

On the fourth night of the spring revival services, a Wednesday evening in April 1986, Manning spoke on this theme: "I Have Sinned; What Shall I Do?" Manning had begun his interim appointment at Cypress Pond the previous November. In his seventies, he had been a loyal Southern Baptist pastor for more than forty years. After his retirement from full-time pastoral work, he frequently served as an interim pastor when churches were in the process of locating a permanent full-time pastor. Manning had entered the ministry in his thirties, after completing a four years of college and three years of seminary in Baptist-affiliated schools. His educational background set him apart from his congregation; he had more training than any of the other persons who preached at Cypress Pond. Sometimes members said his preaching was incomprehensible, but they reacted very favorably to the evangelical sermons he preached during the revival services. These sermons contained more appeals to fear and to the need for an immediate response on the part of the unsaved than the regular services he gave on Sunday mornings and evenings.

This particular sermon can best be described as a "hellfire and damnation" message. Members themselves did not use this term, but as a descriptive label, the characterization fits. In such sermons, pastors make every effort to bring unsaved persons to a realization that they are sinners and need to repent of their sin. In so doing, the pastors constantly and consciously use the fear of eternal damnation as a primary psychological motivator. The sermon content and title is based on Job 7:20, which begins, "I have sinned, what shall I do . . . ?" Manning poses the question in order to dwell on the ramifications of sin in the lives of individuals.

Having quoted this scripture, Manning begins his message with a list of the many accomplishments of humans, including going into space. But he follows the list immediately with the "fact" that sin entered the world "a long time ago," with Adam. Of this, Manning says: "We've resorted to every means known to man to regain the position that Adam lost when sin entered into him. We've tried through education, though philosophy; we've tried through religion, though government; we have tried every means to throw off this yoke of depravity of sin." He gives examples from the Bible of individuals who tried to escape from the consequences of their sin, only to be judged by God. He retells the story of Cain and Abel and the story of Saul, the Old Testament leader, who fell away from God and actually asked the "witch of Endor" to conjure the ghost of Samuel. He uses these biblical references, as well as a number of others, throughout his sermon, as *exempla*, or "illustrative narratives used in the sermon to make a point or draw a moral" (Lawless 1988:121). From these *exempla*, Manning derives his first major conclusion about sin:

> Sin is the death disease of the soul. Again it's sometimes called the cancer of the soul. . . . Sin is the soul's disease, and sin will destroy. What is it? The Bible says that sin is the transgression of God's law. And now, anytime that we invade that forbidden territory of evil, we transgress the law of God. And anytime that we don't live up to the Ten Commandments; anytime that we do not measure up to the Sermon on the Mount; anytime that we are guilty of disobeying God's laws, we are guilty of sin.

From his remarks we can see that this list of sins is all-encompassing; every commandment of God must be obeyed all the time. The remarks also emphasize that no one can escape the consequences of sin. By implication, this retelling of biblical accounts and requirements makes the point that, if these Old Testament people cannot escape, neither can members of the congregation.

Manning continues to enlarge on this theme, speaking of sin as "iniquity" which is always present. That iniquity comes from the inner corruption of "evil thoughts." He also quotes James 4:17, which states: "Therefore, to him that knoweth to do good and doeth it not, to him it is sin." Again, take note of the standards to which Manning is holding the individual: not only must one avoid even thinking evil thoughts, but one must always do good. Furthermore, to be selfish is to trespass on God's divine authority:

> Now, when one prefers self to God, he trespasses into the realm of the almighty, into the realm of divine authority. Egotism and selfishness is sin in the life, it's the mark of sin just the same as theft, just the same as murder. And those who regard their own interest, irregardless of others,

they sin just as much as the drunkard or harlot. And we must know it tonight.

After describing sin as disease and as iniquity, Manning next describes sin as

unbelief, and this is the kingpin of them all. Unbelief is a sin because it is an insult to the truthfulness of God. . . . It is unbelief that shuts the door of heaven for you, it's unbelief that opens the door to hell for you. It is unbelief that rejects the word of God as being, ah, the God for our lives, to bring us to God. It is unbelief that causes one to refuse to receive Jesus Christ into their hearts and lives. And so sin brings results, it has a penalty and that penalty is death. And the book says that the wages of sin is death. No man has the ability within himself to rid himself of sin, but he can come to Christ and have his sins cleansed. He can come to Christ and have his sins forgiven. He can come to Christ and find life everlasting, the free gift of God.

The oppositions in this passage equate sin with death and Christ with life. Christ cleans or removes the "animal" blood that is the human lot in life with his own blood, his own sacrifice. This act changes a person and allows entry into heaven. In this excerpt, and in many of the hymns cited throughout this work, the sinner must be "wash'd in His blood" ("Blessed Assurance," by Crosby and Knapp, in Sims 1956; see also Harding 1987:176); but the individual first must choose salvation.

Turning from the decision itself, Manning spends the next half of the sermon talking about the ways people try to hide or cover their sins so that no one will know. He tells the biblical story of Reuben, the son of Jacob, who tried for over forty years to hide the fact that he had lain with his father's concubine one night. But on his deathbed Jacob revealed that he knew of the sin and had judged his son. Thus "time does not cover sin." Nor can we cover sin with *secrecy*, as had the rich man in Jesus' parable; this man had fed his dogs but failed to help the beggar outside his gates (Luke 19–31). Manning recasts this Bible passage into colloquial language:

The rich man, [he] went out to feed his dogs. He threw the scraps from the table to his dogs. He saw that old man, there in sores, scrambling with the dogs to get a crumb of bread to live. As he brushed off his hands, as he went back toward his sumptuous living in his house, he said, "Pretty soon the old man will die. Pretty soon the community will not remember that he lay at my gate. Pretty soon time will cover this thing."

And pretty soon, he [the beggar] died, but pretty soon, the rich man himself died. And he cried out in those torments of hell for God, to let that one who died at his gate, come with a drop of water on his finger, to touch his tongue. It would've been a little bit of heaven for him, but the angel of God said to him, "Son, remember." He didn't forget; even in hell he remembered how he'd treated that old man at his gate, with the sores on his body, who didn't have food to eat. In hell, he remembered. Time will not cover sin. We try to cover sin with secrecy, and this is the big one. We keep it secret, and we think we've got it encased.

This biblical account of the rich man in hell crying out for a drink of water from the man whom he had treated with disdain is a favorite with pastors who want to emphasize the consequences of sin and the reality of hell. Certainly, from the southern Protestant perspective, this story contains powerful images and associations which cause the individual to *feel* guilty for his actions and to *visualize* the severest possible penalty: unrelieved suffering, to be felt for all eternity.

After painting this scene from hell, Manning immediately moves from the New Testament parable to people he, Manning, has known who tried to cloak their sins in secrecy. First he describes a "fellow out in Texas" who tried to hide from his wife and children the fact that he had an illegitimate daughter now eleven years old. Next Manning tells about a person to whom he had witnessed while preaching a revival several years ago. This man had been identified by the community as a "lost" person. He came to church with his four daughters, but he did not come forward for salvation during the services. Manning had "begged God for his life," but to no avail. So Manning went to visit him after the final service.

I asked for him, and I asked him to please come outside and talk with me. And he came out. And I said, "Sir, I asked God for your life, and you did not come [for salvation], and there's gotta be a reason, and I wanna know what that reason is."

And he said to me, "Sir, when I was a young man I was in the army; I was stationed in the Philippines, and I took a Philippino girl as my live-in wife. I didn't marry her, but I lived with her, and I had a child by her, a son. And that boy now must be twenty-five years of age. But I got orders to come back to the States, and I left the house normally one morning and I just didn't come back."

And he said, "I've done everything I know to do to get that straight," but he said, "I can't get it straight, I can't get it straight, I don't know what to do."

And I told him, I said, "You do what you greatly fear to do. You tell your wife. You write, try to find out about that boy and that woman, and you do what you can, but you straighten this thing out with your family. You straighten this thing out with God, because this secrecy is gonna kill you. It's not gonna help you. It won't relieve you."

I don't know whatever happened to that man because I never did go back into that community, but I often, I've often wondered, whatever happened.

But I stand before you tonight to tell you that secrecy will not cover your sin. If it doesn't come out in you in some way, it's gonna come out in sickness, it's gonna come out. And I'll tell you it will come out because the sense of sin upon the heart is oppressive to the highest degree, and the guilt of sin is depressive to the highest degree, and a man cannot live filled with the sin that's in his life.

From this point to the close of the sermon, Manning is no longer using biblical *exempla*; instead he deals with the personal dimension, drawing on examples that will be familiar to the community. In fact, he makes two further claims which are intended to hit as close to home as it is possible to get in this particular belief system. He attacks those who practice "religious rites" without really believing. So he says that *prayer* alone will not free the sinner from sin. Nor are those who have been *baptized* with the waters necessarily saved: "I think that there are a lot of people who go through the baptismal once, trying to wash sin away from their lives, but I wanna tell you this, that the baptismal waters will not cleanse you of your sins. We try to cover them with those waters, and it won't do it. What should we do?"

He answers his own question with this religion's most frequent plea that the individual accept Christ:

> What am I to do? And the Bible is clear and plain: Confess your sins and seek the forgiveness of God, and that's it. Confess your sins and seek the forgiveness of God. And the Bible says if we confess our sins, he is faithful and just to forgive us our sins and to cleanse us from all unrighteousness. How can God forgive us? Because Jesus went to the cross and died in our stead. . . . By faith in Christ be born of the spirit of God, and know that you are a child of God, and then he'll deal with you as with children. Christ saves us from the guilt of sin, and what a salvation that is. . . . He saves us from the power of our sins. Sin in the life will control the life and ruin the life, and that's the power of sin over a person. He forgives the sin, and then you have the power to control and you do not let the tempter ruin your life as he wants. He saves from the penalty of sin.

Manning concludes the sermon with an "invitation" stressing the need for the individual to make a personal decision for Christ. In it he evokes the crucifixion on Golgotha's hill and contrasts the fate of the two thieves crucified with Christ: one believed and was in heaven that same day, while the other died in his sin and went to hell (see chapter 6 for the full text of this invitation).

Such a sermon obviously intends to bring home to those unsaved, or to those unsure of their salvation, the need for salvation at this very moment. While pastors state that they do not intend to scare individuals with allusions to hell, one of the implied motivations, nevertheless, is fear. Pastors use *exempla* from the biblical tradition to show that there is a scriptural precedent for the judgments, and they frequently invoke the most dramatic of these, such as that of the man crying out for water while in hell, to bring home the "message." Often, as in this sermon, the rhetorical pattern will then shift from the Bible to concrete contemporary instances of sin and its consequences. This linking of the biblical past with the present makes the future, too, real: heaven or hell. Finally, as we shall see in chapter 6, comes the "invitation," posing the choice between salvation and damnation as a question to be decided during the worship service itself: "I Have Sinned, What Shall I Do?" Directed to individuals in the audience, the pastors' voices often change in affective tone as they ask these questions. In quiet tones, they speak of now as *perhaps* the last chance a person will have to *decide*.

This belief system depends on a concrete set of rewards and punishments. Those who fail to repent will dwell in hellfire forever, crying out for a drink of water that always will be denied. Even those who are already Christians are to be punished by God if they fail to excise sin from their lives, and the list of what constitutes sin is formidable indeed. Thoughts and acts of commission and omission all are subject to moral scrutiny. Attempts to hide sin will be of no avail, nor will religious pretenses serve any purpose. This God is an all-knowing, all-judging Old Testament God, mediated only by the saving Grace of Christ. Sin itself is seen as the natural state of humankind. The concluding hymn for this service is "Only Trust Him." How significant that title is. The only thing these Christians can trust after hearing such a sermon is Christ, for their spouses may be concealing terrible sins from them, their neighbors who pray and are baptized actually may be damned. And what of themselves? As this sermon so strongly urges, they must have an assurance of salvation, obtainable in only one way: by accepting Christ as one's savior. No guidelines that go beyond the instructions given in this sermon are available in the belief system; thus, the sermon does not tell the individual how to have this assurance in any way other than "acceptance" of the message.

Motivating Salvation: A Christmas Present for Your Family

On the morning of December 22, 1985, the Reverend Elliott Wayne preached at Cypress Pond. He often filled in as a guest speaker in churches around the region, though his primary job was as a prosecutor in a neighboring town. Close to retirement age, he opened his time in the pulpit with thanks for the invitation to speak, jokes about getting lost ("Like to never found you, though. John Manning doesn't give good directions. I wound up in Hattiesville"), and a joke about preaching to a man whom he had formerly prosecuted. Of his dual roles, he noted, "Best I can tell, I don't see anybody here I put in jail." Before reading the scripture, the story of Nicodemus from John 3:1–15, he justified his choice of a nontraditional Christmas scripture in this fashion:

> I'd like to read a portion of scripture that's not often used in a Christmas message. We think at this time of the year of the birth of the Lord Jesus Christ. We think of Bethlehem. I've been privileged to go there three times in the last years. There in Bethlehem is where they say Christ was born. Today there's a great church built over the alleged manger. And when you go down into the bottom of it there they say Christ was born. How significant that is. And then you can go right outside of the city of Jerusalem to the place that's called Golgotha, where he gave his life that you and I might accept him as our savior. And just a few feet away is the garden tomb, where you can witness an empty tomb where one day a man was buried, named Jesus. But all of that with its great importance is insignificant unless you do one thing, unless you trust as your personal savior. How do you do that?
>
> All of these great and wonderful experiences are of little good until we come to the actual reality of being what? Born again. And I am sure today that we could have no greater Christmas than to see some of our loved ones come to know Christ as their personal savior. Do you have loved ones today that are not saved? I know as I stand here I can think of some that I love very dearly but will not trust, have not trusted Christ, as their personal savior.

He read the story of Nicodemus from the King James Version of the Bible and immediately followed with a prayer invoking the guidance of Jesus and, implicitly, the Holy Spirit.

> Our Heavenly Father, as we come now in this service today, enable us to set aside all that would prohibit the Lord Jesus Christ from speaking to us and through us. We thank you for this church, and we pray that you'll continue to bless them as they carry the message of Jesus Christ in this community and to the outermost parts of the world. Hear our prayer because we pray in Jesus' name, amen.

Subtly, the prayer uses the pronoun "us" to mean both the speaker himself and the audience. It uses the rhetoric of conversion to make the message one that "enlists" or engages listeners in internal dialogues with themselves and at the same time attempts to instill the Holy Spirit in listeners (Harding 1987). This use of a ritual disclaimer overtly says that the words are God's, not Wayne's. Yet the words are used intentionally, to involve the listener in the process. This whole sermon is a form of witnessing that "aims to separate novice listeners from their prior, given reality, to constitute a new, previously unperceived or indistinct reality, and to impress that reality upon them; make it felt, heard, seen, known, undeniably real" (Harding 1987:169). Harding distinguishes between *witnessing* per se, as the informal method of communicating the gospel in the context of a conversation between the saved and the unsaved, and the *sermon,* as the ritual, formal oratory interpreting the gospel. One key difference in context between informal witnessing and witnessing from the pulpit is that the pastor knows that some (and, if he is charitable in judgment, perhaps all) in his audience already are saved; furthermore, most are not novice listeners. In fact, it is likely that all have heard this message most Sundays. Still, Wayne preaches the need for salvation, using the story of Nicodemus to draw in the persons who might not "really" be saved.

Wayne recasts the story into a contemporary account of redemption: a boy lost a boat he had whittled, found it on sale in a pawn shop, and earned the money to "redeem" it. He then shifts back to the biblical *exemplum*:

> In the beginning, beloved, God made you and me, and he has provided his only begotten son Jesus Christ to redeem us. How has this come about? You know the greatest joy in the world today is to be a born-again Christian, isn't it? I see so many people less fortunate in life than we are. You know, I try to witness to them. There's a better way. I tell them that, "You're having difficult times now, but there's a better way."
>
> What is that better way? Christ. He's got the answer. There's a better way for your life than the direction in which you're going. One day a man named Nicodemus came to the Lord Jesus Christ. He had witnessed the miracles of Christ. Whatever he witnessed I do not personally know, but evidently they impressed him and he realized that in his life there was something lacking.

Wayne makes it plain that this "better way of life" is needed not just out "there" in the world, but right "here" in this community:

> I often hear people when they try to answer the question of the preacher, are you saved, and some of them will say, "I think that I am." Others will say, "I hope that I am." Others will say, "Well, my mother was a Christian, my father was a Christian, maybe that makes me a Christian." No it doesn't. Beloved, you in your own hearts, you know whether or not you've been born again. You know whether or not you're saved. You know whether or not your name is written on the lamb's book of life. You know. You may lie about it. And a lot of people don't wanna publicly confess Christ as their savior because of the sins of their lives. They're ashamed of what they're doing and they don't want to make a commitment.

Applying Harding's insights about the rhetoric of witnessing to this form of preaching, we see that the preacher is setting up another kind of internal dialogue about salvation which readily might apply to those persons who have heard this message repeatedly. This dialogue says that thinking, hoping, and tradition do not a Christian make. The text states explicitly that only the knowledge of the "heart" counts and that knowledge is undeniable: "You know whether or not you are saved." Wayne immediately constructs a message that undermines such sure knowledge when he says, "You may lie." As in Manning's sermon, there may be persons who are hiding sins, who are not committed, who are lying about their salvation.

Wayne omits an explicit transition to the next part of his sermon, which focuses on the moment of salvation. The *exemplum* remains the story of Nicodemus. The need to be "born again" is established on the authority of both the scripture and Wayne's personal testimony:

> Nicodemus realized and came to the realization in his life that something was lacking in his life. It was different from those around about Jesus. And he came, he said, "Something is lacking in my life."
>
> I want you to notice just two or three things about this story this morning. First of all, Nicodemus found time to find Jesus. You know we are busy today, aren't we? . . . You might be a Christian but you still need to

find time to sit down, to find out what direction your life is going to be. But if you're one of those under the sound of my voice, you're not born again, you need to come and take time. Just say everything else is not that important, I'm coming to the Lord Jesus Christ.

And then next, notice that he came to the source of authority—the source of authority. Now we Baptists have a Bible, and we say that this is our source of authority, we don't need anything else, we can find God's direction for our lives right here.

I had an experience just a few years ago. . . . [He tells of witnessing while traveling abroad] We asked people to come to the source of authority, come to Jesus. You can find him anywhere at any time. I was born again at five o'clock in the morning on the back porch of a house. When I went out and looked up, said "God, I got the message. You'll forgive me for my sins, I'll trust you as my savior today." And he did. My son had just died in the bedroom. I promised to serve him the rest of my life. Come to the source of authority.

And Nicodemus came and said, "How can these things be?"

And Jesus said, "Nicodemus, you must be born again."

Wayne's rhetorical strategy in this segment of the sermon uses the concept of witnessing to insert a "shock" into his message, one that the listener hardly has time to process. He describes accepting Christ, follows it immediately with the revelation that his son had just died (which he interprets as God having sent him a message). But he does not elaborate this personal account; rather, he shifts immediately to an entreaty that the listener accept Christ.[14] Wayne describes spiritual rebirth as a complete change:

Being born again, beloved, is not remaking the old life. You know a lot of people, they hear a message. They'll go out and they'll say I'm a-gonna quit drinking, quit smoking, quit doing this. I'm a-gonna clean up my house and so forth and so on. . . . Cleaning up your life is not being born again. Stopping this and stopping that is not being born again. You see, born again is a new birth. Jesus tried to explain it: "Except that a man be born of water and of the spirit of God he cannot see the kingdom of God." The water birth is physical birth; the spiritual birth is the birth of the heart, soul, person.

In this Christmas season, Wayne repeats the appeal for spiritual re-birth as the greatest "present" a person could give. Wayne also ad-dresses those already saved, imploring the reborn to become more com-mitted:

> You decide, I'm gonna trust Christ as my savior, I'm gonna turn my life over to him. That's how a person's born again. What greater present could you give to the Lord Jesus Christ today than to trust him as your savior? If you're already a Christian, secondly, to make a commitment that the year of 1986 is going to be the greatest year of my life in Christ.

Finally, Wayne makes a reference to the local church's drive to earn money for missions. In so doing, he links salvation and commitment to the overarching goal of SBC: salvation of the world. This entreaty leads directly to the "invitation," now spoken with the pronoun "you."

> You're giving people because you're a living people, and you're living because you're giving, and you're happy to help those that are less fortu-nate in life than you are. For around this world there are multitude mil-lions and billions of people that are waiting for the gospel. Is the Lord Jesus speaking to you this morning? You have a decision you'd like to share? Would you do it as we sing our hymn of invitation? Would you just ask the Lord, I have a decision that I'd like to make, I'd like to share it with these people, here in this church. We're going to sing our hymn of invitation.

Rhetorically, the explicit purpose of the sermon is to motivate the second birth, the spiritual birth of the "heart, soul, [and] person." Its primary message is intended to be no less compelling than Manning's revival sermon. Its motivation, however, is less the immediate fear of God than a "present" to Jesus at the time when Christians celebrate the birth of Christ. Its secondary message is a subtext running throughout the sermon: there are those who lie about their salvation, and there are those who say they are committed but are not. Both should—indeed, *must*—change. The rhetoric of conversion used here is intended to set up an internal dialogue in which those who cannot claim to know their salvation completely must question if they are saved.

Abstracting the Pattern

At Cypress Pond, time itself sometimes seemed to lose the dimensions of past and future, due to the emphasis given to salvation in the sermons. Pastors echoed the evangelical postulate that the most important moment of each individual's life occurred when he or she heard the gospel message of salvation and made a conscious choice either for or against salvation. Every time one heard the message, the requirement to decide was also present. If one heard and rejected the message repeatedly, evangelicals assumed, then at some point the individual actively and by choice constructed a "wall" between his inner soul and the message of salvation. The imagery was of a "hardening of the heart," as if layer upon layer of conscious choice removed the individual from truth. In a sense, then, this repeated rejection was the worst sin an individual could commit, since it sealed off the possibility of salvation. However, if one did respond, repented of sin, and accepted Christ into one's "heart," Cypress Pond members believed that this was an absolute demarcation which never could be retracted. The saying, "once saved, always saved," captured this point of view.

While Manning and Wayne preached entire sermons on the absolute necessity for this conscious decision for Christ, they provided scant information to show *how* the individual might cross from the negative emotional acknowledgment of being a sinner bound for hell, to the positive emotional assurance of being redeemed by the grace of God and bound for heaven. These preachers said, for example, that the listener should examine his "heart," "pray for guidance from the Holy Spirit," or go to the "authority of the Bible" to learn how to cross this barrier. Such metaphorical treatments are devoid of concrete guidance. Yet these dramatizations of the necessity for a decision for or against the message of salvation brook no equivocation.

Manning followed the sermon on sin discussed above with a handout that members could use. Under the title "The Plan of Salvation," the list summarized the overarching model presented to believers in these sermons:[15]

1. All of us are sinners (Rom. 3:23).
2. Unbelievers are under condemnation (John 3:18).

3. Yet God loves us (John 3:16).
4. And Christ died for us (1 Pet. 2:24–25).
5. He is our only hope (Acts 4:21).
6. Repent of sin (Luke 13:3 and Luke 24:47).
7. Believe on him [Christ] (Acts 16:31).
8. Confess him [Christ] (Rom. 10:9–10).
9. The Great Contrast [death or eternal life] (Rom. 6:23).

In general, pastors and church members did not question these basic guidelines. For example, we have seen that the decision to acknowledge Christ as one's savior involved acknowledging one's sinful nature, repenting of one's sins, and asking Christ for forgiveness. Since the belief system presupposed that individuals were born into a world constituted by original sin, there was no escape from the consequences of sin save through belief in salvation. Sin itself was not open to question, nor did people at Cypress Pond question whether or not humans were innately good. They had been told, and they appeared to agree, that they were abject sinners. Occasionally a person might question how much they had sinned and how bad the sin may have been relative to that of others. They might also question, as Sim did in our introduction, whether or not it was fair for God to consign the more "middle-of-the-road" sinners to hell, but never did they question the basic concept of sin itself.

Pastors and members, however, did question the *results* of the plan of salvation, and in the same sermons they were taught how to question themselves. That is, salvation occurred at the moment in time when they made the decision and were "born again" through God's grace. But, as we shall see in the next chapter, the experience itself was glossed over in order to focus on behavioral changes that should accompany conversion. Standard preaching procedure thus immediately turned the focus from the experience to commitment. Many members questioned this shift.

Belief as an Emotional State of Knowledge

Even though this belief system placed great emphasis on an emotional "knowledge" of salvation, it ironically failed to present a sure method for evaluating that experience. As a result, pastors conveyed both the necessity of salvation and the difficulty of knowing whether one has "gotten" it or not. To answer their own doubts—recall the pastor, described by Sim in the introduction, who decided that he had been mistaken about his own salvation—and the doubts of their congregations, some pastors did offer members guidelines for evaluating the experience itself.

While pastors usually described a prototypical "born-again" person as a Christian who could pinpoint a specific moment of salvation, occasionally pastors were forced to acknowledge that not everyone has such a dramatic religious experience. For instance, Squires, in the sermon "What Is Your Address?," classified the "saved" as being of three types: individuals, like Paul on the road to Damascus, who had had radical changes in their lives; those who had experienced belief shifts which occur when a person leaves the church and later returns to it; and those who always have been a part of the church (Morning Worship Service, May 12, 1985). This list resembles the categorizations of social scientists who have tried to specify the range of religious experiences that constitute Christian conversion. To take one famous example, James (1902) called those who gradually acquired faith the "once born" and those who made radical shifts in belief the "twice born." While individuals in both groups may be committed to their Christianity, in an evangelical belief system which specifies that individuals must be "twice born," the "once born" may need the overt assurances of their pastor and fellow churchgoers that their salvation counts. For if, as is the case at Cypress Pond, one is repeatedly told that the validity of one's salvation experience depends on the emotional experience of a "moment" in which one acknowledges Christ as Savior and "receives" immediate assurance in that "moment," and if the individual cannot actually point to a specific moment in time, then the system sets in motion the constant questioning of an internal believing state. Furthermore, if most people are silent about the content of the experience itself, as was also the case at Cypress Pond, then how can one have a social means of assessing the "truth" of the religious experience?

The "silence" about the content of the religious experience itself can best be illustrated in small-group interactional contexts rather than in the sermons. The "flavor" of the intense longing for that emotional knowledge became clear one night in late March 1986, shortly before the church was to hold its spring revival meetings. Based on geography and family ties, members of the church had been split into small groups which were to meet in the homes of members for "cottage prayer meetings." I was assigned to a home in Southville not far from my own apartment. There were only six of us present that night: Maude and Henry Green (the hostess and host), Deborah Griffin, Mamie Nichols, Ernest Davidson, and myself. Mamie, who led the meeting, began by reading Psalms 51:1–13. This passage starts with a request that God cleanse the speaker of sin and goes on to petition: "Create in me a clean heart, O God; and renew a right spirit within me; . . . Restore unto me the joy of thy salvation; and uphold me with thy free Spirit. Then will I teach transgressors thy ways; and sinners shall be converted unto thee" (Ps. 51:10, 12–13).

Mamie mentioned that she and her husband (who led another cottage prayer group that same night) had discussed what they were going to do in their respective meetings. Both had chosen this passage to set the tone for discussion and prayer. She recalled her own salvation, which had occurred when she was nine, during one of the revival meetings at her church. She had responded to the "invitation" and talked with the pastor. He had decided to talk with her further before "presenting her to the congregation" (that is, telling the congregation of Mamie's decision), because he had wanted to make sure that she really had been "saved." Apparently she convinced him, for he presented her the next night. She subsequently was baptized and had been a loyal churchgoer ever since—she was then fifty. For me, the interesting part of her discussion centered on how any individual can "know." She quoted a former pastor who had said that sometimes "one day is not enough time to know for sure." She went on to say that some people made *"emotional responses* rather than being sure." Since she used to keep track of the church membership, she knew that the church rolls contained names of people she had never even met. Thus, just as the pastors did, she translated the problem of "knowing salvation" directly to action (in this example, church attendance). Beyond noting how happy she felt after her salvation experience, she did not elaborate on its content. Significantly, the only discussion of her points by those present emerged when Maude Green spoke of her own baptism. She too had responded during a revival service and noted that, in the past (she was in her seventies), revivals were the time when most people were "saved." She had been baptized in a creek not far from the church after her response to the revival altar call. After prayers by Mamie and Deborah, the "official" part of the meeting ended, and the next hour was spent in a gossip session covering who in the church was ill, who and how people were kin to each other (partly for my benefit), and even the color of the pastor's suit at the previous Sunday service.

Most small-group discussions about salvation to which I was privy followed exactly this pattern. References made to the emotional experience immediately were placed in the institutional contexts of "invitations for salvation" given during worship services and the subsequent ritual of baptism. In such a system, Mamie's important emotional "decision for Christ" was open to question on the very night she experienced it. Although her age, nine, might have played some part in the pastor's request for postponement, the experience itself had been translated into a larger epistemological framework that made the emotional commitment contingent on later actions. The validity of any given emotional experience always was upheld, not by the intensity and depth felt in the moment, but solely by ensuing behavioral markers.

This cognitive shift was the answer that pastors gave to their congregations. But, as we shall see in the next chapter, even here the assurance of salvation was tenuous. In fact, while I hesitate to use this expression in this context, what resulted was a system in which one was "damned if you do, and damned if you don't." The goal that church members most desired to achieve, salvation, ever remained out of reach.

From the "internal" perspective, this emotional epistemology denied the validity of a psychological state as a criterion of belief. For instance, Mamie could not know if she was "born again" from introspection about her own inner state of being. In this system, her emotional transformation, her conversion, had to be evaluated and sanctioned socially. Her word was not enough. Similarly, as we saw earlier, Sim, who had been coming to church all his life, remained unsure of his own status as a "born-again" Christian. He was "doubtful," "not sure," despite all his efforts to attain certainty.

Other belief systems do provide both the content and the words with which adherents at least may attempt to describe the stages whereby one gains a personal knowledge of the transcendent. The systems that readily come to mind are mystical ones that specify contemplative practices for reaching union with a postulated concept of "God," "the One," or "the eternal" (the labels and techniques vary widely).[16] There are also systems in which the spirit world is made a part of the social world through spirit possession. In such systems, typified by Haitian Vodou but quite common throughout the world, individuals become vehicles for the gods (Bourguignon 1968 and 1991). These gods are thought to displace the personality of the human, to occupy the mind and body of the possessed, and to have their own agency and autonomy vis-à-vis others in the social world. In contemplative systems and in spirit possession, ways to judge the "validity" of a given religious experience generally are more accessible to the seeker than is the case in evangelical Protestantism.[17] Thus, in principle, there is no reason why evangelicals might not also develop means of assessing the religious experiences they seem to desire.

Those in control of the official dogma of the Cypress Pond belief system seemed instead to prohibit such attempts and to preempt the expressed need for such inner assurance. Their primary answer to the question of assurance was commitment to the moral requirements of Christianity. Thus, pastors might vacillate on the requirement that one have a specific moment in time when salvation occurred, but they did not hesitate to assert that the test of salvation itself was morality. As the next chapter shows, pastors suggested that members could assess their probable salvation by looking at the lives of those who professed to be saved. The result was a set of standards categorizing people into slots in a moral hierarchy, in which the truly saved were viewed as the most moral and the most "Christlike."

5

Preaching Commitment

To address the desire for a certain knowledge of salvation, pastors at Cypress Pond preached about overt moral actions by which members could measure their success or failure in living salvation. Especially in sermons directed at how to live the Christian life, pastors offered a set of guidelines and motivations for those who presumably were saved. Such sermons generally concluded with invitational calls imploring the lost to be saved and the saved to confess their sins and draw closer to the Lord. These sermons proposed models by which members could judge their lives. Members were asked to assess the degree to which they as Christians were "growing" toward perfection, how much sin remained in their lives, and how much they lived for themselves rather than for Christ. Pastors also indicated the rewards of achieving a more Christlike life: members, to a certain degree, would receive "blessings"; more importantly, they would become *better* Christians. Pastors encouraged these self-evaluations and urged members to commit to these goals publicly. Since, during some services, they asked members actually to leave their seats and "come forward" to demonstrate commitment, pastors often stepped into the pulpit with that goal in mind.

This chapter shows that the requirement to demonstrate salvation in every facet of behavior was taken as a tendency, or disposition, that should be present in every individual. The existence of this moral imperative meant that one never could rest on one's laurels, secure in the knowledge that one's fate was assured. Furthermore, since the belief system placed upon the saved individual the moral duty to save others, failing to live up to these standards might jeopardize someone else's salvation, if not one's own.

The following analysis of two sermons on how to live the Christian life demonstrates that the dispositional criterion of belief was taken as the only real measure of salvation available to the individual. While the psychological, emotional "moment of salvation" continually was affirmed as the necessary starting point, its significance often paled under the weight of the moral code.

Motivating the Christian Life: Living Perfection

In "What Is a Christian?" Manning skillfully answers his own question with a fairly complex set of teachings. The sermon consists of eight primary points. Manning first defines the term *Christian* and then outlines seven marks of a Christian. He draws on scripture for the definition and the hallmarks of the saved, and he alternates between biblical *exempla* and personal or contemporary *exempla* to illustrate each of his major points. In the context of his discussion, he addresses distinctions between belief and knowledge. Analysis of this sermon provides us with a clearly defined, stringent set of standards for faith. It shows how pastors use language to make the authority of scripture into a plan for living. Finally, in contrast with Manning's evangelical "preaching" sermon discussed in the last chapter, this sermon is an example of one the congregation would label as "teaching."

After citing only three places in the New Testament where the term *Christian* is used (Acts 11:26; Acts 26:28; and 1 Pet. 4:16), Manning immediately shifts to contemporary issues. He tells the following two anecdotes to establish a context for his definition:

> A little boy asked his dad one day, "What is a Christian, Dad?" And the father was thinking about this question, and he thought, "This is an important question. This boy has asked me something that is very important. I must be careful about answering." And secondly, his mind was going as to what he really thought a Christian was. And so he sat down with the boy, and he told him what he thought a Christian was. And when he finished, the little boy looked up at him, and he said, "Dad, have I ever seen one?"

> A lady was cleaning the house, and a knock came on the door. It was

morning. And she opened the door, and a fellow was standing there, and he says to her, "Do you know Jesus Christ?" She was taken aback, to be sure, and, momentarily, just stood there, stunned. And then she just closed the door in his face. And he pulled his foot away in time. She went back to her cleaning. But she didn't get away from his question. It bothered her all day. And when her husband came in later that afternoon, she told him of the incident. And the husband said, "Well, did you tell the young man that you were president of the Women's Missionary Union? Did you tell the young man that you taught a Bible class down at that church? Did you tell the young man that every time the church doors open, that you're down there?" And she said to her husband, "No, he didn't ask me that."

Given the centrality of the theme of salvation, it is no surprise to find that Manning defines a Christian as "one who knows Jesus Christ as his personal savior, and is trying to follow him." The first mark of the Christian is "the fact that one is saved." The scripture reference Manning cites is Ephesians 2:8–9: "For by grace are ye saved through faith, and that not of yourselves; it is a gift of God, not of works, lest any man should boast." Explaining this verse, Manning attempts to define grace and faith.

So what is the grace of God? A difficult question. The grace of God includes the love of God. The grace of God includes the forgiveness of God toward us. The grace of God includes his justification of us when we trust Jesus as our lord and savior. It is the unmerited favor that God bestows upon the person who trusts in the lord.

What is faith? Easier by a mile. Faith is composed of three things at least. Faith is knowledge. Faith is belief. And faith is trust. Let me illustrate. Here is a piece of furniture to my left. I know what that piece of furniture is; that's knowledge. I know that piece of furniture is a chair. I believe that that chair will hold up my weight. Now that is belief. But I've never sat in that chair in all of my entire life. I've been in this one, but not that one. I believe that chair will hold me up. And I proceed to sit in it. I trusted it. I have knowledge of what the chair is. I believe that it will do the job. And now, I've sat in it, and it did do the job. I trusted the chair. That's faith. I had faith in that chair, to hold up my physical weight.

We know who Jesus is. That's knowledge. He is the son of God. We must know that. Do you believe that he has the power to deliver your soul from hell? And from your sins? That's belief. If you believe that, then the ultimate is trusting him with your life, and he will. That's faith. We're saved by the grace of God, through our faith.

This reasoning by example makes knowledge, belief, and grace all components of salvation. Knowledge and belief both are contingent on trust, and both apply equally to salvation. In fact, the literal interpretation of this passage would make knowledge and belief almost identical. One *knows* Jesus is the son of God; that is taken as a given, based on the authority of the Bible. One gains a personal *knowledge* of Jesus as Savior through belief, through trust, and through grace. These all seem to blur together in the context of achieving the ultimate goal.

Manning next discusses the role of repentance in being "born again." While individuals are saved when they repent of their sins, they must also confess them. Manning argues that words are easy:

And so confession has something to do with it. But we are quick with words. We can often just say things we don't mean. But no way can you change the belief in your heart. "If you believe in your heart that God hath raised him from the dead, thou shalt be saved." And we confess to the things that he has wrought in us.

Of the ways the saved testify to their salvation, Manning makes the following crucial distinction:

Now, we can testify of the fact that we are saved by two ways: with the lip, and with the life. As far as the lip is concerned, we're like the Arctic rivers. Too often we are frozen at the mouth. We need to share it, not for our glory, but to help another to come to know him. And if you know Christ, you ought to be willing to share it.

According to this perspective, once saved, a good Christian must "grow," as Manning illustrates with this example:

> A picture, a boyhood picture, that I share with you, that some of you would remember, of course, and maybe you even had it out there on the farm. And that's a ladder leaning against a barn loft. There's the opening for the loft, and the ladder runs from the ground up to the loft. Now if you think of that as a Christian, you become a Christian when you get on the first rung. When your feet are off the ground. When you've been born of the spirit of God, you become a Christian.
>
> But now the Christians that we have trouble with, in our churches and in our communities, are those Christians that are on the first rung and the second rung. They are babes in Christ. And some people just do not bother to move from the first rung or the second rung. They do not want much learning, and they don't seem to want to know about Christ. And they don't care much, but they're touchy. They get their feelings hurt. They are nothing but babies in Christ. Oh, you can't take it away from them that they know the Lord—perhaps. And that's his judgment, not mine. But it's high time that we move on up the ladder in Christian growth and development, so that we will not be causing our fellow man problems.

Each rung of the ladder stands for growth as a Christian. Members are encouraged to move up the ladder, to grow. Judgment of those who fail to move is implied. Manning does reserve the final judgment to God, but the qualifier, "perhaps," after "they know the Lord," conveys his perception of such believers.

Summarizing his argument up to this point, Manning draws on another contemporary example:

> If you were ever pastor, you would know what I'm talking about. We need to grow in grace and in knowledge of our lord and savior, Jesus Christ. And the Bible mark of a Christian, one who knows Jesus Christ as his personal savior, is that he's saved. And as Jimmy Carter made famous, he's born again. And we Baptists believe that.

The second mark of a Christian is "that he is sure" that he is saved:

And I find that a lot of people in the churches seemingly do not know whether they are or not. You ask them. "Well, can't be sure. Joined the church, back yonder. But I don't know if I'm a Christian or not." You can be sure. When his spirit beareth witness with our spirits, we know that we belong to him. We can know that we're saved. And, the Apostle John has said, "These things I write unto you that ye may know that you have eternal life."

Certainty is attainable, according to Manning:

We live in days when a lot of people want to be unsure about everything. They want to stay nebulous. They don't want to be too sure. And some people say it doesn't make any difference what you believe, so long as you work at it. Huh. That's strange, Doctor. The people worked at it down in Jonestown—was it Jonestown? That's what it was, I think. They worked at it. They sure did. They turned over their checks. They turned over their lives. They worked at it. It makes a lot of difference what you believe. And don't you forget that. But, ah, God wants us to be sure. There are two ways of proving that you know the Lord, and that you're trying to follow him. And that's by a testimony of lip, and that's by the life that you live.

Manning stresses these two hallmarks of the Christian, these two ways of "proving" salvation. He returns to these "proofs" throughout the sermon.

Meanwhile, Manning discusses a third mark of the Christian: that one is sound in doctrine. He says, "The blood of Jesus makes safe, but it's the word that makes sure and sound." So one must read the Bible and let "the word speak to you." The fourth mark "of a Bible Christian is that he is surrendered to God." To illustrate surrender, Manning points to Abraham's willingness to sacrifice his son Isaac at God's command. He extrapolates:

Now let me say to you, God wants that ugliness that's in your life—maybe it's temper. Give it to God. He'll help you with it. He'll take it from you. And never give it back to you. Now I know, that's a psychological term, and I know that these things are hard to overcome, but God will help, and God will take away that temper, and make you sound. But you have a good memory, a gift from God. Give that gift to God. He wants all the good things in your lives, and he will give them back to you, glorified for his service.

Of such sacrifices, Manning makes another moral judgment:

> You know, friends, it really bothers me that we sing lies. Does that bother you? It bothers me. Just take, for instance, we sing, "Take my life and let it be consecrated, lord, to thee." And we sing, "Take my silver and my gold." And we sing, "Take my hands and my feet." And we sing all sorta things that we don't really mean. Am I hard, leading people to do that? I don't think we ought to lie behind songbooks. I'm not telling you not to sing. I love for you to sing. But I'm just pointing out that we are singing and not looking at what we're singing. And it's meaningless to us. We sing, "Have thine own way, lord, have thine own way." And knowing, all the time, that we are gonna have our way or bust. And we sing, "More love to thee, oh Christ, more love to thee." And we go from week to week, and we don't really mean it.

Manning gives another illustration concerning a little girl who reaches into a vase, finds something in it, and calls her mother, who discovers that the little girl's hand is stuck. Mom breaks the vase, only to find that her daughter was clutching a penny. The moral: "Sometimes God has to break our lives to get us to give up something that's not even worth a penny. He wants us to be totally surrendered to him. It's the mark of a Bible Christian."

Summarizing the world view of the evangelical, Manning describes a fifth mark of the Christian: separation from the world. He describes America in terms of contradictions. The "world" is "ugly," and the only thing that makes this society worthwhile is Christianity:

> Another mark of a Bible Christian is that he's separated. Now you know, in the early times of Christianity, Christians were persecuted. If that day was upon us today, we wouldn't have as many people joining the church and living for the devil. We wouldn't. Because you don't join

something when you're persecuted. Not just for nothing, you don't. But it's popular to be a Christian today. And we just join our churches, and we really don't live for the lord. This is a sin, and it is a disgrace.

People ask me, "Preacher, don't you believe it's wrong to drink liquor?" It's funny to me. It is. Is there a question about it? "Preacher, is it wrong to smoke cigarettes?" Boy, he's going to stop preaching and going meddling now for sure, for that old habit's got a lot of people. Anything that will tear down this temple that houses the spirit of God, has gotta be wrong. I don't care who you are or where you are or anything about it. He wants us to be separated.

He doesn't want us to be separated from this world; he wants us to be separated unto the Lord. We are leaven in this world. Leaven. That's what I said. Without the Christianity among us, this society wouldn't be worth living in. I wouldn't want to be here. If you were not here, I wouldn't want to be here. This society would be worse than the newspapers and the TV people make it seem. Yes, it would. But Christianity is the leaven of this society. And it makes it worthwhile to live in. I'd rather be leaven, than to be a part of this ugly society. If you're a Christian, you need to be separated unto the Lord. You live *in* the world, but you don't have to be *of* the world. Do you get what I mean?

Even though Manning manages to translate them into moral judgments, the last two points are more upbeat: Christians are filled with spirit and have a song in their hearts. The pastor contrasts the early Christians with Christians today, saying that the latter "are not alive." If members were really Christians, then,

the spirit is going to change your talk. The spirit is going to change your walk. The spirit is going to create a stir. The spirit of God in a man will make him different. There's no doubt about this.

. . . You have a will, you have intellect, and you have emotions. And when you meet your God, all three are coming into play. All of the intellect that you have is going to be challenged. And your emotions are coming into play as surely as I live. You can't meet God and not feel something. And then, it's up to you about the will. Whether you choose to be for him, or to be against him. No neutral ground.

Manning does not summarize the seven marks of the Christian at the close of his sermon. Instead, he makes the invitational call that the unsaved become saved and that those who are not growing in the faith do so. No one responded to this call.

Manning designed this sermon's rhetorical structure to dramatize comparisons between how Christians ought to be living and how many appear to be living. The goal was to stimulate members to reevaluate their lives and respond by becoming better Christians. The changes envisioned by Manning centered on making oneself more like Christ. The model presented was an ever-increasing effort to attain what could not be attained: perfection. In fact, in another sermon on "The Christian Ideal," Manning actually said that he differed from most Southern Baptists on this issue. While most thought the goal was heaven, in his opinion the goal of life was this striving toward perfection, toward the elimination of sin. The God who watched these Christians loved them but hated sin. Since the saved continued to sin, they still had evil within. For that evil, God continued to punish them, since they could not completely eradicate sin from their lives. They had to ask continually for forgiveness, monitoring their every action. In return, God would help them grow as Christians.

In striving for this state of growth, pastors urged members not to be selfish. Selfishness stemmed from following one's own desires. For them, being a Christian meant transforming, through total surrender to God, the individual's innate "sinful" drive for self-gratification. In other sermons, pastors specified the idolatrous gods of sex, money, and one's own way as hindrances to complete surrender. Pastors specified an alternative set of Christian goals in which the individual gave his testimony "with the lip and with the life."

Motivating the Christian Life: "Degrees" of Sin and Salvation

Squires, pastor of Cypress Pond for seven years, was well liked by many in the church, but he also had enemies who stopped coming to church, they said, because Squires was the pastor. Such opposition undoubtedly figured in his decision to leave Cypress Pond in October, 1985. Squires had much less formal education than Manning since his postsecondary work consisted of only two years at a southern Bible college. Having been called in his twenties to be a minister, Squires was a vigorous man in his fifties at the time he left Cypress Pond. A staunch conservative, at the pulpit he took strong stands based on the authority he felt the church assigned his pastoral role. His sermons generally were rated highly by his congregation, whose criticisms had more to do with his failure to "control his family." As the following excerpts show, he had a flair for making personal *exempla* come alive. He also was somewhat less judgmental in his evaluations than Manning, making him more popular with those who were less than perfect.

Squires begins the sermon, "A Committed Christian," with a few announcements overlooked earlier. Then, reading 1 Corinthians 15:10, he makes the transition to the sermon "proper" with a prayer:

> Father, thank you this morning that we have the opportunity to be together. Thank you lord for your presence. Now I pray for the Holy Spirit to lead us, that all that's done and said here today would be for no other purpose than to glorify you. And lord we know when you receive the glory from what is done, then we also receive benefits. . . . Lord help us to be Paul, or like Paul. Help us to understand that by the grace of God we can be all that you want us to be. . . . Father we look back upon the life of Paul and his own testimony, and we see a great change. Lord, help us to make that change in our lives that we might be all that you need us to be. Save those who are lost this morning, bring back the backslidden, and in all that you do, we'll thank you, because we ask it in Jesus' name, amen. (Morning Worship Service, August 11, 1985)

This prayer sketches Squires's intentions for this service. He will discuss the changes that occurred in Paul when he was saved, to demonstrate how members should change. He also will ask members to be saved, and he will exhort the "backsliders" to return to full participation in Christianity.

He opens by asking, "If you were arrested for being a Christian, would there be enough evidence against you to convict you?" He says that murderers, drunkards, and robbers get arrested and convicted based on evidence. With Christians, in contrast, it all involves our act of dedication to the lord as to the extent of how much Christ can be seen through us. How much of ourselves have we been willing to give to the lord? Have we turned over every key of our lives and said, "Lord, you control all of it?" Or have we reserved part of it and said, "Lord, hands off. I'm keeping this under my control. And I'm gonna do my own thing."

Squires asks, "Now what is the proof in your life that you're a Christian? What do we see in your life that would say to the world, I'm a Christian?" To answer these questions, Squires uses the life of Paul, who had undergone a drastic change in his life when "he met the resurrected Lord" on the road to Damascus. "And from that very moment, Paul was a different person. He said to the lord, 'Lord what must I do, what do you want me to do?' . . . Have you said to Jesus, Lord what do you want me to do?"

In discussing Paul's conversion, Squires wants his audience to understand three things about the changes that occurred in Paul's life and that may be expected in the lives of others similarly converted. First, "we'll see a new affection in our lives for Jesus Christ." Now, Squires says, he'll "get personal." He contrasts his own love of the Lord with the attitudes of "those who say they love the Lord and never darken the doors of the church, never do anything that would say to me and to the world around them we love the Lord. I don't think I'm an oddball—some people think that I am—but I don't think I am."

Next, Squires says, the encounter with Jesus causes a "new attitude towards believers." Again, he contrasts God's people with "the world":

> When I was saved, I suddenly found that the loveliest people in the world was the people I had been neglecting . . . that was God's people. . . . They took me under their wing and just helped me to grow and mature in my Christian living.
>
> . . . Now the worldly people won't help you do that. [He tells the parable of the Prodigal Son to illustrate the "world."] . . . When the money ran out, the friends ran out. . . . And so [the Prodigal Son] got up and went back [home]. I wanna tell you something, folks, and I say this this morning with all the love in my heart. The love is still right here in this church. Some of you ought to get back. Now listen to me when I say this. I thought

about it seriously. God has never prepared a sermon in my heart for those who aren't here. What I'm saying this morning, God had for someone who's right here in this building. It may be for you. It may be for you. It's easy to say now, well, he's speaking to that three hundred and something that's not here this morning. No, they may get word of what's being said, but I'm speaking to you. When Christ came into Paul's heart he had a new affection for the brethren.

   I wanna ask you a question this morning. Is there ill feelings in your heart about some person? Have you had words with someone you haven't straightened things out with?

Squires continues to ask similar personal questions, directed to his listeners under the guidance, he claims, of the Lord. Rhetorically, he is setting up a series of queries for listeners to use in constructing another internal dialogue. They are to see if his words are meant for them, if they have been failing in love, failing to grow as Christians.

   The third change that Paul's life illustrates is "a new appreciation for the grace of God." Squires speaks of the grace of God present in Christ's crucifixion, noting that this grace is not something that an individual can achieve; it's a gift. Nor can one be saved by working for salvation. However,

   within each one of us ought to be the desire every day of our lives to say to the Father, Lord I love you. And let him say back to us in so many ways I love you. There ought to be a prayer time in our lives. . . . There ought to be a desire to serve him. There should be some concern in your life about helping with the lord's work. I've only been able to meet with the nominating committee one time so far. But I wonder how many times they have approached some of you already in this, in trying to get people for the new year, when they've had some people say, "No, I can't do it." When you haven't prayed about it. . . . When you love the lord, . . . then you want to serve him.

He continues comparing what many people in the congregation actually do with what they ought to be doing. To prayer and service, he now adds church attendance, introducing the concept of the backslider, or one who is saved but fails to live by the commandments of God.

"Folks, we've got a lot of folks on vacation. And I know this is the time of year for vacations. But we cannot excuse the absentees of this church by saying they're on vacation. Some of them are so backslidden, I don't believe the *devil* could even find them. That's a burden." He recalls conversations he has had with members about the local church's potential and its failure to live up to that potential. He especially asks that young couples come and bring their children to make the Sunday school enrollment swell. Squires repeatedly asks: "But where are you? Where are you?"

He chastises the congregation further, moving from criticisms of their "faithfulness" to criticisms of their "lifestyle." "Now right now you've probably already said, you're going to start meddling. But that's alright, I'm gonna meddle anyway. . . . I'm talking to me, I'm talking to you this morning. We are setting examples before your children." He proceeds with a personal story about a man he knew at a former church who set a bad example for his five-year-old son by drinking and who changed after being saved. But, he notes, "it's not just drinking."

> What about foul language? . . . I said to them, and let me say it again this morning, and listen to how I'm saying this, God's last name is not "damn it." Do you hear me? God's last name is not "damn it." When we've got to where we use it in that connection so much until the name of God doesn't mean anything to the world anymore. It's a curse word, a slang word that we use.
>
> What do young people hear in your voice when they hear you saying that? Like one of the deacons in another town [that] I carried my car to, and someone said my car was giving trouble, and they said, take it to this particular fellow, he'll fix it, he's the best we've got in this town. I knew him, I'd been to his church. I knew he was serving as a deacon.
>
> I walked into that little garage that morning. And he was all down under the hood, fixing something on the car and I walked up there. He didn't know I was on the place and I guess he had a wrench that slipped. And it must have skinned his hand. And he came out of there slinging that hand and saying some of his fifty-cent words. And then when he saw I was standing there, he looked around and went, "Hee, hee, hee."
>
> Let me tell you something, folks, it's not funny. It's not funny. Suppose I had been a lost person and knew that he was serving as deacon in

a church? You know what would happen? It would happen just like I've got a brother-in-law in [a town] right now who won't go to the church that's two blocks from his house because he saw one of the deacons drinking a beer one day. You've got an influence on people around you. It can either be good or bad. What are you doing about it?

In this excerpt, Squires implies that this deacon is failing to live as a saved person. He may jeopardize a "lost person's" chance for salvation by his behavior. As this deacon sins, so too may persons in this congregation.

The closing portion of this sermon establishes not only the need for salvation, but also the need for behavioral changes following that experience. Squires also makes plain that, if there are no behavioral changes, one of two things is going on: either the person never really was saved or the person is a backslider.

Did it change your life when you met the lord? If it didn't, you did exactly what Paul said last week in these verses, we have believed in vain. In other words, the word of God didn't sink into our heart, it was just shallow and there was nothing really happening down in here. And the Bible says if you believed in vain, you are still in your sins.

But I wanna tell you something folks, I believe it is possible to be saved and backslide. I believe in backsliding. It can happen. And that may be the condition you're in this morning if Christ isn't being seen in your life. But you know what the lord said about those who backslide? Come and repent and return to your first love.

Closing with a prayer and the invitation, Squires seeks to draw into the body of Christ both the "lost" and the "backslidden." The former are to come forward for salvation; the latter for rededication. His sermon appeared to have been effective: two women, both "saved" and both hard workers in the church, answered the invitational call in tears, one of them sobbing audibly.

Similar in content but more personally oriented than Manning's sermon, the sermon by Squires establishes a number of moral criteria, or actions, which should "prove" salvation. Among these are frequent prayer, church attendance, service, and witnessing to others by the way one lives one's life. Specific sins mentioned are drinking and cursing. Failing to live as one ought to do imperils the "lost" in general, as well as the souls of children who have not yet "made a decision." In this sermon Squires denotes three categories of people: the lost, the saved, and the backsliders. The latter are saved but are not living as saved. Presumably, the pastor's intent was to cause each member of the audience, first, to hold an internal inquisition—into which of the categories did he or she fit?—and, second, to take appropriate action. This action he specified for them.

In sum, pastors closed these sermons on living a Christian life with appeals for listeners to respond to the workings of the Holy Spirit by walking the aisles during the invitation call. Members of the audience were asked to respond if they desired to be cleansed of unconfessed sins that were preventing them from growing in the Lord, to commit to living more Christlike lives, to renew their desire to know the Lord. Another motivating factor is implied in these sermons. Just as pastors made veiled judgments, so too could fellow churchgoers. If one's behavior was judged as wanting, then questions were raised about one's salvation. One way to show that one was committed and in touch with the Holy Spirit was to respond publicly during the service, in addition to striving to "live as Christ" in their daily lives.

Motivating the Christian Life: The Blessings of God

To the extent that members managed to live in accord with this model, pastors claimed, the Lord would "bless" them in this life. While pastors often mentioned the blessings of the Lord, in the four transcribed sermons discussed in these chapters on "Preaching Salvation" and "Preaching Commitment," the word *blessings* was used only once in a biblical quotation. These sermons stressed the rewards of salvation, but not in terms of concrete "blessings." Squires made one oblique comment, as did Wayne in chapter 4, about the benefits to be gained by being a Christian, while Manning, from my perspective, seemed to avoid using the term *blessings* altogether. However, one of the visiting pastors, the Reverend Mac Jackson, preached an entire sermon ("What Jesus Wants to Do with Us; What Will We Do with Jesus?") that constantly referred to "blessings" (July 28, 1985, Evening Worship Service). Since the goals and structure of Jackson's sermon are very similar to those already discussed, I shall concentrate solely on his use of the term *blessings.*

Jackson was the local head of the countywide SBC Baptist Association. This meant that he primarily coordinated evangelism efforts, and his sermons reflected that aim. This particular sermon, like so many others, stressed the need for salvation and for commitment to Christ. While Jackson did talk about sin, he kept stressing the blessings of God:

> I believe that he wants to do with us so that we will be receiving all the blessings of God. That's what he wants to do with us [so] that we will be receiving every blessing that God has in store for us.
>
> . . . And thirdly, I believe that he wants to do with us so that we might be vitally related to his church and its mission. . . . He wants us to receive all the blessings of God; he wants us to be willing to follow him; and he wants us to be part of the local church, vitally involved in the mission of the church. Which Jesus gave to the church, that we are to go into all the world with the gospel.
>
> . . . I can confidently say, I can forthrightly say here tonight, that I believe a local church congregation like Cypress Pond and the churches across our association are among the greatest blessings that God has given upon this earth.

Jackson's use of the term *blessings* is rather general. God will give his followers blessings if they do what he wants them to do in their lives. Among the things they should endeavor to accomplish, Jackson stresses evangelism. Correspondingly, the main source of blessings is the local church itself, as it sets out to accomplish that goal. Jackson makes no equation between following God and specific, personal blessings.

One reason for such omissions in sermons may have been an unwillingness to correlate salvation with specific lists of "blessings." At Cypress Pond, among the blessings the Lord gives, pastors and members informally included necessities such as food and shelter, and, for those who worked, a livelihood.[1] Health and long life were much more problematic, since many in this congregation were ill. Death, too, was always visible in this kin-based community. Pastors acknowledged that they did not have clear or concrete answers concerning responsibility for suffering; in this area, opinion varied widely.[2]

Another reason for playing down the role of blessings in these sermons may have been that the pastors preferred to focus on other motivating factors. They implored members to become *better* Christians. Becoming more Christlike included personal growth as a Christian, but such development often was overshadowed by the evaluations of behavior made by these pastors. That is, if one were a good Christian, then personal growth would take certain evident forms. If it did not, then pastors implied, "perhaps" the individual was not saved, or was still on "the first rung" of the ladder of Christian life. To assert oneself as a committed Christian, the individual had to draw closer.

What Goes Around Comes Around

All these sermons present verbal models of how to judge beliefs through action. Throughout this chapter and the last, quotations from Manning, Wayne, and Squires showed this judgment in action. In effect, pastors were modeling how to make these judgments in daily life. But in standing behind the pulpit as exemplary models, they also offered themselves as targets of evaluation. Well aware of their congregation's predisposition to judge, pastors played upon and fostered that judgment. In sermons, they referred to themselves and to pastors in general as models. In the sense that they felt called by God to undertake their jobs, pastors concurred with the public perception that they were men set apart by God. As such, when they claimed to be speaking for God, they appeared to feel they could judge with impunity.

In fact, this impunity did not exist, for pastors in turn were judged by church members. They were judged on their speaking abilities, of course. But, because they were so visible, they were expected to exemplify the standard of Christlike living they preached to the congregation. In this small community, many pastors felt the impact of the judgments they themselves preached. Thus Squires, just before leaving, preached a sermon [appropriately titled "God's Call"] criticizing those in his congregation who had been criticizing his family. He asserted that *he*, and not his family, had been called to preach. To expect that his family to be better than other families, he informed the congregation, was unfair.

Manning too devoted an entire sermon to the pastoral role and afterward passed out copies of the sermon to members of the pulpit committee that was searching for Cypress Pond's next full-time pastor. Because he was their interim pastor, his sermon addressed what members should look for in a full-time pastor. He suggested that the congregation investigate these characteristics in prospective pastors: pastoral training and education; grades in school; emotional stability; spiritual life; moral character, including sexual wholesomeness; and credit rating. Members should ascertain whether the pastor tithed, if he visited church members, and how he preached.

Consequences of This Belief System for the Individual

Weber points to one of the major consequences of a religious system that makes the believer attempt to prove the existence of a belief state in the social world: "The ascetic, when he wishes to act within the world, that is, to practice inner-worldly asceticism, must become afflicted with a sort of happy stupidity regarding any question about the meaning of the world, for he must not worry about such questions" (Weber 1963:172–73.) "Happy stupidity," however, hardly characterized the members of Cypress Pond. Often they were far from "happily stupid" as they pursued sure and certain knowledge of salvation in a social context that denied them such certainty. In fact, to achieve any assurance, the believer usually had to reinterpret the system in her or his own terms—a dangerous pursuit in a social system stressing moral conformity. At Cypress Pond, sufficient variation did exist that some few members tried to offer alternative explanations. Pastors, too, were aware of some of the contradictions in their evangelical postulates and sometimes offered pragmatic solutions for themselves and others. For example, Squires did not insist that all in his flock had to have a specific moment in which they were "born again." He also used the concept of the "backslider" to introduce degrees of salvation.

Nevertheless, the path to salvation sketched in the preceding pages is, in Weber's terms, a form of "inner-worldly asceticism." From Weber's perspective, the inner-worldly ascetic focuses on his own conduct as a marker of his saved status, just as the Southern Baptists do. This type of asceticism depends upon a "rejection of the world" in favor of the world to come, while at the same time it demands of its adherents a participation in the world as a "warrior in behalf of god, regardless of who the enemy is and what the means of doing battle are" (Weber 1963:169). As we have seen, Southern Baptists believe that they are engaged in the great work of saving souls from the sins of the world and from eternal damnation, the consequence of that sin. Thus, they participate *in the world* for the sake of the transcendent world to come.

Nevertheless, the system as a whole functions to keep individuals who participate in this world view—and, as we have seen, it is very difficult to escape the world view if one stays in this traditional, relatively closed community—constantly focusing inward, to evaluate their own degrees of salvation and commitment, and also focusing outward, to evaluate the potential degrees of salvation and commitment being shown by their neighbors. As chapter 4 made clear, an emotional knowledge of salvation is not accepted as a valid marker of salvation unless it is accompanied by behavioral changes.

In this chapter, we have seen that these SBC pastors made the major criterion of belief a "spiritual commitment" defined by: (1) the individual's act of will, or choice, which selected this world view as the only true one; and (2) the dispositional state to prove through one's actions that one was committed. Hence actions, especially moral actions, were taken as the most important indicators of salvation.

Problems with this answer, for members at Cypress Pond, were twofold: first, the standards were set so high that members had a hard time coming close to meeting them; second, if members at any time failed to meet the standards, then they were asked to doubt their original salvation in questioning why they had failed. The rhetoric of the sermons reinforced—indeed, it was a major factor in creating—this constant state of uncertainty. Paradoxically, although pastors asserted that one could have sure knowledge of salvation, at the same time they undermined that certainty with a list of questions that seemed to keep the churchgoer perpetually "wallowing" in a liminal state. The professed believer had to ask herself or himself, "Am I really saved, or did I believe in vain? What about the changes in my life—are they enough, or am I backslider? What about my fellow churchgoers—are they really saved, or are they lying?" Though it could be argued that I have overstressed the internal dialogues set up by pastors, it seems to me that, even if one became skilled in tuning out these sermons (as a teen-ager I planned my wardrobe, daydreamed, and so on), their power was great. At Cypress Pond, children were brought to services from the cradle on up, and the messages were delivered at least a hundred times a year. Sunday after Sunday, the genre of preaching in this SBC church made and unmade salvation and commitment as criteria of belief.

Why was this system created in the first place, and why has it en-dured so successfully for generations? The first question lies outside the scope of this work, though Weber's (1958) insights provide clues, and Ellen Rosenberg's analysis (1989) provides insights into the cur-rent political and social agenda of the SBC leaders (though, in my opin-ion, she overstates the degree to which this agenda is a deliberate attempt to perpetuate racism, classism, and patriarchy; see also Ammerman 1990 and 1993). Answering the second question has brought us to the heart of this book, for social systems are perpetuated in social interactions. South-ern Baptist ministers are remarkably skillful in preaching and thus in creating the world view anew each time they speak from the pulpit. Members, in turn, use the worship service as a ritual context for up-holding the world view and for centering their lives in its institutional framework. Community, family, place, and religion become so inter-twined that to question any portion of the system is to question the whole. Thus, to return again to Weber, the "happy stupidity" consists in the rela-tively unquestioned fundamental premise of existence that church mem-bers postulate—namely, that salvation is the goal of life itself.

6

The Altar Call

On the Sunday morning following a week of traditional revival worship services, the Reverend John Manning made an emotional appeal from the pulpit. He lamented the lack of response shown by the congregation at the previous week's revival. Not one individual had been "born again." Manning asked what was wrong. Was it he? Was something wrong in the fellowship? Were members not witnessing correctly or visiting potential converts? He wept as he spoke of the weight of his burden. Even though he personally had witnessed to the unsaved youths in the church who had reached the age of accountability (twelve or older), they had not responded to the invitations for salvation offered during the revival. In fact, many of these young people had not even attended the revival services. At the close of this sermon, Manning gave an altar call asking individuals to respond to Jesus, to confess their sins, and to give Jesus their hearts and lives.

No one publicly answered that altar call for salvation.[1] Instead, one deacon went to the front and spoke with the pastor. Manning reported to the congregation that "one" had come forward with a burden on his heart—with a concern for revival in the church. Manning asked that others who had this same burden on their hearts respond by coming forward. Eleven church members walked up to express their concern.

This incident illustrates that the verbal performance of the sermon features explicit appeals for members to manifest their beliefs in actions. While the previous two chapters examined sermons primarily from the pastor's point of view, here the focus is the *interactional* dimension of the worship service. Recall that, during the sermon, the audience could participate only by listening. But when pastors made the invitation, the audience could respond physically. These congregational actions, or lack thereof, were taken to signify internal belief states.

To understand fully the interactional dimensions of the altar call at Cypress Pond, we first must examine both the traditional pattern of the altar call and why pastors have begun to change this pattern. Manning, for instance, began his altar call with a plea that the lost be saved. When he got no response to that altar call, inspired by the responding deacon, he requested a different kind of action. Responses were forthcoming. In fact, very few responses to altar calls (only 2.3 percent) were linked to traditional expressions of salvation. Rather, 69 percent of audience responses came when pastors changed the altar call and asked members specifically for some indication of their commitment to the church. The patterning of audience responses is examined later in the chapter, along with possible motivations for those responses.

Analysis of data on spoken altar calls and audience responses is based on the following transcriptions and observations. During fourteen months of fieldwork, I attended 111 worship services in which pastors had the option of issuing an altar call. Of these, 46 were tape-recorded. An additional 7 services, which I did not attend, were taped for me.[2] Manning and Squires were full-time pastors at Cypress Pond at different times, and most of the invitations were given by one or the other. Nine other pastors preached "guest" sermons at Cypress Pond; seven such sermons were taped, but only five of their altar calls (given by four different visiting pastors) were recorded.[3] All five of these were transcribed, along with eighteen of the invitations given by Squires and Manning.

At each service I attended, I observed whether or not an altar call was given and who responded to it. While most responses occurred during congregational singing of the invitational hymn, on rare occasions the pastor would ask members to close their eyes while the choir sang and the organist played. Even during these times, I usually was able to see who went forward (since most members peeked), though there were times when it was not possible to do so with accuracy. When I could not identify individuals who went forward, I counted the number of responders by the sets of footsteps I heard. If a member "made a decision for salvation" or for "rededication" during a time when members had their eyes closed, the pastor subsequently would announce the decision to the congregation at the close of the call.

Altar Calls in the Context
of the Sermon Speech Genre

In discussing the sermon speech genre in chapter 4, I noted that altar calls constitute one optional segment of the sermon. Initially, I decided to classify the altar call as a separate speech genre, due to the importance both members and pastors gave to the altar calls. Within the social science literature, however, altar calls are not discussed as a distinct traditional speech genre. Researchers always link them to the sermon. Borker, for example, includes the persuasive "appeal" to the listener given at the close of sermons as one feature of evangelical sermons (1974:177). Baumer classifies the traditional altar call as one feature of evangelically-oriented sermons, regardless of whether or not such a sermon is preached in an evangelical church (1985:80). For reasons of clarity, I elected to treat the altar call as an optional, marked segment of the sermon. While it can be omitted, at Cypress Pond it almost always is performed at the close of the sermon.

Since nonevangelical sermons usually do not include altar calls, and since, analytically, altar calls almost never are considered separately from the sermon, this linkage makes documenting the form of altar calls and changes in them more difficult. Tracing the historical evolution of the altar call also presents many difficulties, since calls were spoken during services and not generally written down. Townsend, in her historical study of South Carolina's Baptists, notes that "the nature of devotional services is difficult to arrive at from the church books" (1935:295). Though she mentions "'doors' opened for experience after business and devotional meetings" and the subsequent baptism of believers, she gives no examples of altar calls (1935:295). The phrase "'doors' opened for experience" may refer to some established ritual period, such as an altar call, in which the individual could declare salvation, but the inference is uncertain. Hill (1966) and Mathews (1977) describe the southern style of preaching in general terms, including its emphasis on salvation and rededication, but they fail to provide examples. Morland discusses calls as features of Baptist religion, presenting them as integral parts of every Baptist worship service (1958). However, he observes that few go forward in response, because everyone in the congregation already belongs to the church (1958:113). A few transcribed examples of contemporary altar calls are to be found in Borker (1974), Lawless (1988), and Peacock (1975).

Even though social science writings on southern Protestantism emphasize the orientation towards salvation, they usually omit analysis of the ritual contexts calling for salvation (Bryant 1981 and Peacock 1975 are exceptions; see Golding 1981; Greenhouse 1986; Hill 1966; Hudson 1972; Morland 1958). Although a person may be saved in contexts other than the call, usually the experience of salvation does come during a worship service (see Hudson 1972; Morland 1958), or at least it is publicly acknowledged then. A few social science studies have examined large-scale mass media evangelical altar calls, such as those sponsored by the Billy Graham Evangelical Association (Altheide and Johnson 1977; Lang and Lang 1960; Wimberly et al. 1975). However, none of these studies is interactional in nature; researchers have focused on how to determine whether those who responded during the altar call actually were converted. In contrast, this research portrays the patterns associated with altar calls in a kin-based, circumscribed, small-group setting as they occurred over a year-long period.

Because members of Cypress Pond included the "invitational call" as a separate folk category, I was able to gather information about changes in altar calls that had taken place over the past two generations. These changes were reflected in the use of altar calls both to invite salvation and to mark specific commitments to the church. While I suspect, based on observations in other churches in the local community, that these changes were widespread,[4] the present work documents the usage and reported changes found at Cypress Pond during the study period.

Congregation members told me what invitational calls were like prior to 1950. At that time, altar calls were given only during revival worship services rather than as part of almost all worship services. Most older church members recalled experiencing salvation during revival meetings held at their church once a year during "laying by time." This period in the annual church cycle coincided with a period of rest in the late summer, after plants were too big to plow but were not yet ready for harvesting. Then members attended revival meetings over week-long periods, and the youth made decisions for salvation. Congregation members frequently told me that they had considered the decision well before the actual revival, or that they had thought about salvation during the week of preaching, going forward on the last night.

A marked change occurred in the frequency of the calls beginning in the 1950s, after Cypress Pond hired a full-time pastor. In 1985–86, the invitational calls were given at most worship services, including those held during two weeks of revival services each year. This increased frequency apparently caused pastors to search for additional means to ensure audience participation. As Morland asks (1958:113), if a pastor preaches to a congregation of believers, who can respond to a call for salvation? If no one responds, Sunday after Sunday or during a week of revival meetings, then the altar calls may seem redundant to both the pastor and his congregation. At Cypress Pond, members still expressed uncertainty concerning the incorporation of an invitational call into every worship service. For example, Alex Finch, a former Methodist who now was a member of Cypress Pond, criticized the practice one night while I was visiting in his home. Talking with me while his wife Pat put the children to bed, Alex claimed that Southern Baptists have too many invitational calls. He had noted that the Baptists gave them often, but, he said, "nobody goes forward." Puzzled by this state of affairs, he had questioned a former pastor about why Baptists had so many altar calls. The pastor had explained that the calls were given every Sunday so that people could respond whenever they felt the need and not just at set times. But he seemed unconvinced, for he asked my opinion of the practice.

Variation in the Content of Altar Calls

If altar calls were seen as a part of the sermon, how did the congregation know when the altar call began? Viewing the calls as sociolinguistic phenomena reveals several criteria by which the altar call was framed, or "keyed," in the verbal performance of pastors at the close of the sermon (Bauman 1977). Two features marked the shift to altar call: the manifest content of the invitation to respond, and the actual announcement by the pastor that the congregation now would stand to sing the

invitational hymn. While these features indicated to the listening congregation that the sermon was almost over and the ritual time to respond was at hand, pastors varied in the speech styles they used to key
the call and in the types of calls they gave.

With respect to content, I have indicated that two main types of
calls were given at Cypress Pond, readily distinguishable by the kind
of response they solicited from the congregation. How did the congregation learn what actions each type of call demanded? The first type of
call was the *traditional call for salvation and rededication*. In a somewhat
expanded form, this type remained the call type most prevalent at Cypress Pond; all but eight calls were of this type. While these calls included a request that persons come forward to indicate their salvation,
they also incorporated a more general request that listeners make "the
decisions they need to make." At the time of this study, the church
taught that there were many decisions which could be made during
this ritual. For example, during one Baptist Association meeting preparing for the "Good News America Simultaneous Revivals," held in
1986, various Salkehatchie County Baptist church members who were
interested in counseling responders discussed the use of a printed form
to be given to responding individuals. It included the following categories:

1. I accept Christ as my Savior and Lord.
2. I reaffirm my commitment to make Christ the Lord of my life.
    [Rededication]
3. I want to explore opportunities in church vocations.
4. I feel definitely that God is leading me toward a church vocation.
5. Other.[5]

Another response pastors sought with these traditional altar calls was
the formal transfer of membership from one church to another. A person who wanted to shift membership had to do so by asking that a "letter" be sent from her or his former church to the new church. A person
announced his intent to make this change during the invitation by walking to the front of the church and telling the pastor of the decision.

Pastors at Cypress Pond, in order to maximize the number of responders, nearly always included some general "invitation" in their al-

tar calls. For example, in the following request, given during the announcement of the invitational hymn, Squires asked members to respond in this fashion:

> Now, we're going to ask you to stand with us as we sing Hymn Number 240 ["Just As I Am"]. Perhaps there is someone this morning who needs to come in dedication of heart and life or to come for salvation. Whatever your need is, we encourage you to come at this time as we stand and sing. May we stand please. (Morning Worship Service, June 2, 1985)

Squires frequently abbreviated the invitational call even more, knowing that his congregation understood the types of responses they could make. Thus, he would conclude a sermon with a simple plea such as this:

> Our Hymn of Invitation this morning is Number 248 ["Almost Persuaded Now to Believe"]. We're going to stand in a moment and sing. I trust that as the lord has moved upon your heart, you'll make the decision that you need to make. May we stand please as we sing. (Morning Worship Service, June 30, 1985)

A visiting local pastor, the Reverend Mac Jackson, presented a series of invitations illustrating the various types of responses possible:

> Let us pray. . . . We pray that if there is one here today [who is not saved] that this would be the day that they are born again by the power of God through Jesus Christ our lord. We pray in his name and for his sake, amen.
>
> The invitation of this church, of your pastor, would be indeed to invite you to come receiving Christ as lord and savior, being born again by the power of God. As we sing together we invite you to come. If there are others here today who would come in rededication, recommitment, or seek to unite with this church by movement of letter or statement, we invite you to come. This is a time that—on the mind of Christ—is upon our mind that people be born again and this song is the opportunity for someone to respond. It is Number 240 as we sing together. (Morning Worship Service, July 28, 1985)

Table 1. Altar Calls for Commitment

Pastor's Name	Service	Action Requested	Number of Responders
1. Hammet, Revival Guest Speaker (along with Squires)	Revival Service	Parents were asked to come indicating their desire for Jesus' guidance in raising their children	8
2. Hammet, Revival Guest Speaker (along with Squires)	Revival Service	Members were asked to come forward to thank their pastor or to ask for his forgiveness. Hammet widened the invitation to include all who had anything on their hearts which might keep them from being the right kind of Christian.	18
3. Squires	Sunday Morning Service	Members were asked to pledge support to the new pastor and his family that God will provide for the church.	35
4. Manning	Sunday Morning Service	Persons were invited to respond by coming nearer to the light symbolized by a candle at the altar.	23
5. Manning	Sunday Morning Service	Members who tithed were asked to respond by coming forward on the first verse of the invitational hymn. Members who wanted to commit to becoming tithers were to come forward during the second verse.	31
6. Manning	Sunday Morning Service	Members who were dedicated towards working and praying for revival in the church were asked to come to the altar.	18
7. Manning	Revival Service	Members who were concerned about persons not saved were asked to come forward.	7
8. Manning	Sunday Morning Service	A deacon came forward during a traditional call for salvation. Manning reported that "one" had come forward concerned about the need for revival in the church. He asked others who shared this concern to come forward.	12[a]
Total			152

[a]The number 12 includes the "one" (a deacon) and the other eleven who responded.

This call explicitly lists the types of responses looked for: salvation, re-dedication, recommitment, and movement of church membership.

The second type of call given at Cypress Pond was *the call to demonstrate commitment through specified actions*. By shifting to a commitment call, pastors could ask those who presumably were already saved to show exactly *how* much they were committed to the church fellowship. During the course of the fieldwork, three pastors who preached at Cypress Pond gave altar calls of this type a total of eight times. Table 1 summarizes all eight. Though given rarely, these calls were marked by large-scale congregational responses.

One of the most stirring of these calls was given by Manning during a Sunday morning worship service. In my fieldnotes (the service was not recorded on audiotape), I recorded this commitment altar call given on January 19, 1986, during the morning worship service.

Manning first lit a candle on the Communion table in front of the church to symbolize the light of Christ. He next "drafted" six people from the congregation to stand in the center aisle of the church. Some were directed to stand close to the front, others near the rear of the church. The pastor used this graphic illustration to talk about persons near or far from the light of Jesus. If you were near to the light, you tithed [gave the church 10 percent of your gross income], you went to church frequently, you prayed frequently, and perhaps you taught Sunday school. If you only came when it was providential, you were further from the light. If you only came "once in a blue moon," you were even further from the light. The person at the very back of the church, the venerable Deacon Lancaster, was labeled as a person unsure of his salvation, who wanted to know Jesus.

To demonstrate being drawn to the light of Christ, Manning went to the back of the church and escorted Deacon Lancaster to the altar at the front of the church. He asked the other five standing in the aisle to come forward to the altar, too, and they did so.

After completing these actions, he invited all who would to come forward to the light. Manning recited by heart a verse from the invitational hymn, "The Light of the World Is Jesus," and asked that only those come forward who were truly moved. He did *not* want people coming for "show." All those at the altar joined in the singing of this hymn as the organist played. During the invitational hymn, an additional seventeen people went forward to join the six members already at the "light."

This call asked responders to indicate their commitment to the church by literally moving closer to the light of Christ, symbolized by the burning candle. The behaviors commitment should entail were spelled out: congregation members should give 10 percent of their income to the church; attend church regularly; help in the work of the church; and pray frequently. If one did all these things, then one was a committed Christian. If one did not do these things, one was not a committed Christian. Very little ambiguity, either for the congregation or the pastor, was found in this type of call.

These calls to demonstrate some specific form of commitment (for instance, support for one's pastor) sometimes were tied to the kind of sermons discussed in chapter 5—that is, sermons dealing with images of the committed Christian. However, this link was not essential. For example, such calls were not included after the two sermons discussed in chapter 5. Yet, in "The Price of Consecration," Manning did connect the need for revival in the church with a general plea that members be more committed and commit less sin. This sermon led to the specific "invitation" in which members were asked to draw nearer to the "light." In the other seven sermons that preceded commitment calls, the pastor preached sermons targeted at one particular Christian action (see table 1). Manning, for instance, preached about the need for revival before asking persons committed to revival in the church to come forward ("Power Failure Produces Crises!," Morning Worship Service, March 2, 1986). Manning's sermon, "How Much Shall I Give," was followed by an altar call emphasizing the necessity of tithing (Morning Worship Service, January 19, 1986). The Reverend Bill Hammet, guest revival speaker, followed up a sermon on parenting with an invitation asking any parent come forward who wanted "Jesus to help me be a wise parent" (Revival Worship Service, September 24, 1985). These examples show that variation existed in the rhetorical devices and content of the sermons used to motivate salvation and commitment. Variation also existed in the typical forms of delivery.

Variation in Pastoral Speech Styles

Pastors usually ended their sermons with a pastoral prayer in which the altar call was embedded, following that prayer with the announcement of the invitational hymn. Squires, pastor at Cypress Pond for the first six months of fieldwork, always used this format in making invitational calls when he preached. This closing prayer and the announcement of the invitational hymn illustrate his style:

> Would you bow your head with us please? [pause]
> As our heads are bowed and as we pray, in just a moment we're going to have our invitation, the lord speaking to your heart, you'll have the opportunity to make the decision you need to make. But right now as every head bowed and every eye is closed, as the Holy Spirit deals with our hearts, have you let Christ come into your life? Or is he still locked out, because doors are closed? What about the door of fear? What about the door of doubt? What about the door of shame? Perhaps that you've committed sin in your life, he may find that you're unclean if he comes into the heart or if you let him in through the open door. What about the fear of doubt, wondering if he can forgive you of your sins and save your soul? What about fear itself? [The organist now was playing softly in the background.] The fear that he may blame instead of comforting. Christ wants you tonight to come, he wants you to come by opening the door and letting him into your life, to be a central part of it. If you're not a Christian tonight we encourage you to be saved. If you are a Christian, if you're not living as you know you need to be living for his glory, then you dedicate that life for him and live for him from this day forward.
> Our father, we thank you tonight for your presence, thank you lord for the opportunity to share from your word. Thank you lord that you do come into our lives, thank you that you have forgiven our sins, and you paid the debt on Calvary's cross. Thank you that you are a resurrected and living savior. And thank you that because you live, we also live. In these moments, speak to hearts and may a decision be as you would have it to be made. Because we ask it in Jesus' name, amen.
> Our hymn of invitation tonight is No. 219 ["Pass Me Not, O Gentle Savior"]. Hymn No. 219. We're gonna ask you to stand with us, and as

we sing, you make the decision the lord is leading you to make this very night. May we stand please. (Evening Worship Service, June 23, 1985)

In this passage, the altar call is woven into the closing prayer, and persons present are encouraged to respond to the urgings of the Holy Spirit. The opening of the prayer is marked by the announcement that members are to bow their heads, while the closing of the prayer is marked by an "amen." Other altar calls embedded in prayers followed the same general pattern, regardless of which pastor preached. Five of the seven pastors taped giving altar calls (including Squires) used this format. The only variation in overt style was the phrase used to introduce the prayer. Four of the five used the phrase "let us pray" to mark the transition into prayer, while Squires used "would you bow your heads, please."

Though a prayer at the end of the sermon clearly marked the transition to the altar call, not all pastors used this style. An alternative method of keying the altar call used by some pastors was to weave the invitation into the closing portion of the sermon. The shift to the call occurred when the pastor began to ask the congregation personal questions calling for a response and/or began to stress the immediate need for personal salvation. Placement and content signaled the shift to the altar call, confirmed when the pastor asked members to stand to sing the invitational hymn. Manning preferred this style of invitation. While less common, this style was used by one other visiting pastor.

Manning's revival service, discussed in chapter 4, contained a call illustrating this format. Its overt goal was conversion. As his sermon drew to a close, Manning invited persons to come forward who wanted to be saved.

Now I want you in your mind's eye in these closing moments to see Golgotha's hill. There are three crosses there, there are three men there. One man dies in his sin, going to hell. One man dies for sin, delivering all those who cry out to him. One man dies confessing his sins and calling upon the lord to save him. And Jesus hears him and Jesus saves him.

Now the miracle took place on Calvary. And that's where my sins were handled. And that's where your sins were handled. And that's the good part of preaching. And I praise the Lord that I can stand before you tonight and say that if you will confess your sins openly, and if you will confess Jesus openly before men, and you want to receive him, he will receive you. And he will forgive your sins and cleanse you of the power and guilt and penalty of those sins and give you life everlasting, eternal. We just need to trust him.

And that's our hymn of invitation, "Only Trust Him," 235. We're gonna stand and sing it. And the invitation is open to you to trust Jesus and come confessing your sins, trusting in the Christ and he will save you. 235. Let's stand as we sing. (Revival Worship Service, April 9, 1986)

This passage shows no sharp boundary between the text of the sermon and the call to respond. The sermon topic on the subject of sin has been carried forward into the visual images of the crucifixion of Christ and the choices made by the two criminals crucified with Christ. Once this illustration is in place, Manning asks members to receive Christ and announces the invitational hymn.

Pastors sometimes skip the altar call altogether. This omission occurred in 9 instances out of the 111 services I attended. Of these 9, 3 were services in which pastors did not give sermons. In 5 of the other 6, pastors preached sermons, but other forms of audience participation existed besides the altar calls. These 9 services are summarized in table 2.

All nine of these services were "special" in one way or another and supplemented the traditional sermon with additional elements. In eight of the nine, members participated in ways they would not have during an "ordinary" service. Yet pastors could elect to include calls even in these special types of services. For example, on Mother's Day, 1986, the altar call was given. The altar call also was given after a Communion service, after another song service, and after another sermon preached by the departing pastor concerning the search for a new pastor. Time constraints might be one factor causing pastors to omit the call. After all, the call was the last major item of the service and could be deleted if necessary. But, since most pastors did not omit the altar call when they preached over the allotted time, audience participation in the service apparently counted most in pastoral decisions concerning whether to omit an altar call.

Table 2. Services in Which the Altar Call Was Omitted

A.   Services with Sermons and Audience Participation

1.   On Mother's Day, 1985, the oldest and youngest mothers present were recognized.
2.   In May 1985, three babies were dedicated by their parents; that is, the parents promised to raise their children in the church.
3.   In June 1985, "Lord's Supper" was held; all who so desired could take communion.[a]
4.   In October 1985, a joint baptismal and "Lord's Supper" service was held in which five people were baptized and all present who so desired could take communion.
5.   In April 1986, "Lord's Supper" services were held; all present who so desired could take communion.

B.   Services with a Sermon and No Audience Participation

1.   In November 1985, the interim pastor preached a sermon telling the pastor search committee and the congregation what they should look for in a fulltime pastor.

C.   Services with No Sermons and Audience Participation

1.   In July 1985, after a week-long series of Bible classes known as "Vacation Bible School," the children presented a program in evening worship service.
2.   In September 1985, an informal congregational song service was held during the evening worship service, in which congregational members requested their favorite hymns and then sang them.
3.   In December 1985, the children of the church presented a Christmas pageant during the evening worship service.

---

[a]The Communion service was always referred to as the "Lord's Supper" in the Order of Worship. In informal conversation, the ritual was known as both Communion and the Lord's Supper.

Responding to Altar Calls

We have seen what the pastors intended to do with their altar calls, but how did the congregation respond? For 64 of the 102 services observed, no one went forward. The other 38 services witnessed a total of 220 responses. Such a large number of responses might have suggested that the church was rapidly growing, adding many saved persons to the congregation; however, this was not the case. The majority of responses, 152 of the 220, came during the eight services in which special pleas were made for members to show commitment to the church itself in one way or another (see table 3). It was relatively easy to tabulate audience responses to these altar calls and to see a one-to-one correlation between the pastor's intent and the overt audience response.

Making sense of the responses to the traditional altar calls was not easy for me—nor, I suspect, was it easy for church members. The problem stemmed from the fact that members did not always know *why* any particular individual was at the altar. Pastors always screened the responses of those who came forward from the congregation. That is, all could see who went forward, but the congregation *heard* only what the pastor chose to relay publicly after talking privately with the responder. For instance, when John Lee went forward in response to a traditional call, he spoke briefly with Squires, who then asked him to be seated on a pew in the front of the church. After the singing of the hymn, Squires asked him to stand and relayed this information:

> The church doors are open to receive members as is the custom of Baptist churches. We have tonight presenting himself as a candidate for baptism, John Lee, 101 Cypress Lane in Southville. John, as you know, has been coming to our church now for several months. And right after he started coming out here, I questioned John about his relationship with the lord. I found out that John had made a profession of faith at First Baptist Church Southville, but had never followed through on baptism. Tonight John came and dedicated his heart and life to the lord, seeking to walk in closer fellowship with the lord. And wants to come and offer himself as a candidate for baptism into the fellowship of this church.
>
> What's the pleasure of the church concerning this request? (Evening Worship Service, September 8, 1985)

Table 3. Responses to Altar Calls, May 1985–June 1986, by Type of Call

Type of Call	Number Responding	Percentage Responding
Traditional Calls	68	30.9
Salvation	5	2.3
Rededication	2	0.9
Moving Letter	7	3.2
Other	54	24.5
Commitment Calls	152	69.1
Totals	220	100.0

Because this is a congregational church, permission to baptize John into the fellowship at Cypress Pond required that the church vote on whether to receive him. Following what appeared to be Roberts's *Rules of Order,* a motion was made and seconded that John be accepted for baptism; the church then voted that John be baptized. Those present were invited to come forward after the benediction at the close of the service to welcome John into the church. John's private religious experience, disclosed to the pastor, now had become a matter of public knowledge.

While some motivations for responses were relayed to the congregation, as John's was, the intent behind most responses to traditional altar calls remained private, between the pastor and the responder. My notes on these services indicate that only fourteen of the sixty-eight responses to traditional altar calls were categorized by the pastor in terms corresponding to the types of requests usually made in such calls—that is, salvation, rededication, or "movement of letter" (see table 3). A large residual category, fifty-four responses, was labeled "Other." The category "Other" included responses by members who went forward during the traditional call but whose purpose in going forward was not announced to the congregation. Responders in this category already were members of Cypress Pond and already had been baptized. Possible motivations for their responses are considered in the section entitled "Congregational Assessments of Altar Calls."

Single and Multiple Responders

During my fieldwork, 111 persons responded to altar calls. Since 220 responses to altar calls were observed in this time period, some people obviously responded more than once. In examining the patterning in responders, I separated the one-time responders from the multiple responders (see table 4).[6] Of the one-time responders, most (43 of 65 responders, or 66 percent) answered commitment calls. The 46 multiple responders had from two to ten responses (see table 5) and accounted for 70 percent of the total responses. Most multiple responders went forward for special commitment calls and/or under the traditional call subcategory "Other." Only three multiple responders went forward for "Other" responses alone.

These patterns in single and multiple responders indicate that it is acceptable to go to the altar many times in response to commitment calls and, more rarely, to respond multiply to traditional calls.

Congregational Assessments of Altar Calls

The preceding section presented statistics on responders to altar calls and described patterns in their responses. Counting, as a means of measuring religious experience, is widely practiced in both social science and evangelical traditions. Evangelical preachers count numbers and types of responders to determine the success of a revival, the skill of the evangelist who preached, and the spiritual viability of the audience. For example, Billy Graham has developed an elaborate system for count-

Table 4. Typology of Responders

Type of Responder	Number of Persons	Total Number of Responses	Percentage of Total
Single	65	65	29.55
Multiple	46	155	70.45
Total	111	220	100.00

Table 5. Multiple Responses

Number of Multiple Responses	Number of Persons	Total Number of Responses	Percentage of Total
2	5	50	22.7
3	5	15	6.8
4	5	20	9.1
5	3	15	6.8
6	5	30	13.6
7	1	7	3.2
8	1	8	3.6
10	1	10	4.5
Totals	46	155	70.3[a]

[a]Totaling and rounding off percentages results in a discrepancy between 70.45% in Table 4 and 70.3% here.

ing responses during his mass media "crusades for Christ" (Altheide and Johnson 1977). Within the SBC, similar examples demonstrate how pervasive this method of evaluation has become. During my fieldwork, the SBC held simultaneous revivals in local churches over much of the country, advertising these worship services on television, radio, and in newspapers. Afterward, the number of people who attended and the number baptized were tabulated and published (*Baptist Courier*, April 23, 1987).

Though the SBC publishes tallies of revival results and of baptisms within its constituent churches, social scientists have concluded that many of those who respond to mass-media "crusades for Christ" do not have the experience of being "born again" that they report (Altheide and Johnson 1977; Lang and Lang 1960; Wimberly et al. 1975). We have seen that, at Cypress Pond, pastors structured their sermons so that the congregation members constantly were induced to ask themselves if they "really" were saved. Thus, we might expect that "numbers" do not necessarily tell us much about how a congregation actually interprets what happens during any particular altar call response.

At a simplistic level, we could conclude that pastors make commitment calls to increase audience participation and that data from this
study indicate that pastors are successful in their efforts. But what did
the observed responses mean to the participants? I suggest that responses to the invitations constituted one outcome measure used by the
congregation to resolve some of the dilemmas about salvation present in
this belief system. While these ritual actions did not fully resolve the
problem of "knowing whether one is saved," they at least provided a
formal context in which to demonstrate both *what* one believed and *that*
one believed. Given the emphasis at Cypress Pond on judging one's
own and others' salvation, and given the prominent attention accorded
altar calls, it is hardly surprising that members watched the patterns in
responses and assessed the status of responders.

Due to the sensitive nature of the subject, it was somewhat difficult
to gain access to these assessments of altar calls. As we saw in the description of a cottage prayer meeting in chapter 4, members usually
were *silent* about the content of the salvation experience itself. They felt
that this was a private matter, not one to be discussed with others, despite pastors' endeavors to have them testify with "the lip" (prosely-
tize). An apparent insecurity about their status as saved also manifested
itself in discussions of responses to the altar calls. Many responses to
"invitations" were tied intimately to the salvation experience itself and
to its public validation in the community.

At Cypress Pond, in the absence of information to the contrary,
those who proclaimed their salvation during altar calls and who were
subsequently baptized were assumed to have been saved. Additional
self-report sometimes occurred which indicated that this assumption
was erroneous. For example, I spoke with two members who had been
baptized as youths. These women later came to question their salvation, to the extent that they asked for another baptismal service. One
actually was rebaptized; the other was not. Members then must have
been fully aware, from pastoral sermons as well as requests for rebaptism,
that ritual proclamation alone might not be sufficient.

Another source of information about how one could assess one's
own experience of salvation came from the socialization process. Those
youths who had not yet answered the call were encouraged to do so by
their families and pastor. Before responding, a child had to have an un-

derstanding of her or his own sinful nature. In practice, children were deemed able to make such judgments about themselves as early as age six. Church members considered that the child, by age twelve, knew how to make the requisite distinctions. Those children who had not joined by age twelve were visited by the pastor and other lay leaders and encouraged to respond. When these people urged children to respond, they conveyed information about how one knew one was saved. However, even in this context, communications about how to be saved appeared not to be well developed. The best advice I heard during my entire field-work period was that given by Shirley Thames to her *adult* grandchild, Sarah. In a Women's Missionary meeting, Shirley told how she had answered Sarah's questions about salvation. She told Sarah that she needed to listen to the Holy Spirit. When the Holy Spirit moved her, all Sarah had to do to respond was put one foot forward. The Holy Spirit would do the rest. Later, Sarah did take that step. She walked forward to the altar to indicate an experience of salvation. This action on her part was met with tremendous relief and rejoicing by Sarah's family, for she was close to thirty years of age at the time, and, while she had attended church, her failure to make a profession of faith had concerned her family deeply.[7]

One further example demonstrates the way members incessantly questioned the relationship between altar calls and salvation. Pat Finch— one of the women who had thought about being rebaptized—cited two young boys in the church who had answered an altar call for salvation and had been "saved and baptized." Since both were very young (under age ten), she wondered if they could know if they had been saved? She felt that the church, by accepting these professions of faith, had paved the way for the boys' own questioning at a later date.

From such accounts and from the analysis of sermons, we know that members also were encouraged to evaluate the Christian status of those around them. These evaluations concerned members for several reasons. First, they wanted to know if family members and friends had been saved, especially since they assumed that, after death, they would be with their families in heaven. Second, they did not want to be led into sin or kept from salvation by the devil, acting through the machinations of the unsaved. Pastors frequently spoke of having the "world" (the unsaved) in the church fellowship itself. When the unsaved posed

as the saved in the church, then congregation members might more easily be led "astray."

Since knowing who was saved remained problematic, the dispositional criteria of belief gained weight. According to these criteria, the
saved had to follow the moral code. If a member lapsed, then he could
ask for forgiveness and begin anew. In this community, just how much
one could lapse, or "backslide," before the status of one's salvation
came into question was unclear. Since members believed that one could
not lose salvation, a dilemma occurred when a person who claimed to
be saved acted like an unsaved person. Then members began to question whether the individual was saved in the first place.

While answering altar calls formed one ritual, institutional means
of indicating one's saved status and commitment to the church and its
fellowship, going forward to the altar could be a risky proposition if it
highlighted a discrepancy between one's action in going forward and
one's actions in the community. For example, during traditional altar
calls, one young man went forward several times, crying, to speak with
the pastor. That same young man was known for his repeated consumption of alcohol. An older man, Jonathan Green, evaluated Billy's
proclaimed religious experiences in light of his continued "sinful" behavior. In a Sunday school class, Jonathan talked about those who kept
responding to God's call and then failed to live up to this commitment.
He specifically mentioned Billy's responses to recent altar calls and said
that Billy simply did not seem able to change his ways. Jonathan had
prayed with Billy's father and had talked with Billy, too. Jonathan remarked that those who kept going forward time and time again, but
who did not change their behavior, made him question whether they
"really meant it."

A joke I heard told in many contexts at Cypress Pond epitomized
this skepticism. The following telling occurred in a Training Union
class. Ray Smith, a deacon, told of a comment he had heard about Billy
Sunday, a famous evangelist. A man who was drunk came up to Billy
Sunday and stated that Billy had saved him the week before. Billy Sunday replied, "It must have been me, it sure wasn't the Lord [who saved
you]." The implication, of course, was that if the drunkard had had a
true experience of salvation, then he would have been able to stay sober.

How often should a person go forward to the altar and for what reasons? These questions continued to concern members, who found the multiple responses to traditional calls difficult to evaluate. As reported above, only fourteen responses to traditional calls were announced by the pastor as definitely being for salvation, church membership, or rededication. Reasons for the other fifty-four responses were communicated privately to the pastor. Since members knew that it was possible to question one's salvation, they knew that this was a possible motive for such a response. But, since they had no way of "knowing" that this was the motivation, they could only infer. Another motivation known to spur responses was the need to "share a burden," or concern, with the pastor. Still other motivations included repenting of sin and/or communicating a religious experience of recommitment which was not relayed to the congregation by the pastor.

Since everyone knew each other, they could identify each responder by name and family connections and might have some knowledge of the individual and her or his life situation. Many problems related to sickness and other family "burdens" were well known to the community. For example, Joseph Davidson, a member of Cypress Pond, was dying of cancer. Since the congregation knew of his illness, the motivations for his multiple responses to the altar call readily could be deduced. Let us explore his example in detail, to see how motivations other than salvation entered into altar call responses.

The morning Joseph Davidson responded once more to a traditional altar call, Squires's sermon, "The Capstone Truth" (August 25, 1985), stressed the need for salvation in order to lead a moral life. Squires closed by saying that Christ lived in his own heart; "how about yours?" Joseph responded by going forward (his third such response during the fieldwork period) and speaking to Squires with his arm over the pastor's shoulder. Squires apparently asked him to sit down on a pew because Joseph did so, while Ted squatted down and continued talking quietly. As the last words of the last verse of the "hymn of invitation" died away, Squires stood up and asked if any others had come to the altar during the refrain. No one had, so he, with tears in his eyes, remarked that we all knew about "Joseph and his situation." Squires added that he wanted to call the congregation to "an altar of prayer" for Joseph, because he, Squires, believed in the power of God's healing. About two-thirds of the church congregation left their pews to join Squires and Joseph at "the altar." Squires asked those still in their pews and "visitors" to also pray. He was quiet for a while, allowing people to pray silently, and then he prayed aloud, asking members to join hands with "loved ones" next to them. Many—men and women, members of Joseph's family and others—cried during this time.

As this example shows, sickness (and possibly a concern about salvation) could influence who went forward. However, unless the trouble was reported by the pastor or was known widely in the church, responses of this type could be determined only from self-report.

Self-report concerning motivations for responding to altar calls was rare. One faithful member, Eunice Nichols, told me that she had to assess the depth of her feelings before responding to an altar call. She said that, as far as making a new beginning and being repentant went, she did these activities all the time. So all the sermons could apply to her, and she could be down at the altar repenting every Sunday. However, she thought that she should go to the altar only when she was moved in some special way. She felt that going forward too often raised doubt about the sincerity of an individual's actions.

Since one of the most frequent responders had gone forward yet again on that same Sunday, I took Eunice's comments to imply indirect criticism of that individual. It appeared that too frequent responses certainly could call into question one's sincerity and perhaps even one's salvation.

From listening to such assessments, I deduced that, while responses to traditional calls sometimes might be difficult to evaluate, members apparently felt that they could go forward as many times as they wished to indicate specific forms of commitment to the church. No one was criticized in my presence for answering too many commitment calls. The 69 percent of responses falling into this category reflected this prevailing view. Some members went forward for six or seven of the eight commitment calls.

Members who responded frequently to specific commitment calls generally were church leaders or faithful attenders. Such persons could respond time after time without criticism because members already acknowledged their behavior as being close to the church's stated ideal.

While the committed might be criticized—for instance, some members accused deacons and church leaders of hypocrisy—this criticism revolved around their abilities to fulfill their leadership roles with the right Christian "attitude," rather than their failure to live by the moral code.

Thus, repeated responses to altar calls for commitment tended to validate or enhance one's status within the church as a committed Christian. In examining persons who responded three or more times, I found that eight of the nine males responding in this category were either current or past deacons of Cypress Pond. These eight men accounted for forty-four responses, or a total of 20 percent of the *total* number of responses. For these men, responding may have been be one way of enhancing, or fulfilling, their leadership positions in the church. It also may have been a factor in how one became a deacon. Since deacons were elected by the congregation, being visible as committed, dedicated Christians affected how others perceived a deacon or potential deacon. All those who were deacons in the church were multiple responders, and the two new deacons elected during the fieldwork period also were multiple responders.

Considering the multiple responders as a group, I found that thirty-five of the forty-six multiple responders were members of the families of deacons. Some of these family members were church leaders in their own right, and others were not. But even if they were not leaders, they had ties with someone in a leadership role. The other eleven multiple responders did not have close family ties in the church. All were, however, active in church affairs and held one or more church leadership positions. In summary, multiple altar call responses constituted one means to acquire and maintain committed status within the church.

Conclusion

A response during an invitational call could signal many things to the congregation: religious experience, commitment, validation of status. It could also signal uncertainty and ambiguity. Interpreting the responses and evaluating the statuses of the individuals who made the responses required more than simply knowing who attended church. To make sense of altar call responses, members had to take into account individuals' past behaviors and anticipate their future behaviors, according to community standards of what it meant to be a Christian.

The altar call itself reflected this variability in the two major forms it took at Cypress Pond. Since responses to altar calls provided the pastor and his congregation with tangible outcomes of services, pastors strove to increase participation. Recently pastors had added to their repertoire a form of the call which asked for specific forms of commitment. They utilized it to bring forth audience participation on a level not possible in the past. Calls for commitment allowed for more responses by more people. They were, in the words of Squires, a "symbol of your willingness to cooperate and your desire to understand."

Altar calls allowed members to assess their own salvation and the salvation of others. They also allowed members to assess relative degrees of commitment and even provided an arena within which members could demonstrate commitment. With the invitational calls, we can see that verbal attestations of religious belief never could be sufficient in this community. Members had also to act upon their beliefs. Because they had to act, members could assess belief through actions. Watching the responses to altar calls Sunday after Sunday allowed those attending to observe ritual performances indicating belief. At Cypress Pond, members did not stop evaluating when the church doors closed. Their judgments of salvation through the ongoing "works" (the dispositional state) of the professed believer embraced the individual's entire life span, the subject of the following chapter.

7

Conversion, Self-Transformation, and Conflict

In previous chapters, we saw how pastors and members alike communicated beliefs about salvation during the worship services at Cypress Pond. But the cultural theme of salvation, as expressed there, extended beyond this ritual context. At the personal level, members attempted to make the message of salvation their own. They interpreted what salvation meant to them and evaluated how they should express salvation throughout their lives. Because members had learned to define certain verbal and behavioral actions as markers of belief, they could, in practice, make certain assessments of their own beliefs and those of others. When members had committed themselves to live as saved individuals, these assessments facilitated an ongoing process of self-transformation. This chapter examines how members accomplished this self-transformation. After looking at the process itself, we examine three short case histories of adults seeking to transform themselves in light of their stated beliefs; finally, we look at sources of conflict inherent in the cultural theme of salvation.

Salvation and Commitment

The perspective of members socialized at Cypress Pond constituted one localized, evangelical interpretation of the process of self-transformation through salvation, or what is frequently called *conversion*. We must be cautious in equating salvation with conversion, however, because church members and social scientists may not understand the concept of salvation as conversion in the same way. From William James (1902) to the present, social scientists have attempted to pinpoint a definition, and describe the causes, of conversion. Despite years of research, no single definition of the term has emerged. Snow and Machalek summarize four kinds of changes that traditionally have been associated with conversion:

> the commonplace kind of role changes, called alternation, that occur without disrupting the individual's existing world view (Travisano 1970); the consolidative variety, illustrated by "a person raised in a southern Baptist church, who rejected those beliefs for drugs and perhaps Eastern religion, and who then became a Jesus Person" (Gordon 1974:166); the regenerative type associated with St. Augustine, whose mother's deep religious convictions influenced his early years; and the dramatic, metamorphic sort of change exemplified by the Apostle Paul's embrace of Christianity while on the road to Damascus. (1984:170)

Such varied definitions of conversion have made it impossible for researchers to agree on any systematic approach to studying the causes of conversion, as each definition may imply a different set of causal forces (Heriot 1982; Kilbourne and Richardson 1989).

My own research on conversion began in 1980 while I was doing fieldwork with a group of Mormons in Los Angeles. That research, and my research with the Southern Baptists at Cypress Pond, led me to question the ways in which social scientists conceptualize conversion and also their explanations of it. Heirich's (1977) critique of social science research on conversion remains illuminating. He tested three of the most prominent social science views of conversion: (1) conversion as a "fantasy" solution to situations of psychological and social stress (e.g., one joins because one's spouse has just died); (2) socialization theories which claim that the convert is influenced by prior conditioning (e.g., one joins because one was raised in a particular group); and (3) the analysis of interpersonal influences as significant factors in bringing converts into the group (e.g., one joins because one's friends also are in the group). Heirich found that none of these notions was sufficient to explain what actually happened in the group of Catholic Pentecostals he studied. As a result, he argued that, since social scientists could not then "explain what lies behind the religious quest and response to it," they should ask different types of questions (1977:653).

Most social science research undertaken since publication of Heirich's study has done little to improve the situation. For example, Richardson (1985) argues that a new research paradigm has emerged, stressing the active role of the convert in bringing about his own conversion, in contrast to an older, passive research paradigm that stressed the role of forces outside the individual in causing the conversion. But Kilbourne and Richardson (1989), extending this argument, conclude that further research is needed because all possible explanations have not been tested. They suggest that scholars researching conversion seem to be guided by their own preconceived questions (1989:17).

Although emerging from vastly different agendas, the questions Cypress Pond members and social science researchers seek to answer are the same: how one is converted, what causes the conversion, and if indicators exist to enable the individual (believer or researcher) to "know" that the conversion represents a true change in belief (whether such changes are simply alternations in belief systems or radical shifts in world view). Such questions allow no ultimate, absolute answers, but only socially constructed ones.[1] Therefore, the best that researchers and believers alike can do is to look to the social system itself and observe how cultural members construct the phenomenon socially. Since so many different groups construct the phenomenon in so many different ways, it is difficult to find elements of causality that apply across groups. It also is difficult to compare what happens in one group with events in another, not simply because their constructions of reality differ, but because the basis for the constructions of reality usually is not portrayed by social scientists. That is, to echo Heirich, the latter ask the wrong questions.

My own portrayal of the social system of salvation has important limitations, of course. Despite familiarity with the system and despite careful fieldwork, I cannot say with assurance that I asked the right questions. As Harding notes, those who research conversion tend to be highly skeptical—indeed, to think that "nobody in their right minds would believe this stuff" (1987:168). I had often suspected that other social scientists had not spent much time listening to what their informants had to say about the phenomenon in question; because Cypress Pond members approached the question of salvation with intense seriousness, I tried to listen well and to keep an open mind.[2]

As I listened and observed the community, I heard the messages of salvation and commitment and saw the rituals of "invitation" that I have discussed in previous chapters. That level of analysis—dealing with what was said and done in institutional, ritually defined contexts— was relatively clear. Discussing how individuals tried to make sense of what often were competing and contradictory messages, roles, and expectations, however, has been more problematic. In this chapter, I convey the richness of my informants' lives and the very real problems they faced, especially as their difficulties seemed to be both alleviated and compounded by the religious belief system to which they so passionately wanted to belong.

The Social Construction of Conversion

Even though "the new conversion paradigm" has given converts' self-descriptions a larger role, most social science researchers remain skeptical of the convert's own words. Such skepticism is reflected in the continued analytical separation of the "converted" Christian from the "lifelong" Christian.[3] With this analytical separation, many researchers define their research question in terms that would not be endorsed by those they study; in so doing, they refuse to listen to their informants (see Beckford 1979; Scobie 1973; Snow and Machalek 1984). The picture of conversion painted by Cypress Pond members was much more complex than a dichotomy between "convert" and "lifelong member" could capture. Indeed, if I had defined a "convert" as one who had experienced a radical change in belief, I might have found, in this entire evangelically-oriented congregation, no one who fit the criterion.

The problem stems from the different definitions given to the term *conversion*. Social scientists have been drawn to the notion of a "radical" change in belief as denoting the phenomenon of conversion, although the term has been used in many other senses in social science and in folk terminology (Gerlach and Hine 1970; Heirich 1977; Kilbourne and Richardson 1989; Lofland and Skonovd 1981; Staples and Mauss 1987; Straus 1979 and 1981). Kilbourne and Richardson (1989) find an underlying consensus, arguing that a socialized conversion experience entails "claims of special experiences, claims of special self-effects, and a normatively relevant social audience reaction" (1989:16). They speak of the convert either as gaining a new identity within a given social group or as changing social group. This broader definition more closely accords with definitions given at Cypress Pond. That is, at Cypress Pond, *conversion* involved the claims a person made when he or she gave a profession of faith, as well as the interpretation of such a profession within the context of the local group. At Cypress Pond, the ideal religious experience involved both special experiences and resulting special changes. Every walk down the aisle to profess salvation was taken as an explicit statement that such experiences did occur. But, in reality, few members reported such personal experiences, pointing up the notorious discrepancy between ideal norms and actual norms. However, neither members nor I could readily question the reality of the "ideal" without serious consequences for the continuance of the belief system itself. Thus, to separate analytically what believers themselves did not separate would have been to negate the social construction of conversion as they enacted it. Conversion, for them, involved the normative acknowledgment that a special experience had occurred, and the convert, the born-again person, was required to affirm this publicly, despite any personal doubts.

At Cypress Pond, the social construction of the convert's identity as a saved person also entailed the concept of commitment. Although social scientists usually try to keep the concepts of conversion and commitment separate, believers may claim that the two are inseparable. We have seen that, according to Cypress Pond belief, one could not be converted and fail to live as converted. In this milieu, profession of faith entailed actions demonstrating conversion to others. If behaviors did not match stated beliefs, the individual's profession of salvation was questioned and might actually be invalidated socially. In religious systems where conversion is an integral part of the world view, then, analysis of the phenomenon must consider not only the place of conversion in the belief system and conversion as a reported personal experience, but also how members construct the reality of conversion in others.

This approach to salvation, as conversion demonstrated through commitment, presents a view of the seeker that is both active and passive at the same time: the individual is told that salvation depends on conformity to the belief code (passive) and that she or he must make herself or himself conform (active). To be sure, the individual is seen as doing so under the guidance of the Holy Spirit, of God, but that guidance is socially constructed so that the interactional dimensions of belief come under the control of the social group. This means that, at one level, the conversion experience at Cypress Pond had been made into a routine process, with the preservation of the status quo as its primary, overt function. At another level, though, the conversion experience, the goal of the entire belief system, had been made into a contested domain.

I seek to convey the shared, consensual aspects of the process of salvation—a process that apparently takes as given both a certain moral order and an institutional context that defines the world view of the saved. In addition, I emphasize the active role of the seeker, who selects among the available alternatives to construct her or his own process. While the parameters are largely given, the process itself is not predetermined (or even predestined). Members of Cypress Pond might elect active and/or passive roles; that, of course, was one reason why causality, with regard to any particular social actor, was so difficult to determine.

Morality as a Contested Domain

The image of the converted, committed Christian presented thus far has been that of a condemned sinner who accepts Christ as savior and who strives to live as perfectly as possible, according to the demanding guidelines of a particular moral code. Members did not question these basic premises. To lie, cheat, commit adultery, and harbor anger against one's neighbors all were condemned as wrong, as sins. But, just as contradictions existed for the person who wanted to know if he really had had an experience of salvation, the moral code itself gave rise to two sorts of contradictions. The first entailed neglect of the social gospel. Christ said such things as "If thou wilt be perfect, go and sell that which thou hast, and give to the poor, and thou shalt have treasure in heaven: and come and follow me" (Matt. 19:21); and "Thou shalt love thy neighbor as thyself" (Matt. 22:39). Since the social gospel was preached only through the medium of conversion—conversion being seen as resolving all further problems—members were not taught to concern themselves with righting social injustice.[4] All social problems would be resolved by Christ and his Second Coming; until then, "ye have the poor with you always" (Mark 14:7). Meanwhile, members occasionally pointed out the discrepancies they saw between the social gospel and the implementation of charity in their own neighborhood—though usually not in the larger world.

A second concern, of more immediate importance in the daily life of Jingletown, stemmed from the linkage between the institutional moral code with social roles, particularly gender roles within the family. Work outside the home, as noted earlier, was not taken as an important context for living salvation. The world of work was seen as being "out there," where the world of the unsaved predominated, while the world of the family and the church institution itself were the primary contexts for maintaining the saved world view. Family was important because there one showed one's salvation daily, and there parents socialized their children into the faith. If one's family was not saved, then the "world," in the form of the devil himself, had entered what should be sacred space. In that case, too, the continuity of the family was threatened both from the institutional point of view (because group maintenance would suffer) and from the ideological point of view (because the family would not be together in heaven).

According to Greenhouse's study of a Southern Baptist community in Georgia, the family:

> is understood by people not primarily as a set of relationships (as anthropologists might see the family, for example) but as a set of interlocking roles, or identities. Thus in the local view, family life becomes perfect not as individuals perfect their knowledge and appreciation of one another but rather as individuals perfect their senses of themselves. (1986:48)

Greenhouse here refers to a tendency to see individuals in terms of how they fulfill their roles as husbands and wives, fathers and mothers. Cypress Pond members sharply divided members according to gender roles similar to those Greenhouse describes. She notes that a woman was "expected to maintain her household in cleanliness, style, and good health" (1986:55–56). In contrast, men ruled the public, business domain (1986:57). However, the gender-role separation she chronicles with respect to suburban Baptists of Hopewell, Georgia, is mitigated at Cypress Pond by the rural lifestyle and by the existence of large kin networks. While close friends nearly always were of the same sex, often they were kin as well. Such friendships often endured across the individual's life span and provided tremendous personal support. I recall sitting with two women, both retired, as they discussed their school antics fifty years ago. Still friends, they brought out their high-school yearbook to show me images of this shared life. From my perspective, their relationship portrayed the richness of "spirit" found among those who through the years have developed a tolerance and appreciation of each other's strengths and weaknesses.

At Cypress Pond, gender-role expectations defined men as financial and spiritual heads of both the household and the church. Women were expected to accede to male authority in both contexts, since this was their place, as this system interpreted the Bible. Since both men and women were subject to sexual temptations, this social system appeared to take literally Paul's teaching that it was better to be married than to "burn" (1 Cor. 7:9). As a fellow scholar said of another southern community, humans were expected "to go about two by two," just as the animals did in Noah's ark. Ideally, men and women got married, had children, established a Christian family, and brought that family and its roles with them into the church institution. Together, in gender-specific roles, men and women worked towards salvation.

Once again, the ideal was rarely the norm, and sources of conflict arose concerning the linkage of gender-specific roles with salvation. Researchers and church leaders long have observed that in America women attend church more than men, while men traditionally occupy leadership roles. Utilizing structuralist oppositions between men as leaders in the "secular, outside world" and women as keepers of the "hearth, home, and religion," Lawless analyzes some of the contradictions inherent in this situation (1988:156).[5] Among the contradictions are the tendency for men to want to dominate *all* worlds (rather than leave home and religion under the control of women). Thus, men tend to establish religious affairs as hierarchical and political arenas under their patriarchal control (1988:161). Men may *say* that women have primary responsibility for religion while attempting to usurp that responsibility and to define its content.

This tension between men and women was acknowledged and defined from the pulpit at Cypress Pond. Pastors often decried the fact that many males failed to fulfill their roles within church and family. For example, Manning preached a sermon in which he criticized men for failing to function as spiritual heads of their households and for leaving the task to women. Today, he claimed, even women were failing to live up to this calling. At one point in this sermon, he actually challenged men who were "living for the devil" to stand up and say so publicly in the church. No one did.[6] In fact, women frequently functioned as spiritual heads of their households, especially if their husbands failed to attend church regularly. In another sense, women *already* were the spiritual heads of households, by virtue of their roles as primary caretakers of the home and children. Women were expected to bring their children to religious services and to church social events. They also were expected to witness to their children and help guide them on the path to salvation. At Cypress Pond, women in their late twenties and early thirties had special difficulty fulfilling these roles. Due to economic pressures, most of them worked outside the home and, after work, faced the tasks of cooking, cleaning, and childcare. With responsibility for bringing children to church also on their shoulders, most of them reported being tired and wanting some time to themselves. They often resented the fact that their husbands had much more free time. As children left to set up their own homes, the pressures eased somewhat. But even older women retained responsibility for maintaining the home, while the emphasis shifted to the expression of salvation for the sake of one's grandchildren.

Some exceptions to these generalizations about male and female roles existed. I observed fathers who routinely brought their children to services while a wife worked. Some male volunteers taught the youth of the church in Bible classes. I observed men who went on church trips with their wives and children. However, many men attended only Sunday morning worship services and left to their wives the task of bringing their children to all the other services. This phenomenon did not necessarily imply that men were uninformed or uninterested in church affairs. Masculine influence in this church, exercised through kinship ties and male leadership, was stronger than pastoral criticisms suggested, but men generally took on key leadership roles in the church as they neared late middle age or retirement.

During the period of my fieldwork, all the deacons in the church were men fifty years old or older, whose children were grown. These men interested themselves in the sacred and secular affairs of the church and controlled most church business transactions. Their authoritarian roles as deacons made them the object of much criticism. For example, they were frequently criticized for their decisions in handling church finances, for being resistant to change, and for being unaware of significant political issues. Sometimes they also were criticized for some breach of the moral code, such as cursing, or for failing to provide adequately for their families. Nevertheless, they could maintain their *elected* positions only by controlling their own images as saved people. Too many complaints easily could translate into defeat in the next round of elections. Members apparently demanded of their male leaders a certain degree of conformity, especially in coming to church and being involved in local affairs. Perhaps because of his position of strength as a deacon, Sim Davidson was able to express doubts about his own salvation in so public a context as a church meeting (see introduction). Certainly no one else at Cypress Pond during the fieldwork period did so with anything approaching such audacity.

When individuals at Cypress Pond were judged, it was on the basis of their conformity to the world view of salvation. That world view emphasized the need not only for the experience of salvation, but also for the expression of salvation through adherence to the moral code *and* these "God-given" family and gender roles. If people wished to be taken as saved, they must try to conform to all these specifications. The women in their thirties who are discussed below, and many others as well, found it nearly impossible to fulfill these requirements. Yet these women, whom I knew well, made the effort. Ralph Turner's concept of the "institutional self" provides one way to conceptualize their attempts to transform themselves.

Institutional Self-Transformation

In general, at Cypress Pond the ideal transformation of self from sinner to saved could be achieved only via an institutional pathway. Turner (1976) suggests that, in American society, the process of transformation in the "real" self moves along a continuum from the "impulse" self to the "institutional" self. Using a symbolic interactionist framework, Turner defines the "real" self as the self which the individual identifies as the embodiment of the true self. It is the self for which the individual takes responsibility and to which the individual attaches significant sensations and actions (1976:989). The real self can be anchored in either institutions or in impulses. He describes the polarity between the two as follows:

> [Regarding the institutionalized self:] To one person, an angry outburst or the excitement of extramarital desire comes as an alien impetus that superficially beclouds or even dangerously threatens the true self. The experience is real enough and may even be persistent and gratifying, but it is still not felt as signifying the real self. The true self is recognized in acts of volition, in the pursuit of institutionalized goals, and not in the satisfaction of impulses outside institutionalized frameworks. [Regarding the impulse self:] To another person, the outburst of desire is recognized—fearfully or enthusiastically—as an indication that the real self is breaking through a deceptive crust of institutional behavior. . . . One plays the institutional game when he must, but only at the expense of the true self. The true self consists of deep, unsocialized, inner impulses. (1976:991–92)

While both types of anchorage probably are found in the average person, the expressed view of "proper behavior" characteristic of some groups of people tends to stress one or the other type (1976:997).

As Turner characterizes the institutional self, "the real self is revealed when an individual adheres to a high standard, especially in the face of serious temptation to fall away" (1976:992). The self is something to be "attained, created, achieved, not something to be discovered" (1976:992). The time orientation is towards the future when achievement will be recognized. All of these characteristics stress the active will of the individual in adhering to a moral code and achieving self-fulfillment by living according to its tenets. All the stated information communicated about the belief system of these evangelicals would indicate that a "good" member of the church would have to identify with an "institutional" self.

Earlier, in chapters 4 and 5, we saw how pastors characterized humans old enough to know right from wrong as sinful and destined for hell, unless they were saved. In this view, humans, by the very fact of being human, were subject to temptation. Only through salvation, through God's grace, could individuals hope to transcend their inherent sinfulness and achieve a more "perfect," relatively sin-free existence. Thus, members believed that only through acceptance of this institutionalized pathway and commitment to it could they transform their "true" selves into "saved" selves.

While church attendance figured prominently as one marker of salvation, one could endorse the moral code without attending the institution itself. According to Turner (1976), the identification of the "true" self with institutional goals does not necessarily entail membership within, or attendance of, any actual institutional setting. Certainly there were nonattenders in the Cypress Pond community whose "true" self-identities could be considered as located in the institutional self. But, due to the nature of my research design, I collected much less data on those who manifested their salvation completely apart from church attendance. Most nonattenders who identified with the institutional ideal, however, seemed to have been intensively socialized in the religious system when younger.

For instance, Lester, who came to church only a handful of times during the fieldwork, told me of his strong belief in Jesus Christ. As a youth, he had attended Cypress Pond with his parents and sisters. As an adolescent, he participated in church activities, singing in the choir. Now divorced, he said he had stopped coming to church because of the things people said to him and the questions they asked, which he did not want to answer. His sister felt that Lester had a strong belief in God; she reported that he wrote down scripture verses and memorized them, and that he felt the Lord was calling him to do something—what, he did not know as yet.

Despite such anomalies, members continually endorsed church attendance as one of the major means by which they could manifest salvation. For those who professed to subscribe wholeheartedly to the institutional ideal, the comparison between a true believer who came to church and one who did not could be resolved only by a reformulation or a modification of the image of an ideal Christian.

Personal Expressions of Salvation at Cypress Pond

To see how Cypress Pond members attempted to transform themselves in conformity with the institutional ideal, let us look briefly the lives of three women, each a wife and mother in her early thirties. These three, from similar life circumstances, illustrated the variety of ways in which Cypress Pond members internalized the belief system, manifested it in daily activities, and handled the inevitable evaluations of their choices.[7] These women, like most church members, had been socialized in the Baptist church from birth. They followed the paths traditional for women in this milieu, marrying in their late teens or early twenties and subsequently bearing or, in one case, adopting children. As mothers of children ranging in age from five to thirteen, they had primary responsibility for the socialization of their children and constantly worried about that responsibility. Though they had no postsecondary education themselves, these mothers valued education for their children and agonized over the latter's school performance. Beyond their roles as wives and mothers, they contributed to their households though full-time employment. Two worked in local service or manufacturing jobs, while the third took care of the children of friends and relatives for pay.

Let us examine these women's lives in terms of three factors: the individual's decision to live by and identify with the institutional ideal, beliefs the individual had learned about the ideal expression of salvation in various local cultural settings, and the impact of personal life experience. While social science accounts of conversion tend to focus on factors leading to and involved in converts' decisions to join a group, members socialized at Cypress Pond saw salvation as something to be lived throughout life. To this end, members spoke of high and low periods in their commitment to the ideal. In crises such as illness or death, individuals might respond with increased commitment to, or with partial or full rejection of, the belief system. In a sense, Cypress Pond members "graphed" the high and low points of their Christian lives when they talked of the impact of life crises on their lives and those of others.[8] Throughout their discussions, those who identified with the ideal institutional self interpreted their life events, feelings, goals, values, beliefs, and relationships with others in terms of their own understanding of this ideal. In making these interpretations, they sometimes questioned certain aspects of the system, especially their gender roles. They also usually answered each other's questions by presenting one or more of the same types of answers: answers that affirmed the belief system rather than the process of questioning. Such tactics are referred to in the social sciences as "blocks to falsifiability"—ways adherents of any belief system keep from questioning the latter's basic assumptions.[9]

In addition to struggling with their self-identities as Christians, the three women had to deal with the church community's evaluations concerning their status as saved. They were expected to demonstrate salvation, not only for their own benefit but also for the sake of their families, especially their immediate families.

Samantha Green Richardson: Conflict over the Institutional Ideal

One of the days I remember best from my time at Cypress Pond was spent in Samantha's company, though not in any traditional religious context. It was a day in early February, with the mild weather of a southern winter beckoning folks outdoors. Sunday morning services had ended around noon, and I had gone out to lunch with Samantha's cousin, Denise. Having returned to Denise's home, we then walked over to Samantha's. We sat around for a while, chatting about current church affairs and our work, and complaining about the pastor's sermons; but our goal was enjoying the outdoors. Samantha loaned me a sweatsuit, and we left for a walk. Our group consisted of the three "grown-ups," Samantha's two children, and two children of her first cousin, Leslie Harris (Samantha had charge of them for the afternoon). As we walked, Leslie and her teenage sister Ginger met us down the road, coming to pick up Leslie's kids. They joined us.

Feeling a bit overwhelmed by the family context, I nevertheless joined in the games initiated by Samantha. We walked along a set of railroad tracks until the we hit a place where the tracks crossed red clay hills. Railroad engineers had sliced the hillsides flat to lay the line, and I looked up to see pine trees cresting the tops of the slopes about twelve feet above. Samantha had grown up here and had loved to slide down the cut-away hills on a cushion of pine straw. Forbidden to do this as a child, she would return home with a muddied, red "behind"—undeniable "evidence" of her activities. Duly punished for disobeying her parents' strictures, she went again and again. Now a parent herself, she brought the children with her to play at the activity that once had been forbidden. We all joined in, adults and children alike, and had great, good fun sliding down the banks.

Continuing our walk for perhaps two miles, we went down another steep slope, with more mud, and into close forest cover encircling a creek on the other side of Samantha's home. Samantha located a clear patch of flowing water and helped her children to a drink from cupped hands. In all these activities, she was the clear leader, the strong one, the one who knew what to do next. She understood how to have fun and how to encourage others to have it, too, bursting into laughter with the sheer joy of living.

That afternoon was a "time out," a time away from daily cares. As I left to get ready for the evening services, Samantha and her cousins all had decided not to go themselves. I felt then that the decision reflected, in part, a reluctance to give up recreational time before Monday's tasks, as wells as discontent with the current church institution.

Over the course of my fieldwork, I had learned that Samantha had been raised in the church community but had drifted away from the church for a time in her early adulthood. Partly as a result of encouragement from the Reverend Ted Squires, she and her husband had begun to take an active role in the church several years before my arrival at Cypress Pond. During the first months of my fieldwork, Samantha's family attended many church services. She and her husband, Bruce, took an active role in youth affairs. They went together on church trips arranged for the young. Bruce drove the church bus and grilled hamburgers at parties. They both played on church softball teams, and Bruce helped coach the youth.

Samantha and Bruce had become friends of Ted Squires and his wife Rachel. They actively supported him in the church and were quite upset over his decision to leave in October 1985. They blamed others in the church for criticizing Squires and felt that these criticisms had influenced his decision to leave. As part of the conflict surrounding Squires's leaving, Samantha and Bruce themselves came under heavy fire by church leaders.[10] The nominating committee had selected Samantha and Bruce as nominees to serve on the church "Youth Committee." At the same time, the gossip network claimed that the couple had been leading the youth "astray." The story went that Samantha and Bruce returned from a church youth trip and invited several teenagers over to their home. Another church member showed up unexpectedly that night and later reported that she had seen the youth pouring beer down the drain to avoid discovery. This member also asserted that those present were watching "X-rated" movies on the VCR.

The gossip spread to the nominating committee, which decided to talk to Squires about the suitability of the couples' nomination. Squires was upset and immediately asked Samantha and Bruce to speak with members of the committee. They heatedly defended themselves, calling members of the nominating committee "fuddy-duddies." Shortly thereafter, the chairperson of the nominating committee resigned, while Samantha and Bruce, despite the talk, were nominated and approved. However, the controversy did not die.

Even before this incident, Samantha had claimed that the church did not support the youth. She often observed that there was tension between the older folks and the younger people at Cypress Pond, especially on the issue of church spending. The conflict was expressed as generational; the deacons (who were responsible for church finances) were all older and were "tight." (The deacons, in response, claimed that church funds were being used in an inappropriate fashion to "feed the youth.") After the party incident, I observed Samantha siding with the youth and actively working with them to achieve a concrete financial goal. Since Squires had supported the youth in their projects and now was leaving, Samantha helped organize a project to purchase a used bus to replace an older, irreparable bus. She stated that this bus, a gift from the youth, was to be a *symbol*, expressing gratitude for all that Squires had done. To that end, Samantha and other supporters began to help the youth raise money for the bus by organizing doughnut sales. Their initiative was taken by some as an insult, implying that the church would not support youth activities. Eventually, members voted to authorize the purchase of a used bus with general church funds. The youth were allowed to keep the "bus" money they had raised for use with other projects. Even the doughnut sales were criticized. Some members asked whether the church should sell doughnuts at all. Others found fault with the organization of the project, claiming that they were excluded or uninformed.

In response to these negative evaluations, Samantha noted that she easily became upset. She also spoke out. In one Sunday school class, she reacted strongly when the teacher, her Uncle Jonathan, observed that it was hard to love those who found fault all the time. Samantha interjected emphatically, "Some people look for the least little thing." She felt that people criticized her more than was necessary. While criticisms upset her, she refused to change her behavior. Instead she commented unfavorably on the critics, calling them "hypocrites." Despite her self-avowed emotionalism, she also referred to herself as strong and able to withstand criticism. This strength apparently enabled her to continue coming to church in the face of strong opposition.

For example, on several occasions even before Squires left, Samantha recounted an incident concerning visiting young people that symbolized her perception of internal membership strife. Several years earlier, while bringing a friend, Jane, and her children with her to church, Samantha invited Jane's children on a church hayride. She later had been told that these children could not come since they were not members of Cypress Pond. This, she said, citing one of Squires's sermons, was "like hanging up a sign saying you're not welcome here." This attitude affected Samantha deeply. On other occasions during my fieldwork, she related incidents in which teenagers she was befriending had been told by members of Cypress Pond that they were "not welcome." Those persons who found fault with Samantha's actions claimed that these teenagers were not living by the moral code. They thought that the teenagers were a "bad influence" on churchgoers' children. Samantha, in contrast, seemed to feel that it was both a duty and an expression of Christian charity on her part to help out those whom she felt really needed her.

Before Squires left, Samantha faithfully attended church, brought her family with her, and participated in church events. Since Squires supported her efforts with the youth, she mourned his departure. She responded to several altar calls once she learned of his decision, sobbing as she talked with him during the hymns of invitation. After he left, she continued to attend church sporadically, commenting loudly and unfavorably on those who suddenly had decided to reappear in church. She told me that she had tried to like Manning but found his sermons, his altar calls, and his way with the youth all unpalatable. She stopped coming to every church meeting. Instead, she would drop her children off at church for Wednesday night services and pick them up afterward. Or she would come to Sunday school and leave with her family before the main worship service, to avoid having to hear Manning preach. She even considered switching Baptist churches but, in the end, decided that this would "set a bad example for the youth."

Despite this decline in church attendance, in the day-to-day occurrences of her life, Samantha continued to apply Christian principles as she understood them. Although she never prayed aloud in church or talked publicly about her salvation experience or about the need to witness verbally to others, she demonstrated how she attempted to put Christian beliefs into action. For example, during a Sunday school class focusing on helping others, Samantha stated that often people did not stop to help someone out because they had become hardhearted. Recently, she said, she had been driving home from work with four or five coworkers. She had seen an accident in which a driver had run into a deer and wanted to stop to see if the driver was okay. Her coworkers said, "No, don't, he's okay. Let's drive on." She stopped anyway. Everyone got mad at her and would not speak to her the rest of the way home. Samantha also took actions such as requesting prayer for coworkers who were sick and visiting them in the hospital. She occasionally mentioned talking about her religious beliefs with coworkers.

Still, in her behavior, Samantha did not conform completely to the moral code advocated at Cypress Pond. For instance, she enjoyed dancing. While no one could force her out of the church, older members, who remembered when dancing had been a cause for expulsion from the church, felt that such behavior was wrong. Samantha's cousin told me that an unnamed church member had told Samantha that "every time she danced she was sinning." Since her husband occasionally drank alcohol and expressed discontent with the church leadership, Samantha and her husband continued to be criticized.

This brief account of Samantha's life at the time I knew her points to major sources of conflict in "living as saved." While she was criticized in the context of the moral code for her failure to give up "dancing," I never heard anyone actually question her salvation, as they did

Billy Burke's in connection with his drinking (discussed in chapter 6). People did, however, make references to Samantha's failure to attend church throughout her life; people recalled that, as an adult, she had started to come only when Squires recruited the family and that her attendance had fallen off sharply after he left. As discussed earlier, many members and pastors claimed that members who did not come to church regularly might not be saved. Anyone who did not attend, including Samantha, might view such conjectures as veiled doubts about their probable salvation.

Another source of the negative evaluations of Samantha came from her husband's actions. Because Bruce was known to drink an occasional beer, his status as a good Christian husband was suspect. Since both males and females were evaluated on their reciprocal family roles, criticism of Bruce also meant criticism of Samantha.

After Squires left, Samantha pointed out the discrepancy between the harmony and warmth that were supposed to characterize a Christian context, and the disharmony that existed at Cypress Pond. She attributed the discord to generational differences and hypocrisy. But she herself contributed to the conflict by making accusations. I never clarified the "facts" about Samantha's and Bruce's alleged actions in leading the youth "astray." However, Samantha's kinship ties in the church, much stronger than those of her husband, may have helped her withstand criticism. In this milieu, with its dense network of family ties, interfamilial rivalries may have been a source of such disagreements in this church. Interfamilial rivalry, however, could not have been the *only* reason for the disagreements, since familial ties cut across so many of the extended families in the church.

Samantha's self-identification with the institutional ideal, then, was called into question by others in the church who claimed to live more in conformity with institutional goals and behaviors. In spite of these negative evaluations, however, she seemed to remain committed to the institutional ideal. This commitment could be seen in her decision to stay at Cypress Pond despite the continual conflict. She identified herself as someone who attempted to live her life as an example to others, specifically the "youth." Even though she failed to live as the "ideal" Christian, as defined at Cypress Pond, she continued to attend and to defend her positions. She even tried to redefine the ideal, when she stressed helping others despite the cost to her own reputation. She had been told that the path to self-transformation lay in changing certain of her behaviors—dancing, attendance patterns, and treatment of the "youth." She preferred instead to live by her *own* interpretation of that path, in the face of opposition. By self-definition, she pursued self-transformation through commitment to this particular church institution, an institution that also was home to most of her extended family. Whatever her future decisions about commitment to this church might be, the social construction of her identity as a saved individual on the path of self-transformation remained, at the time of this study, somewhat shaky.

Deborah Griffin: Committed to the Church Institution

The first time I talked with Deborah, she conveyed to me many of the themes that concerned her deeply. I had just attended my very first service at Cypress Pond and then stopped at the local McDonald's. Deborah was there with her two young daughters, Joan, ten, and Elaine, six. I recognized her from church services and went over to chat. She told me that she had moved to the Southville community thirteen years ago, when she married Michael Griffin. She said she still missed her former home and would drive the forty miles to visit every chance she got. There, in contrast to her situation in Southville, she had a wide kin network. She told me about the job she had recently taken and about her involvement in the local church. She had charge of the three- and four-year-olds on Sunday nights and played softball. Of the latter, she said that she and others had to watch how competitive they got, because she felt it was not right for Christians to want to win too much. She quoted words from Squires's sermons to that effect.

In truth, Deborah's life seemed to revolve around church and family. As one of the "faithful," she attended church for almost all services. The qualifier "almost" was due to the fact that her job sometimes required that she work on Sundays or Wednesdays. She described her commitment to the church as a constant factor in her life.

When Deborah, the youngest of four children, spoke of her childhood, the impact of her family's religious training came through strongly. Residing in a nearby community, Deborah's mother walked with her four children to attend a Southern Baptist church in that locale. Her husband was an alcoholic and did not attend church. Deborah's life changed dramatically at an early age, when her father reformed, becoming a staunch supporter of the church and a deacon there. After his transformation, he imposed a number of rigid rules concerning conduct. For example, Deborah was not allowed to date or wear makeup until she was a junior in high school. She could not wear pants, a prohibition that caused her much grief since she was an avid participant in sports. Only in this area did she disobey, sneaking out of the house with pants and changing so that she could play ball. Apart from this minor rebellion, Deborah generally obeyed her father. She had always attended church regularly. She was saved at age seven and told me that, of all the pastors she had known, the only one who stood out as special was the one who had led her church at the time she was saved.

Deborah married at age twenty and moved to Southville to live with her husband. She started attending Shenandoah Southern Baptist Church in the area and stayed there for ten years, bringing with her to church the two children she bore during this period. Eventually she left this church, because the church could not "keep" a pastor. She wanted her children to have a stable church environment; they had been asking her why the pastors kept leaving. She began attending Cypress Pond because she had heard it was a "friendly country church" and because her husband had relatives there. She moved her membership about three years ago and stated from the pulpit in a testimony that she looked up to the "older" folks at Cypress Pond. She felt that Cypress Pond provided her with what she needed at this point in her adult life, when she needed the church the most. She added that the older people at Cypress Pond were the right kind of people, people she could look up to, who did their work well.

Apparently the church community was especially important to Deborah because she had limited kin and friendship ties in this community. Though she had lived in Southville County for thirteen years, she still felt like an outsider. She was not alone in this perception; others who had married into the church reported feeling isolated and not accepted, even after thirty years of regular attendance. Deborah expressed these feelings to me, another "outsider," on many occasions. Though I found her quite friendly, she had had difficulty in making friends, especially among those her own age. Her tendency to judge others against the same rigid code by which she had been reared doubtless affected how others perceived her, whether they actually "misbehaved" or committed "sins" themselves. For example, she often vocalized strong, unbending judgments of these behaviors: failure to attend church, failure to witness, any consumption of alcohol, or cursing. Since she explicitly linked all such behaviors to the status of an individual's salvation and not to "backsliding," she faced isolation by peers inside and outside the church setting who either did not subscribe so wholeheartedly to the belief system or who found themselves prey to "temptation."

At the time I left the field, Deborah was involved in the following church activities: she played on the church softball and basketball teams; taught the Mission Friends on Wednesday nights (children aged five to seven); assisted in teaching the ten- and eleven-year-old class for Training Union; and was substitute teacher for the Ladies Sunday School Class, aged twenty-five to thirty-four. She also regularly attended the Women's Missionary Meeting for older women, held once a month. In short, she attended any and every church meeting. She sang in the choir and loved singing so much that she went to hear gospel singing groups at various *other* churches on Saturday nights when a possibility presented itself.

Deborah not only attended church activities constantly, but she also participated in prayer speech events marking her as a committed Christian. She skillfully prayed aloud whenever called upon in worship services or classes. In addition, she frequently responded to altar calls. During the fieldwork, she responded to calls that showed she tithed, to calls asking members to be better parents, to calls that members be drawn closer to God, and to calls to support the pastor, among others. Sometimes she responded emotionally, with tears running down her face.

Through such actions and through her personal accounts, Deborah defined herself as a committed Christian and interpreted all life events in the context of her belief system. She sought resolution of all problems through the church. In connection with her extended family, her immediate family, and her job, Deborah related situations in which she attempted to apply Christian principles. For example, many in Deborah's extended family were ill at the time of the fieldwork. Her husband's mother was paralyzed and "confused" due to a brain injury. Her husband's father had great difficulty coping with the situation and was threatening to divorce his wife. Her mother, Deborah suspected, had Alzheimer's disease, because she became confused and could not be left alone. Her father, while his mind was still intact, was now in his seventies, had a few minor operations during the fieldwork period, and refused to acknowledge his wife's declining mental capacities. Deborah would ask others to pray for these family members. Good at public prayer herself, Deborah often included her family's illness in her public prayers. Never did I hear Deborah question the efficacy of prayer, though she had many burdens to bear.

Deborah's more immediate concerns had to do with her family, especially her children. She objected to the values her children were learning in school. In addition, her oldest daughter, Joan, was failing two school subjects. She began seriously to ask about Christian schools in the area that she might possibly afford. Though encouraged to continue training the children at home in Christian beliefs, as she was doing, she felt she was fighting a battle that she was not sure she could win.

Though Deborah failed to acknowledge it, she compounded her family problems by insisting on bringing the children with her to all church meetings. Often they were the only children there. At six and ten, respectively, Elaine and Joan were expected to behave in church, following Deborah's instructions. Once she "wore them out" (spanked them) when they disobeyed her by playing outside while she was at choir practice. Though other members criticized her in my presence for bringing them to functions inappropriate for children, she seemed to feel that the church exposure enhanced her children's lives. Furthermore, if she wanted to attend these services, she had few other options. Her husband worked shifts, which meant that he often was unable to care for the children during church affairs. She had no relatives in the area who could baby-sit, and the church had no childcare arrangements for activities other than the three regularly scheduled services. Her children dealt with the constant churchgoing by drawing during church services, going to sleep, and, occasionally, disobeying her. Joan, the oldest, once confided to me that she hated revivals because they entailed coming to church every night and not having any time to play.

Another problem Deborah faced in her immediate family concerned her husband, Michael. Though he had agreed to attend church with her before she married him, he failed to live up to that promise. He attended a few times a year but asked Deborah, "Why come to church where there's no unity, no harmony, and people are just trying to get recognized for a position in the church?" She worried about her husband's behavior when he invited friends over on Sunday afternoons and criticized Deborah for leaving to attend Sunday evening services. Still, she left him at home and came to church Sunday after Sunday.

With respect to her beliefs about salvation, she stated in one Sunday School class that, when you are saved, you accept the responsibility to live the right kind of life. She believed that Jesus came so that we could have the opportunity to accept him, and that the only sin for which a person cannot be forgiven is the sin of not accepting him as savior.

As part of living the right kind of life, Deborah spoke in both church and nonchurch contexts of the importance of witnessing to others. For example, she was aware that she sometimes offended people when she told them they were doing something wrong. On one occasion, she asked how she could point out others' wrongdoing to them without irritating them. At another occasion, she talked about the real need to have Jesus with us, so that this would show in how we lived our lives. Deborah also noted that it was important to share Christ's message in the context of the family. This, she asserted, was difficult to do with loved ones, because she became afraid that she would lead them further afield. For instance, by constantly confronting her husband for his failure to attend church, she risked his anger and refusal to listen. Such responses were taken in the community to signify a refusal of salvation. She specifically mentioned in yet another context particular members of her family who needed to hear the gospel.

Interestingly, Deborah confided that she became nervous when she went on church visitation, a form of witnessing to others. At Cypress Pond, visitation involved meeting at the church, deciding on people to visit, and pairing up with one other person before driving to the selected homes to "visit." Members usually visited people who had stopped coming to church, who were sick, or who never had made a profession of faith. She felt uncomfortable with this aspect of her Christian life for several reasons. First, she had found that few women come to the church for organized visitation. If there were only men, she went home because "no matter how innocent it looks, people will talk." She could not pair with a man to go on visitation from the church, because the two of them would be going alone. In fact, members of opposite sexes almost never paired together for activities as a couple unless they were dating, married, or close kin.[11] Pairing of the sexes implied sexual interest. Second, Deborah felt she did not know what to say. She thought that you should wait before witnessing about salvation until *asked* to witness. She knew that others believed that one should witness immediately and that some did so.

She came so much and undertook so much at Cypress Pond that members criticized her efforts. Some criticism probably stemmed from the fact that she had married into the church community and subsequently assumed an overtly committed role. Since she was so willing to undertake church tasks, she was perceived as usurping leadership roles. People said she "tried to do too much." This comment pointed to a duality in the way members evaluated themselves and others. Deborah was one of three adults under fifty that I classified as core members of the church. For this reason, she ought to have been highly praised. In fact, she was not. Members seemed to feel that she had gone beyond her capacity to achieve all she set out to do, and they questioned the sincerity of her motives. These evaluations suggested that jealousy existed when an individual claimed to live so closely within the constraints of the belief system. Also, an upper limit may have existed on behaviors designed to demonstrate salvation.

The lack of support accorded Deborah was remarkable, considering her years of residence in Southville and her degree of commitment to the church. For example, she once attempted to organize a women's missionary group oriented toward the younger women in the church. Only four women attended the meeting, including Deborah, who had volunteered to teach the class.

On one or two occasions, women in the church made remarks about Deborah's enthusiasm for sports and her willingness to play impromptu basketball games with the men of the church. No one ever overtly grumbled that Deborah was not fulfilling her gender role expectations; after all, she was a wife and mother, brought her children to church, was concerned about their salvation. Yet, some of Deborah's problems may have stemmed from her assumption of masculine leadership roles in this male-dominated church. Only deacons prayed as often or as well in public. Only deacons were more involved in the public business of the church. Deborah certainly never expressed to me any gender-related conflicts save issues she and her husband disagreed about. Indeed, if he had come to church as much as she wanted him to, she probably could have enjoyed a more legitimate leadership role and faced less criticism.

From this glimpse of Deborah's life, we can see how well she had internalized the Christian principles as articulated in this community. She came regularly to church; she gave of her time, talents, and money; she openly demonstrated her salvation through prayer and altar calls. Her search for self-transformation guided the judgments she made of herself and others. She openly asserted that the major focus of her life was her responsibility to live as saved. Her self-identity was expressed through her actions. She attempted to live salvation through her commitment both to the ideal and to the church institution as the embodiment of that ideal. In terms of the types of self Turner distinguishes, her identification with an institutional self seemed quite high, since all actions and all behaviors were interpreted in this light. She herself remained bewildered as to why she had not reaped the rewards of such complete identification.

Leslie Harris: Struggling in the Face of Circumstance

Leslie, Samantha's first cousin, also grew up attending Cypress Pond. Her parents brought their children to church most Sundays, sitting on their "family pew" near the front of the church. Speaking of this experience, Leslie commented in a Sunday school class discussion on the harsh discipline enforced when she was a child. Barbara, another member of the class, had begun a discussion of church attendance and discipline by citing Laura Ingall Wilder's book, *Little House on the Prairie*. She recalled how at that time children had to sit in church with their hands folded in their laps, not moving. Leslie, Jennie, and Barbara each reported the number of spankings they had gotten because they had failed to behave in church. I too recollected being spanked if I misbehaved; even chewing gum could elicit wrath.

Leslie said that she'd had to sit up straight in church, with no giggling or talking. Their family always sat on their family pew near the front of the church. Right behind them sat an older woman, now dead. Since Leslie's mother frequently stayed home to cook dinner for the family, this woman would watch Leslie and her siblings in church. Then she would call Leslie's mother to tell her how they had behaved. Sometimes she said the children were "angels." Usually, though, one or more had misbehaved. Misbehavior was followed by punishment.

In the past, Leslie's father had served as deacon of the church; her mother had taught Sunday school classes for years. Both still attended Cypress Pond, with as many of their grown children and grandchildren as would come. Saved as a young girl, Leslie had attended Cypress Pond until, in her twenties, she married. Thereafter, she lived in Southville and in successively larger towns in South Carolina and Georgia. She returned to the Cypress Pond area when her husband got a job at one of the local plants. While I was at Cypress Pond, she and her husband moved their church membership back to Cypress Pond. Leslie first accepted a "call" to act as substitute teacher of the Ladies Sunday School Class for ages fifty to sixty-four, and then agreed to teach the Ladies Sunday School Class for ages twenty-five to thirty-four. Both positions required that she prepare and teach lessons on Sunday mornings. At first her attendance had been good, but as pressures at home increased, Leslie stopped coming regularly. Sometimes she even failed to notify others so that a substitute could be found. Eventually she resigned from the teaching positions, as her involvement in the church diminished. Despite her erratic attendance, Leslie, like her cousin Samantha, conceived of her true self as identified with the institutionalized ideal. Her struggles to live by the code she learned and endorsed as a child were occasioned by life circumstances related to her marriage.

Assessing her commitment patterns, Leslie said, "As long as I was single, it was easy for me to put God first. Now that I'm married and have kids, sometimes it seems as though God comes after the children and this isn't right. He should come first." Not only did she have trouble coping with the demands of her two foster children, but also she had many difficulties early in her married life. Shortly after her marriage, before the couple decided to keep foster children, her husband had a good job. They financed a home and two cars. He lost his job; subsequently, they lost the house and the cars. Of this experience, Leslie commented, "It doesn't do to be too proud." While she asserted that the

Lord wanted people to have nice things, she also felt that, if things came too easy, then the Lord would remind you of his presence. On other occasions, she made similar claims that the Lord would "get your attention if you forgot about him." She felt that one reason she and her husband had been able to recover from this experience and regain their home was the way they reacted to the Lord's reminder. She prayed constantly, they continued to tithe, and both she and her husband took concrete steps to resolve their financial plight.

These troubles seemed so overwhelming that she once likened her life to that of Job.[12] She noted that when she got to heaven, the first person she wanted to see was Jesus, and the second was Job. She wanted to pat Job on the back for all that he went through.

With any given problem, Leslie reported, she tried to pray and to remind herself of her initial salvation experience. Unlike most others at Cypress Pond, she could remember the exact time of night and the exact day on which she was saved as a child. At that time, everything seemed fresh and new, but the experiences of her adult life clouded things over. Leslie believed that when she accepted salvation, she also accepted an obligation to work at maintaining God's favor and blessings: "If you forget to thank God, then comes trouble." She also said, "If you obey God, then he will bless you."

One of the ways in which she attempted to obey God was by witnessing to others. For example, she once told how she had felt "the hand of God" directing her to witness to a young woman who had moved in across the hall in her apartment building. Leslie had asked her if she was saved. Probing further after the woman asserted her saved status, Leslie discovered she was a Catholic and, as such, had thought that baptism ensured salvation. Leslie witnessed to her, marked passages in a copy of the New Testament, and gave this to her. The woman cried and listened but refused "to give in." This upset Leslie, and she called her pastor to ask what she should do. He assured her that she had "planted a seed and now it was up to the woman. You can't force a person to be saved." Despite this overt demonstration of her commitment to the "Great Commission" (to evangelize the world), she also noted her failings. At times she had stopped attending church, especially when she lived in the larger cities. She said of this experience, "It's hard to keep our commitment to witness when we're with non-Christians. Nine times out of ten, one just goes along with the crowd." She added that it was easier for the bad to lead the good astray, than for the good to lead the bad.

With respect to home life, Leslie urged fellow Sunday school classmates to witness. She herself believed that one witnessed to one's husband on a daily basis by one's actions and words. Nevertheless, "it's hard to witness to your own family," she asserted. "They know you so well and can point out your faults. You can read Bible stories to your children, but you witness to your husband. Our lives are a witness to others." Hinting at her own familial strife, she spoke of how one's husband could pull at one's loyalties—for example, when he preferred that one stay home from church on Sundays.

In fact, Leslie's husband rarely came with her to church. An underlying family discord appeared to be pulling Leslie in several directions. Her husband's mother clung to her grown children, demanding their attendance at family get-togethers. Leslie cried in bed one Thanksgiving morning because she had agreed to "celebrate" the holiday by going to dinner at her mother-in-law's home. Her husband's parents were fighting and finally agreed to a separation; the mother-in-law allegedly threatened suicide. Leslie, when asked by her cousin Samantha, on several occasions refused to discuss these difficulties. (My knowledge of the situation came from Leslie's father.)

These family problems were further compounded by Leslie's difficulties with her foster children. Leslie had the care of two children, Bob and Mindy, a brother and sister aged ten and five respectively. Since she could not have children herself, she had planned to adopt these two and had been caring for them as her own. Their backgrounds, however, allegedly included severe abuse in an alcoholic household. Bob remembered the abuse, though he refused to talk about it; his social worker termed him a "walking time-bomb." Since Mindy apparently did not remember, she adjusted to her new home more easily.

The situation came to a head when Bob stole two of his foster father's rings and set fire to Sunday school books in the bedroom. Leslie was distraught, not knowing how to cope. She turned to those of us present in one Sunday School class, telling us about her predicament and her feelings. Bob's social worker had decided that he needed to be placed in a psychiatric hospital to determine his current mental state and the best type of treatment for him. Leslie was afraid that he would be taken from her and that, if he were taken, Mindy also would be taken. Of her attempts to deal with the situation, Leslie said that she had prayed about it and had felt that her prayers had gone no further than the ceiling. Members of the class assured her that God had heard her prayers. A sister whom she had turned to earlier had offered similar assurances. Leslie prayed that, if it was God's will that Bob go into another home, she would be able to accept it.

Denise (a member of the class and Leslie's first cousin) asked if Bob knew the Lord as Savior. Leslie replied, "No." Denise said that his conversion was the first step in changing the situation. If he could know the love of the Lord, that could really help him. Leslie had tried loving, and she had tried hollering; she did not know what else to do. Denise later told me that the class should have prayed for Leslie at this point, but no one initiated prayer during that class.

Problems of such severity provide major tests of faith. Leslie turned to the religious solutions she had internalized. She prayed, she asked fellow church members for support, she tried to witness to her foster children. While Bob remained unresponsive, Mindy, the five-year-old, told Leslie that she wanted to be saved so that she would not go to hell. At the time the fieldwork ended, the family situation was unresolved. When I returned to visit several months later, I heard that Leslie was separating from her husband and moving to another small town in the same general vicinity.

As I have argued, individuals' lives do not always reflect a steady progression towards the institutional ideal. Life events such as those affecting Leslie can impinge on one's ability to live according to the beliefs and actions required to fully exemplify this ideal. Although she did not always attend church, Leslie nevertheless remained committed to seeking religious solutions to her problems. This was true despite the fact that the application of the religious solutions of prayer and salvation at times failed to produce the results she desired. Speaking of her doubts elicited overt reaffirmations of the belief system from her peers.

With separations and impending court decisions concerning her foster children, the future would carry Leslie past important milestones in her career as a Christian. She would have to decide whether she still believed. At the time of writing, I cannot know the outcome. Nor could Leslie's fellow Christians know the *ultimate* outcome, for her or for themselves, at the Final Judgment. But they could look to the patterns of their lives, to their self-definitions, for guidelines.

Leslie herself was not without doubt about the church as an institution. Nor was she free from criticism. When she failed to appear for a class she was supposed to teach and did not call anyone, members understandably were annoyed. She in turn retaliated, saying that not everyone who came to church was truly saved. More than once she remarked that it did not matter whether one came to church or not; it only mattered whether one was saved. She also commented on members who failed to greet visitors to Cypress Pond, in effect turning the visitors away. These unfriendly members were "self-satisfied," in Leslie's opinion. She claimed, "They're in church but don't care about others." With respect to the hypocrites at church, she asked a former Cypress Pond pastor what she should say to people who said they did not want to attend church with the hypocrites. He replied, "I'd say I'd rather go to church with the hypocrites, than go to hell with them."

Leslie's life, like Samantha's and Deborah's, reflected the problems of living by the moral code as saved, at a time when family conflicts undermined the desire to be fully committed. These women could not "control" their husbands' actions and so suffered in community evaluations. Many other factors also were beyond their control: shifting economic fortunes which propelled them into the labor force, familial and generational tensions within the church, and cultural subordination to masculine authority in a patriarchal system.[13]

But these women did not frame their tensions in those terms. Rather, as in Leslie's case, they were expressed as a tension between an individual's self-defined commitment to live as saved and the social construction of that identity. Leslie's story suggests how the impact of life events, over which she likely had little control, affected how she could come to terms with the Christian ideal. How she worked through the stress would determine whether others saw her as being committed to the institutional ideal. She, on the other hand, might redefine that ideal in much the same way that Samantha did. That is, she might decide that she was saved, no matter what the evaluations of her behavior were. She also might come to question herself and her commitment to that ideal.

Who Is Truly Saved?

After reading about Samantha, Deborah, and Leslie, the reader surely is tempted to point out that these accounts of conversion blur the experience of salvation, morality, and gender roles, so that conversion cannot be discussed as a separate phenomenon. That certainly is the case and, I would argue, *precisely* the point. Salvation is a world view, a way to interpret all one's actions in light of cultural codes with which one identifies. Though a central cultural theme, it is not the *only* cultural theme present in the South; there also exist conflicting themes of individualism and materialism—to name two prominent alternatives. But "believers," those socialized into this world view who continue to profess its centrality in their lives, interpret their actions in light of its tenets. In the cases we have looked at, the women were not completely powerless, and they did perceive some of the sources of tension in their lives. More important to them, however, was the fact that they knew their actions were constantly judged on the basis of this world view and that their very definition of themselves as saved, as converted, was contingent on the actions they took within the community context. At Cypress Pond, in other words, conversion was socially constructed based on the actions an individual takes throughout his or her life.

The examples of Deborah's, Samantha's, and Leslie's lives show that it may not always be simple to apply the standards for evaluating the actions of the saved. The pathways to self-transformation in practice may become blurred. In none of the cases discussed was there a complete rejection of the belief system. Such rejections obviously do occur, as, for example, in declared atheists. Within this milieu, however, most Cypress Pond members said they could not even *imagine* what it would mean to be an atheist. Whenever the question was raised, members said that people who were atheists were not *really* atheists. Members asserted that atheists *had to believe in God*, despite their statements to the contrary. Such enmeshment with the belief system places all serious doubters either on the fringes of noncompliance or in danger of being excluded. Denial of the belief system entails exclusion not only from the church community but also from one's kin networks. Readers likely have noticed that, whenever doubts were raised, most members responded by reaffirming the belief system.

In theory, when paradoxes about beliefs are recognized, individuals become uncomfortable, dismiss them, reject one or the other of the competing beliefs, or make some choice, even if it is to ignore the paradox (McMillan 1988:328–29). Festinger's original formulation of cognitive dissonance assumed that when individuals were faced with discrepancies between what they claim about the world and what actually happens, they would experience conflict. Such individuals would, he argued, seek to resolve the resulting dissonance (1957). Snow and Machalek (1984), however, argue that some individuals apparently simply ignore the potentially disconfirming evidence.

Pastors and members offered various means for dealing with paradoxes and doubts, answers which usually served to keep believers from questioning too closely. To understand the tactics they used, let us first look at Prus's study of pastors (1976). He examines the ways ministers deal with doubts on the part of their members and notes that ministers operate within the framework of the belief system, assuming that members share the same "taken-for-granted reality" (Schutz 1953, cited in Prus 1976:129). Prus discusses the strategies ministers use to counsel those who have doubts. Many of these tactics also were relied upon by Cypress Pond members, especially the use of prayer and the necessity of salvation.

Members of Cypress Pond thus demonstrated that they, like the ministers Prus studied, have internalized the belief system to the extent that even doubting takes on a certain "accepted" quality. The response most likely to be given when doubt is expressed is advice that the individual pray. This answer was given to Sim when he expressed his doubts (see the introduction) and to Leslie when she agonized over her foster son Bob's condition. She said, with very real anguish in her voice, that she was afraid her prayers had gone no farther than the ceiling. Those present were quick to assure her that God would hear her prayers. To all situations of conflict, or doubt, prayer is one of the standard responses advocated by Southern Baptists (see Greenhouse 1986; Heriot 1993).

The other major strategy for dealing with problems also was illustrated in connection with Leslie's difficulties. When she expressed her need for help with Bob, Denise asked her if Bob was saved. When Leslie said he was not, the conversation immediately shifted to talk about how a mother could witness to her children about Jesus. The implication was that Leslie's and Bob's problems would be resolved if Bob were saved. Similarly, if a woman in these conversations had problems with her husband, all seemed to feel that the problems would be resolved if the husband made a clear commitment to the belief system. Domestic problems, as well as national and international problems, all were transformed into questions of salvation.

In such a milieu, the process of self-transformation is envisioned as a lifelong, relatively unquestioning commitment to the church, in which the final outcome cannot be known absolutely. Constant vigilance is required to transform the self. As I have shown, members linked commitment to conversion, because they held the conversion experience to be spurious unless it was manifested in behavior. In order to be considered saved, one had to show continually, in words and deeds, that one's real self was identified with institutional goals. Only through behavioral manifestations of that experience was the conversion process validated as "true."

In closing, I would like to return briefly to debates in the social sciences concerning the definitions and causes of conversion. Since at Cypress Pond conversion was deeply embedded in the social context, assessments of one's own and others' experiences of conversion through salvation became part of the ongoing daily actions of members. Those social scientists who limit definitions of conversion to the radical transformation of self at a particular moment in time cannot credit these informants' own definitions of this process of self-transformation. Results also are skewed when researchers fail to investigate informants' claims that true conversion must be manifested in a *lifelong* process. When conversion is joined to commitment, as was the case at Cypress Pond, separating the two analytically yields a distorted view of the meaning of conversion. In this milieu, assessing the process of conversion of necessity takes into account how conversion is socially constructed by members through their evaluations of action.

Let me end with a series of questions that were asked of me. A divorcee was struggling with the negative evaluations she was receiving. She thought of herself as a committed Christian but knew that others were questioning her status. She wanted to know if an entire life living in conformity to the moral code could be wiped out in one night of debauchery. That is, what happens if one dies that same night, while living "in sin"? What happens if the self-transformation is not complete? In a milieu of constant assessment, who is truly saved?

8

Belief and Action

As a central cultural theme presented in sermons and stressed on a daily basis by those who identified with institutional goals, salvation formed the primary frame within which Cypress Pond members interpreted their lives. In effect, they participated in a centuries-old tradition of Protestant evangelism in which members are first socialized into the world view of salvation and then given the task of evaluating their salvation daily through actions. On the one hand, their folk epistemology equates belief with undisputed knowledge of the transcendent world—a world they postulate as "truer" and "more real" than the social world in which they live. On the other hand, the expression of this "true" belief in social contexts is problematic. To that end, members claim that the emotional experience of salvation, a psychological criterion of belief, is the only way to attain "born-again" status. Once "born again," however, the individual must prove that experience through moral actions adhering to the stipulated code of conduct—a code involving such things as keeping the Ten Commandments; avoiding the "barroom" vices of drinking, fornicating, and gambling; and conforming to "God-given" gender and family roles. Living by this code is taken as "proof" that one is saved; such conduct presupposes dispositional criteria of belief. That is, one ideally must have within oneself the will to commit to the belief system initially and then commit to it through one's actions over and over again, in every context in which its tenets conceivably might be invoked. Spiritual commitment thus can be measured and evaluated by members of the community—in principle, at least. We have seen that such measurements are context-specific and actually create contested definitions of salvation within the church institution itself, as members try to interpret these guidelines and apply them in their own lives.

The Expression of Salvation through Belief and Action

Weber characterized Protestant salvation as a state that could not be attained through individual good works and claimed that proof of salvation came only with "a specific type of conduct unmistakably different from the way of life of the natural man" (1958:153). These Southern Baptists took to an extreme the principle that salvation should be manifested through the actions of their lives. Their ongoing evaluations of behaviors thought to demonstrate salvation seemed to encompass all social contexts and, indeed, the totality of life. The message of salvation portrayed at Cypress Pond made certain specified actions the key in evaluating inner subjective states of being. Conrad succinctly summarizes this world view, stating, "For Southern Baptists salvation does not come through works, but works reveal salvation" (1988:350).

The metaphorical linkage of the religious experience of salvation with the outward expression of salvation was made even more powerful because believers were told that the testimony of their "lips" and "lives" helped, or hindered, the salvation of everyone else on earth. The prescriptions for that testimony entailed continuous striving toward an unattainable perfection, a perfection that the Reverend John Manning, for example, claimed was the goal of the saved Christian. Since the posited goal could never be attained, members always could criticize themselves or others. Thus, to identify with the institutional goals usually meant some degree of uncertainty regarding one's performance. Members depended upon others to validate their experiences and their commitment and had consciously to redefine them when their behavior fell short of the ideal.

The paradox of knowing the unknowable squarely places the burden of proof in the realm of social action. Since internal believing states cannot be accessed directly, these Southern Baptists solved the dilemma by making actions criteria of belief. For Cypress Pond members, it was inconceivable that one could believe and not make that belief known to others. The stress on an overt demonstration of an internal state meant that individuals constantly were told that the expression of their true self could be attained only through institutional goals, by conformity to what Turner has characterized as an institutional self. This emphasis apparently caused committed individuals to try to fuse their self-identities with the institution itself.

Such fusion was not without its own problems, since members displayed differing degrees of adherence to that institutional ideal. Variation existed with respect to types of saved individuals and with respect to whether one publicly questioned one's own inner state of salvation. Some members never publicly questioned; others did. The degree to which members allowed such questioning appeared to be tied to community evaluation of the reputation of the person speaking; i.e., persons who revealed salvation through action occasionally might bring up the problem of subjectively knowing belief. Variation also existed with respect to the question of how to live salvation by a moral code that also contained gender and family role directives. We have seen that women in their thirties, for example, might not be able to square institutional goals with the realities of their responsibilities.

When questions and paradoxes came to the attention of committed churchgoers, they dealt with them in terms of the belief system of salvation itself. That the system created its own set of tensions about the problem of knowing salvation served to keep believers focusing on the local context of salvation, asking over and over again: "Am I saved? Is my family saved?" With the fate of their souls preoccupying believers, other concerns and problems receded in importance. I do not mean to imply that members had no other concerns. Rather, they framed those concerns in the context of the cultural theme of salvation. As such, their gaze was directed inward, often in fear and often in uncertainty, as they strove to gain that "blessed assurance" of salvation.

Epistemological Considerations

Since members questioned their own and others' beliefs, the answers they gave formed one means of establishing the social construction of salvation. This consideration returns us to the epistemological question I raised earlier: how can an outside observer infer belief? Referring to the work of Goodenough (1981) and Holy and Stuchlik (1983), I argued that believers in fact can infer from words and actions the existence of a belief state. Furthermore, the ultimate reality of such a belief state

does not matter in terms of social interactions, if members cite the belief system as a motivator and act "as if" they believe. The outside observer can, in practice, infer beliefs through actions.

Much of the substantive portion of this work documents that Cypress Pond members have established a precedent for making such
judgments. Based on my own observations of the socially agreed-upon
evaluations of belief, I have offered one translation, a portrait of the
means by which believers gained access to belief. Of course, no portrait
can substitute for the belief itself, a fact that doubtless always will remain the strongest argument against the feasibility of complete translation.

Individuals always manage the world through contextual living,
whether or not they manage, or even notice, the paradoxes of their
lives. They know what to do by the context, which is created not only
by the setting, but also by the people in the setting, and by the knowledge the individuals carry of what to do in such settings—either because they have been in similar settings before, or because they use familiar cultural patterns to interpret a new context. From that perspective, the
received knowledge directing social conduct in specific settings can appear to have a life of its own, creating a kind of "social force." In social
interactions, the expressions of these beliefs reinforce their existence
over and over again, so that they come to form a world view.

What I examined at Cypress Pond was the maintenance of a sacred
social order in the face of forces—weaker here than in many places—
representing modernity. In contrast to the situation in much of the modern Western world, here the larger social community was not clearly set
apart from the religious community. To an extent far greater than in other,
less culturally bounded regions of America, people here included both
sacred and secular in the world view they agree upon. As Salkehatchie
County was representative of white rural southern culture, its residents
overwhelmingly, in numbers at least, identified with a Protestant tradition. For generations, in a relatively homogeneous social milieu, these
southerners had been heirs to the Protestant Reformation. I have called
members of this Southern Baptist community traditional evangelicals,
rather than fundamentalists, because they reside in a locale where their
belief system is not called into question by direct exposure to compet-

ing belief systems. These very classifications imply that I subscribe to some form of modernization theory, since that theory assumes that conflicting belief systems are a fundamental aspect of the "modern" world (Bellah 1972). That theory also assumes that, when Cypress Pond is faced with ever-increasing outside encroachment from the "modern" world, its consensual world view probably will change. But *will* believers compromise the sacred explanatory model in the face of a competing secular world view?[1]

To say that this world view can exist only in a milieu in which the modern secular world is minimized is to view Cypress Pond as a small island or a bulwark against the onslaught of modernity. Certainly, as a heuristic device this is convenient, but in these last pages I question the presuppositions underlying such categorizations. The impact of alternative world views on any given sacred world depends, in part, upon the processes creating and maintaining world views themselves.

Most social scientists conceive of alternative world views as competing in a kind of ideological "market" system. For example, according to Berger and Luckmann, plausibility structures (or world views) are learned by the individual in social interactions and internalized, so that the individual chooses to identify with that structure (1966:154). If a person leaves his primary world view for another, he must commit to the new world view. Berger and Luckmann term this process of change "alternation," stressing the role that commitment plays in maintaining a changed subjective reality. Speaking of religious conversion (as a form of such alternation), they write: "To have a conversion experience is nothing much. The real thing is to be able to keep on taking it seriously; to retain a sense of its plausibility. This is where the religious community comes in. It provides the plausibility structure for the new reality" (1966:158). Commitment to the religious community is required in order to maintain a sense of identity with the institution. Berger later describes how, in the modern world, religion has changed so that it has to market its plausibility structures among others competing for voluntary individual affiliations. He argues that "the religious tradition which previously could be authoritatively imposed, now has to be marketed. It must be 'sold' to a clientele that is no longer constrained to 'buy'" (Berger 1969, cited in McMillan 1988:326).

This vision of competing plausibility structures which must be "marketed" underlies many of the assumptions made by modernization theories. These theories subtly influence many social scientists' evaluations of modern religion, because the theories usually assume that the sacred comes into conflict with the secular, or modern "scientific," world at some level and that each competes for the "soul" of the individual. Earlier predictions that secular world views would replace sacred ones have proved erroneous, in the American religious tradition at any rate (Marty 1983). This situation has left those social scientists who were committed to "science" puzzled about the reasons for the enduring appeal of the sacred. They had assumed that religion could not withstand the forces of modernity, because "science" would outperform and outpredict religion in the marketing of plausibility structures. These social scientists' utilitarian vision of the world, though not as rigidly laudatory of science as Frazer's forecast that science would totally usurp the place of religion (1922), had predicted that religion would function only the realm of meaning and as a social institution. As a meaning system, religion would answer the questions science could not, until science itself found the answers (Skorupski 1976). As social institutions, religious systems would function much as any other social system; therefore, their foundations could be exposed "scientifically." But these Western views, of science as the purveyor of knowledge and of religion as the irrational knowledge system serving functions that finally could be taken over by science, do not accord with the current world situation. For instance, in the market of competing world views, the worldwide resurgence of fundamentalist religious movements indicates that believers are rejecting secular world views for a sacred vision of the world. These religious movements, however, do not necessarily reject the capitalism and consumerism of the modern world; instead they redefine them in sacred terms.[2]

Why has the secular "science" presupposed by modernization theory been unable to subvert religious systems completely? There are many possible answers,[3] but the one that I want to discuss here pertains to the maintenance of world views. As I noted with respect to conversion theories, the answers provided may reflect the kinds of questions researchers ask. As I have shown throughout this work, those who hold a sacred world view have powerful means of transmitting that same world view to the next generation. Among these means are the language of persuasion, which communicates the belief system to followers and urges them to adopt it as their own (Berger 1966). One function of the language of persuasion, which seems to be acknowledged by social scientists and then dismissed, has been the subject of this work. That is to say, the folk epistemological system of this Protestant group fuses belief and knowledge in a way that science does not. While anthropologists continue to act as if the line separating belief from knowledge exists at some absolute epistemological level, I drew the reader's attention to the arguments of Needham (1972) and Mary Black (1974), who assert that this boundary has not been proven and instead is a function of Western thought patterns. The refusal of Cypress Pond members to distinguish clearly between belief and knowledge is at the heart of the Western confrontations between science and religion. Social scientists often seem to wear blinders when they approach religious systems, acting as if only crazy or irrational people could believe that the knowledge participants gain from a religious system constitutes a form of reality. Social scientists seem to think that, if believers accept religion as *a* reality, it is a *social* reality based upon faulty assumptions. Yet their very denial of the "reality" of religion means that, at the same time, they deny the means and methods whereby members of the social system construct that reality and live as if it transcended the social.

If, in contrast, knowledge and belief are taken as equivalents in the folk epistemology, the question of "believing" may be hard for the individual to avoid. As members of this social system say to each other and to outsiders, all the individual has to do to believe is to listen and to accept as true what one has heard. The starting point in the process is the language of persuasion, and how can a member of any social system avoid the language of persuasion? Individuals may reject its truth, but evangelicals are correct when they assert that individuals must engage in the dialogue as soon as they begin to hear. As such, the language of persuasion forms an especially powerful means of engaging the self with the social constructions of the belief/knowledge system. Failure to adopt the belief system and make it one's own in a given social context would make the individual's life "subjectively empty of 'living'" (Berger and Luckmann 1966:155). That is, if one does not identify with one plausibility structure, then one must endorse another, presumably the one(s) the individual most frequently encounters—or live without meaning.[4]

Furthermore, since, in the social system examined in this book, belief/knowledge is so inextricably tied to action, separating belief from action would undermine the entire social reality these Baptists affirm in worship services and daily interactions. Competing world views may challenge this powerful linkage, but thus far they have done so without success. This linkage exists, in part, because a large proportion of community members have been socialized into the sacred and carry it with them when they encounter the secular. When members equate belief with action, they bolster the essential dualism of their belief system. One is either saved or damned, and the test of one's status is the way one lives. This test makes the boundary between the sacred and the secular relatively clear-cut, since the saved are expected to manifest their saved status in the secular world. If they fail to do so, then their salvation is called into question—a powerful method, indeed, of constructing a sacred reality.

While this sacred reality can be threatened by exposure to other world views, its equation of saved status with overt actions renders it, to a certain extent, impenetrable and stable. Such a world view provides answers to its own questions and defines a truth that is not readily falsifiable. Beliefs expressed through action are a dynamic truth repeatedly played out in social contexts, both expressing and continually creating a view of the world in which salvation is evaluated through actions.

Epilogue

I left Cypress Pond in 1986 to return to graduate school in California. I have not been back in the intervening years. When I was in South Carolina for my grandmother's funeral in the spring of 1992, however, I encountered a woman who had once been a member of Cypress Pond. What she told me about my role at Cypress Pond has haunted me since.

What did she say? Merely that Cypress Pond accounts of my time there defined my role in Cypress Pond terms: *I* had helped to keep the church community together during a period when it was experiencing difficulties.

Appendix A.

"What Is Sin?"

This sermon was preached by the Reverend Ted Squires during a Sunday evening worship service on July 14, 1985, and broadcast over the Salkehatchie radio station.

False starts made by the speaker are marked in parentheses, and interpolated comments are enclosed in brackets. All nonstandard verb forms and colloquial expressions have been included as uttered by the pastor.

Transcribed Text

Truly, there is no one else who could do for us what the Lord has done, and we are grateful for that tonight, the message in song. And I trust all of us will think seriously about that situation.

I ask you tonight to turn with us to Genesis, the third chapter; Genesis, chapter 3. We are gonna begin with verse 1 and read through the entire chapter, speaking tonight upon the subject, sin, and what it is, and what it does. What is sin? Where'd it come from? How did it originate? What does it do for us, the individual? Or what has it done to us, as individuals? Genesis, the third chapter, beginning with verse 1.

[Reading of Genesis, chapter 3]

And that concludes the reading of chapter 3, speaking tonight upon the subject of sin, what it is, and what it does to us. Would you pray with us, please.

Our Father, we thank you for your word tonight. And in these moments I trust the Holy Spirit will be our guide. Let us yield ourselves into his hands, and, may he use this service to speak to our hearts. Draw us closer to you. Save those who are lost, and bring back the backslidden. And we'll thank you for it, because we ask it in Jesus' name, amen.

The Bible is the number one book of life. It is also the number one bestseller. Has been for a long time. I trust, will be for a long time. I know that you respect the Bible; all of us do. We hold it in reverence. We know that it is God's word. It does not contain God's word; it *is* God's word to man. It is the way that God has chosen (to spoke to us) to speak to us in these days. The Bible says that oftentimes in times past, the Lord used many ways to speak to us. But in the last days has spoken to us through his son. And in this word we have the spoken word of (only) not only the prophets of old times, as God used them to speak to our hearts, but also the recorded words of his own son, as he spoke to us.

And in this book, in the book that we just read from tonight, in Genesis, describes on its opening pages, the origin of life. In Gen. 2:7, the Bible says, "And the Lord God formed man of the dust of the ground, and breathed into his nostrils the breath of life; and man became a living soul." So the Bible tells us where life begins for man. It also declares that the gift of God is eternal life through Jesus Christ, our Lord. We know the Bible has told us that we, in sin, have fallen away from the Lord, as we read a few moments ago. Sin entered into the heart and life of man in the Garden of Eden. Fellowship with God and man was broken, and man had to be cast out of the Garden of Eden, to till the soil, to make his living from hard work. The soil will also bring thorns and thistles that will make it that much harder. And so man has had to live in that condition because of sin.

I want us to look tonight at sin, and see what it says to us. Now, as we think about it, (we, we) we call it many things. We label it many things. We dress it up. We make it look good. Even the devil himself makes it look good. Even the Bible itself says there is pleasure in sin for a season. And that's part of the attractiveness of it. But I want us to notice tonight what God calls it, and what he has always called it, and that is sin. His estimate of wrongdoing has never changed. It has always been sin; it always will be sin, in his sight, when man does that which is evil, does that which is in contrast—or is contrary—to his will for our lives.

So let's notice sin tonight, and see what it is. First of all, sin is disbelief. Now we find this right in the very beginning. Adam and Eve were given dominion over everything. They were placed in the garden (that) where everything was there for them to enjoy. All that they could ever want or desire [or] need in life, was placed at their disposal. And in the midst of all this beauty and pleasure and joy and peace and contentment, God placed one tree, and he said, "Don't eat of this tree, don't even touch it, lest you should die." And you know, the Lord—the devil came along and used this situation, and he planted the seed of doubt in Eve's mind. He caused her to doubt the word of God. And he has been doing this ever since.

Now the devil uses many ways to attack the church, to try to stop the word of God from going forth, or (for) the work of God from going forth; but the primary way that he attacks and has always attacked, is to attack the word of God. If he can cause us to doubt what God has said, he has won the victory. And so we see from the beginning that the Bible tells us that disbelief is sin.

You looked in Genesis 2, chapter 2, verses 16 and 17, and we find the words, "And the Lord God commanded the man, saying, 'Of every tree of the garden thou mayest freely eat: but of the tree of the knowledge of good and evil, thou shalt not eat of it: for in the day that thou eatest thereof thou shalt surely die.'" Now that's what God said. But yet the devil came along when he asked Eve about it, and she says, "Well, the Lord says we can have anything we want of any (other) other tree in the garden, but don't eat of that one tree. If we did, we would die." And he says, "Now surely you don't believe that God meant that you would die." Planted that idea of doubt, and Eve fell to his old tricks. So sin is disbelief in the word of God.

Secondly, sin is disobedience. And I think we could say that doubt, or disbelief, is always the forerunner of disobedience. Now there is first a thought, and then the deed. I've often wondered, when we commit sin in our lives, is it something that just happens? Is it something that we just woke up one day, and there was a sin that we could not overcome the temptation? Or is it something that there was a seed planted some time ago, and little by little this seed begin to grow, until one day we could not overcome the temptation that faced us?

You remember David? With his sin with Bathsheba? You would look—as you look into the Bible there, you'd find, you'd think if you just read the Scripture as it's written in that one place, you'd think that there came a time when David left the leadership of his army in control of someone else, and went home and walked up on the roof to his house, and just happened to look over to the courtyard of a neighbor, and there saw the neighbor's wife taking a bath, and it was tempting to him, and he commanded that (he) she be brought to him. But if you look at his life, and go back a number of years before that, you'll begin to find that David beginned to do some things that God said he should not do. He should not have concubines, and he had concubines. And it goes on and on. Little by little these things begin to fall in place until David got to the place that it didn't seem such a bad thing to do. And I think that's the way sin is, and when sin, when that doubt comes into our minds, it always leads to disobedience. First the thought, and then the deed.

Now ever since the human race has been in existence, ever since the fall of man in the Garden of Eden, there has been rebellion against God. It hasn't ceased even to this day. We look around us today, and you'll find that the majority of the human race was not in church to-day, not only in one service, but in no service. Not just in Southern Baptist churches, but all denominations. And there is a majority of the population of this world that don't even acknowledge the existence of God. And so we know today (that) that rebellion of man against God is still in its heyday. And I guess the greatest picture of rebellion we find in the Bible is the illustration of the prodigal son. Here was a man who had everything he could want at home, but he was a person who wanted to throw all restraint aside, and he said literally to his father, "I wish you were dead, that I could have what's coming to me. Give it to me now." It was the custom of the Jews that at the death of the father, (the) the property was divided among the sons, and that son was saying in a sense, "I wish you were dead, so that I could have my inheritance right now." He got it. He rebelled against the father. And that is a picture of the man—of the human race, mankind itself, rebelling against God the Father.

Sin is first of all disbelief, secondly it is disobedience.

The third thing we notice in verses 5 through 7 that we read tonight, is that sin is defilement. Look in the verse 5 that we read in chapter 3. "For God doth know that in the day ye eat thereof, then your eyes shall be opened and ye shall be as gods, knowing good and evil." But instead of being like gods, they saw themselves as beasts. What did it do immediately? When their eyes were opened the first thing they saw was that they were naked. And they hid themselves, and sewed fig leaves together and tried to cover (the) their body. Sin is defilement. Immediately upon the commitment of that sin or disobedience against God, they were ashamed. Now, before their sin, they were like little, innocent children. I think we could almost say like angels themselves. Not knowing sin. Not knowing anything wrong. Just living in perfect harmony with God. Complete innocence. Suddenly because of sin, the tragedy was that they did not see the ugliness of sin before it had happened. They didn't see what was going to happen on down the road. All they saw was the tree was beautiful, and they desired to eat of that tree.

We may mention the number of times, and I'm sure you've heard it many times, that when we see the commercials that we find on television, and the things we are tempted to do, the devil never shows us the black side. He never shows us the penitentiary. He never shows us the death and the disease that can be brought about by these things. And that's the tragedy of it. Sin is defilement. It defiles our bodies. It breaks the fellowship.

Then also in verses 8 through 10, you'll find that sin is division. Look at those words, "And they heard the voice of the Lord God walking in the garden in the cool of the day: and Adam and his wife hid themselves from the presence of the Lord God amongst the trees of the garden. And the Lord God called unto them—unto Adam, and said with him, 'Where art thou?' And he said, 'I heard Thy voice in the garden, and I was afraid, because I was naked; and I hid myself.'"

Now can you imagine this? You know, (this is) this is a beautiful time of the day. And especially after a cloud has come over and (we) we have the coolness in the air, it's just a beautiful time to sit out on the porch or to walk in the yard or through the fields and enjoy the coolness of the day. And to fellowship, one with another. And this is the picture that we get with the Lord (and) and with Adam and Eve. That he would come down in the cool of the day and commune with them. In other words, walk with them, and take a leisurely stroll with them. Talk with them. Perhaps in this time of the day. Or early morning. But then because of that sin, suddenly a wedge is driven between man and God, and that wedge is man's sin. Sin that man has committed. The Bible says that God cannot fellowship with sin, God cannot communicate with sin. God will not have anything to do with sin. And so, when that happened, there was a wedge driven between man and God.

Adam and Eve tried to hide themselves by making clothes of fig leaves. But nothing that man can do can hide sin in our lives. I think it was last week, perhaps, in one of our studies, or a week before last, in our Bible study on Wednesday night, that we talked about how men like to do things that are wrong at night, under the cover of darkness. We slip around and do our bad deeds at night, when we think no one can see us. But the Bible distinctly says that daylight and darkness are the same to the Lord. He doesn't have any problem seeing at night. You don't hide anything from him. And so Adam and Eve was not able to hide anything from the Lord through the flabby, or the flimsy clothes that they might have been able to make from the fig leaves.

Another thing that we find is that sin is a destroyer. It destroyed God's plan for man. His plan was that God and man could live in communion and fellowship together forever. Now we see that plan destroyed. It also destroys man's happiness. We think of David a few moments ago as we mentioned him (as) after his committing the sin, he would not confess that sin, (and) and we believe that perhaps went for a period of time, and maybe as long as twelve months before he would commit, or confess, his sin. And we find in Psalm 32, verse 3 and 4, as he describes his feelings while he went during that time of not being able to confess his sins. He says, "When I kept silence, my bones waxed old through my roaring all the day long. For day and night thy hand was heavy upon me: my moisture is turned into the drought of summer."

I think I know a little bit about what David went through. And I'm sure that there's been sin in your life that you haven't been able to confess, there you have also known that same feeling. Until we come to the place that we can confess our sin, it destroys our happiness. It destroys our peace. It destroys our fellowship between God and man. And also, sin destroys fellowship between man and man. When there's sin in life, most of the time there's a fellowship that's broken, even between man and man. So sin is a destroyer.

Then another thing that we find in verse 21, sin can be defeated. Look in verse 21 that we read tonight. "Unto Adam also and to his wife did the Lord God make coats of skins, and clothed them." Now sometimes we perhaps think of that just being a slight little thing that God took time out to do. I've heard the question asked, "Well, where did God get the skins?" He got it from slaying an animal. It cost some animal its life, and its life blood, to provide those coats of skin for Adam and Eve. There had to be a covering, and God provided that covering. We don't understand it all. But I do know this, that that sin that we inherited because we are descendants of Adam, every one of us tonight need our sin covered.

And there came the lamb of God into the world, so that he could be slain and shed his blood, so that our sins could be covered. That lamb of God was Jesus Christ himself, the son of God. You remember John the Baptist who was baptizing one day and looked up and saw Jesus and said, "Behold the Lamb of God, that taketh away the sins of the world" [John 1:29]. Jesus has been slain. He has shed his blood. He has paid the penalty so that your sins could be covered, and my sins could be covered.

The question tonight, have you realized the awfulness of sin in your life? Have you realized what it is? And what it has done to you? Have you realized it to the point that the Holy Spirit has convicted you of the sin in your life, and you've confessed it, and it's Christ who is your lord and savior? If not, tonight during this service, we encourage you to accept Christ, to confess your sins, and to have them covered by the blood of the lamb.

Would you bow your heads with us please.

Sin destroys, sin is disbelief, sin is disobedience, sin is defilement. But sin can be defeated through confession, through knowing Jesus Christ as our Lord and Savior. I trust that you know him tonight. But perhaps someone is listening by radio, or even here tonight in the building, that has never accepted Christ as lord and savior. We don't even want you to go through this hour without knowing him. If you are in your home, or perhaps on the road in your car, or maybe in a hospital room or somewhere, and you're listening, if you want Christ to save your soul tonight, the Holy Spirit dealing with your heart at this moment, all you need to do is confess your need of Jesus. Commit those sins that you have committed unto him and ask his forgiveness and ask him to come into your heart and to save you. Upon the authority of his word, we say that if you will do these things—first of all, repenting of your sins which means turning away from them, confessing them unto the lord, and asking him for forgiveness and that you might be saved, he said he would do it, "Whosoever shall call upon the name of the Lord, shall be saved" [Acts 2:21]. Have you asked him? If not, wouldn't you do it tonight? We're waiting for you in just a moment.

Father, thank you for your word, thank you that you have taught us what sin is all about. It begins with disbelief, and it leads to disobedience, and rebellion, it defiles us, it destroys our fellowship. But it also can be defeated. Because Christ already has provided the covering for our sins. We're so grateful for that tonight. And we pray now in these moments that you might lead, (the) the Holy Spirit might lead in this service. Should there be one lost, this would be the time of salvation. And as it's done, we'll thank you because we ask it in Jesus' name, amen.

Our hymn of invitation tonight is Hymn Number 240. If you'll turn with us and as we stand and sing. The Lord moving upon your heart you make that decision tonight that he's leading you to make. As we stand please.

[Congregation sings four verses of Hymn No. 240, "Just as I Am." Two teenage girls responded to the altar call.]

We are grateful for those who did move tonight. I trust that you will pray with any decisions that they are making. And I trust that you will pray one for another. Remember those who are sick tonight as we leave. I'm gonna ask John [a deacon] if you will dismiss us please.

[John gave the benediction.]

Appendix B.

"What Is a Christian?"

This sermon was preached by the Reverend John Manning during a Sunday evening worship service on February 23, 1986, and broadcast over the Salkehatchie radio station.

False starts made by the speaker are marked in parentheses, and interpolated comments are enclosed in brackets. All nonstandard verb forms and colloquial expressions have been included as uttered by the pastor.

Transcribed Text

Take your hymnal and turn to responsive reading number 47. And we're going to let you remain seated as you read responsively. You will read the dark-printed part, and I will be reading the light-printed part. The title is "Christian Discipleship."

[Responsive reading by congregation and pastor consisted of: Matt. 10:24–25; John 12:24–25; John 8:31–32, 12; John 13:34–35; John 15:8; Heb. 12:1–2.]

We come tonight to speak to you on the subject, "What is a Christian?" What is a Christian?

Now, first of all, I would tell you that the word *Christian* appears in the New Testament only three times. You will find it first in Acts 11, verse 26, (ah) where it is recorded that the disciples were first called Christians at Antioch. And then, in Acts 26, verse 28, (ah) the Apostle Paul is testifying before King Agrippa. And Agrippa replies, saying, "Almost thou persuadeth me to be a Christian." And then in First Peter 4:16, you find the word, "If any man suffer as a Christian, let him not be ashamed; but let him glorify God."

A little boy asked his dad one day, "What is a Christian, Dad?"

And the father was thinking about this question, and he thought, "This is an important question. This boy has asked me something that is very important. I must be careful about answering." And secondly, his mind was going as to what he really thought a Christian was. And so he sat down with the boy, and he told him what he thought a Christian was. And when he finished, the little boy looked up at him, and he said, "Dad, have I ever seen one?"

A lady was cleaning the house, and a knock came on the door. It was morning. And she opened the door, and a fellow was standing there, and he says to her, "Do you know Jesus Christ?" She was taken aback, to be sure, and, momentarily, just stood there, stunned. And then she just closed the door in his face. And he pulled his foot away in time. She went back to her cleaning. But she didn't get away from his question. It bothered her all day. And when her husband came in later that afternoon, she told him of the incident. And the husband said, "Well, did you tell the young man that you were president of the Woman's Missionary Union? Did you tell the young man that you taught a Bible class down at that church? Did you tell the young man that every time the church doors open, that you're down there?" And she said to her husband, "No, he didn't ask me that."

A Christian is one who knows Jesus Christ as his personal savior, and is trying to follow him. Now, if you come up with a better definition than that, I want you to share it with me. I don't say that that's the best. But I say that that's the best I can do, right now.

A Christian is one who knows Jesus Christ as his personal savior, and is trying to follow him. Now if we look at the Bible, we can find there marks (of a) of a Christian. The first mark of a Bible Christian that I would mention is the fact that one is saved. Now the Scripture tells us that he is saved by the grace of God through his faith. "For by grace are ye saved through faith; and that not of yourselves; it is a gift of God; not of works, lest any man should boast" [Ephesians 2:8].

So what is the grace of God? A difficult question. The grace of God includes the love of God. The grace of God includes the forgiveness of God toward us. The grace of God includes his justification of us when we trust Jesus as our Lord and Savior. It is the unmerited favor that God bestows upon the person who trusts in the Lord.

What is faith? Easier by a mile. Faith is composed of three things at least. Faith is knowledge. Faith is belief. And faith is trust. Let me illustrate. Here is a piece of furniture to my left. I know what that piece of furniture is; that's knowledge. I know that piece of furniture is a chair. I believe that that chair will hold up my weight. Now that is belief. But I've never sat in that chair in (my) all of my entire life. I've been in this one, but not that one. I believe that chair will hold me up. And I proceed to sit in it. I trusted it. I have knowledge of what the chair is. I believe that it will do the job. And now, I've sat in it, and it did do the job. I trusted the chair. That's faith. I had faith in that chair, to hold up my physical weight.

We know who Jesus is. That's knowledge. He is the son of God. We must know that. Do you believe that he has the power to deliver your soul from hell? And from your sins? That's belief. If you believe that, then the ultimate is trusting him with your life, and he will. That's faith. We're saved by the grace of God, through our faith.

We're also saved through repentance. Now repentance is something that's quite easy to understand. It is turning about. It's turning from self, and turning unto God. Repentance is turning upon the old way of sin, and turning to a new way of righteousness. That's what repentance is. And you have not repented if you turn but you go right back and you keep on going in your sins. That's not repentance. You repent when you turn away from what is wrong in your life, and you turn to that which is right in your life.

Now we are saved by confession, and belief, and Romans 10:9 tells us, "that if thou shall confess with thy mouth the Lord Jesus, and believe in thine heart that God has raised him from the dead, thou shalt be saved." And so confession has something to do with it. But we are quick with words. We can often just say things we don't mean. But no way can you change the belief in your heart. "If you believe in your heart that God hath raised Him from the dead, thou shalt be saved." And we confess to the things that he has wrought in us.

Now, we can testify of the fact that we are saved by two ways: with the lip, and with the life. As far as the lip is concerned, we're like the Arctic rivers. Too often we are frozen at the mouth. We need to share it, not for our glory, but to help another to come to know him. And if you know Christ, you ought to be willing to share it.

A picture, a boyhood picture, that I share with you that some of you would remember, of course, and maybe you even had it out there on the farm. And that's a ladder leaning against a barn loft. There's the opening for the loft, and the ladder runs from the ground up to the loft. Now if you think of that as a Christian, you become a Christian when you get on the first rung. When your feet are off the ground. When you've been born of the spirit of God, you become a Christian.

But now the Christians that we have trouble with, in our churches and in our communities, are those Christians that are on the first rung and the second rung. They are babes in Christ. And some people just do not bother to move from the first rung or the second rung. (They) they do not want much learning, and they don't seem to want to know about Christ. And they don't care much, but they're touchy. They get their feelings hurt. They are nothing but babies in Christ. Oh, you can't take it away from them that they know the lord—perhaps. And that's his judgment, not mine. But it's high time that we move on up the ladder in Christian growth and development, so that we will not be causing our fellow man problems.

If you ever pastor, you would know what I'm talking about. We need to grow in grace and in knowledge of our lord and savior, Jesus Christ. And the Bible mark (of a) of a Christian, one who knows Jesus Christ as his personal savior, is that he's saved. And as Jimmy Carter made famous, he's born again. And we Baptists believe that.

Now another Bible mark of a Christian is that he is sure. And I find that a lot of people in the churches seemingly do not know whether they are or not. You ask them. Well, can't be sure. "Joined the church, back yonder. But I don't know if I'm a Christian or not." You can be sure. When his spirit beareth witness with our spirits, we know that we belong to him. We can know that we're saved. And, the Apostle John has said, "These things I write unto you that ye may know that you have eternal life" [paraphrased from John 20:31].

We live in days when a lot of people want to be unsure about everything. They want to stay nebulous. They don't want to be too sure. And some people say it doesn't make any difference what you believe, so long as you work at it. Huh. That's strange, Doctor. The people worked at it down in Jonestown—was it Jonestown? That's what it was, I think. They worked at it. They sure did. They turned over their checks. They turned over their lives. They worked at it. It makes a lot of difference what you believe. And don't you forget that. But (ah) God wants us to be sure. There are two ways of proving that you know the lord, and that you're trying to follow him. And that's by a testimony of lip, and that's by the life that you live.

Now the third mark of a Bible Christian that I would bring to you tonight, is that you're sound. What if you called me over here, and there was a very serious flaw in my doctrine. And I was ever up here a-talkin' about that flaw. Would you be stable enough to stay on your own? That's what I'm asking. The person, or the Christian, who is sound, is not going to be blown around by every wind of doctrine. I'll tell you now, God wants us to be steadfast. God wants us to be immovable in our faith. You gotta know what you believe. Because people preach many different doctrines.

What do you believe? That's somethin' to think about. God wants you to be sound. Now Paul, in writing to Timothy, said, "Give attention to doctrine" [paraphrased from 1 Timothy 4:13]. And that's what I'm preaching. Now you know, and I remind you, that it's the blood that makes safe. The blood of Jesus makes safe. But it's the word that makes sure, and sound. So you feed upon the word to be sound in your doctrine. You let the word speak to you. He wants us to be sound. He wants our all on the altar of faith.

Another mark of a Bible Christian is that he is surrendered to God. The Apostle Paul, in writing to the Romans, said, "Yield yourselves to God" [Romans 6:13]. We ought to yield everything, holding back nothing. For instance, God said to Abraham, "That boy, (ah) Ishmael, that boy born of the bondswoman. Give me that boy." Abraham was faithful. Abraham gave God Ishmael. God took Ishmael, never to return him to Abraham. But Abraham finally had another son, Isaac. And God said to Abraham, "Give me that boy. I want him too." And I can see the old prophet, almost, in the mind's eye, as he trudged up the mountain with the boy, Isaac. And there on the mountain top, he built the altar. And it came time for the offering. And he took the boy, and he raised the knife, and he was going to give a living sacrifice unto his God. But God stayed his hand. And the offering was caught in the brush. God took Isaac from Abraham, but he gave him back, glorified for service.

Now let me say to you, God wants that ugliness that's in your life— maybe it's temper. Give it to God. He'll help you with it. He'll take it from you. And never give it back to you. Now I know, that's a psychological term, and I know that these things are hard to overcome, but God will help, and God will take away that temper, (and) and make you sound. But you have a good memory, a gift from God. Give that gift to God. He wants all the good things in your lives, and he will give them back to you, glorified for his service.

You know, friends, it really bothers me that we sing lies. Does that bother you? It bothers me. Just take for instance, we sing, "Take my life and let it be consecrated, Lord, to Thee." And we sing, "Take my silver and my gold." And we sing, "Take my hands and my feet." And we sing all sorta things that we don't really mean. Am I hard, leading people to do that? I don't think we ought to lie behind songbooks. I'm not telling you not to sing. I love for you to sing. But I'm just pointing out that we are singing and not looking at what we're singing. And it's meaningless to us. We sing, "Have Thine own way, Lord, have Thine own way." And knowing, all the time, that we are gonna have our way or bust. And we sing, "More love to Thee, oh Christ, more love to Thee." And we go from week to week, and we don't really mean it.

A little girl was walking around in the home, and she saw a vase— a va-a-ase, if you want to call it that—on the table. And she had to tip- toe to reach up to get it. And she turned it over, and caught it with the other hand. And then she ran her hand down in there, and she found something. And then she tried to take her hand out. And it wouldn't come out. And she got a little excited, and she called mama. And mama came in and mama tried to get her hand out of the vase, and it wouldn't come out. And the mama got excited. And she broke the vase. And she found the hand balled up in a little fist. And slowly she pried the fin- gers open. And there was a penny in her hand. Sometimes God has to break our lives to get us to give up something that's not even worth a penny. He wants us to be totally surrendered to him. It's the mark of a Bible Christian.

Another mark of a Bible Christian is that he's separated. Now you know, in the early times of Christianity, Christians were persecuted. If that day was upon us today, we wouldn't have as many people joining the church and living for the devil. We wouldn't. Because you don't join some- thing when you're persecuted. Not just for nothing, you don't. But it's popular to be a Christian today. And we just join our churches, (and) and we really don't live for the Lord. This is a sin, and it is a disgrace.

People ask me, "Preacher, don't you believe it's wrong to drink liquor?" It's funny to me. It is. Is there a question about it? "Preacher, is it wrong to smoke cigarettes?" Boy, he's going to stop preachin' and going meddlin' now for sure, for that old habit's got a lot of people. Anything that will tear down this temple (where) that houses the spirit of God, has gotta be wrong. I don't care who you are or where you are or anything about it. He wants us to be separated. He doesn't want us to be separated from this world; he wants us to be separated unto the Lord. We are leaven in this world. Leaven. That's what I said. Without the Christianity among us, this society wouldn't be worth living in. I wouldn't want to be here. If you were not here, I wouldn't want to be here. This society would be worse than the newspapers and the TV people make it seem. Yes, it would. But Christianity is the leaven of this society. And it makes it worthwhile to live in. I'd rather be leaven, than to be a part of this ugly society. If you're a Christian, you need to be separated unto the lord. You live *in* the world, but you don't have to be *of* the world. Do you get what I mean?

Take Simon Peter, for instance. Jesus, one day, walking along the beach, called Simon and said, "Follow me." And he left his nets, and he followed him. But it was about three years later before Simon Peter gave up Simon Peter. And sometimes we find it awfully difficult to give up the old self, and be totally separated unto the lord. But that's a mark of a Bible, mature Christian.

Now another mark is that he is spirit-filled. Now it's almost surprising today to find a person that's filled with the spirit of Christ. You know, in the early days, they thought the Christians were drunk. It was the spirit in them. Today, it seems to me, that Christians appear more to be doped. We're docile. We're not alive. We're not ready to go with our faith. If you're filled with the spirit, the spirit is going to change your talk. The spirit is going to change your walk. The spirit is going to create a stir. The spirit of God in a man will make him different. There's no doubt about this.

And I heard of the college professor who said, "Well, my religion is above emotions. Emotions are dangerous," he said. "I'm afraid of them." You catch that same college professor out in the football field when his team is winning, and you watch him. And you're talking about letting go with his emotions—he does. You raise the United States flag to the top, and let me be standing there at attention and watching it. Something happens—up and down—my spine. I love this country of ours. I thank God for this enlightened country. You have a will, you have intellect, and you have emotions. And when you meet your God, all three are coming into play. All of the intellect that you have is going to be challenged. And your emotions are coming into play as surely as I live. You can't meet God and not feel something. And then, it's up to you about the will. Whether you choose to be for him, or to be against him. No neutral ground.

Another mark of a Bible Christian, I think, is that he has a song in his heart. He is a singing person. Now the clouds hang low on some days, and the clouds are dark and ominous. But the Christian, who knows Jesus Christ as his personal savior and is trying to follow him, he has a song deep down in, and he's claiming a promise. "All things work together for good to those who love the Lord, to those who are called according to his purpose" [paraphrased from Romans 8:28].

Dr. Pace, a cartoonist, has said it best when on his poster he said, "CHRIST dash IAN." IAN stands for I Am Nothing. Christ is everything. Christian. A Christ follower. Are you one? Do you know him in the pardoning of your sins? Have you been born of his spirit? Are you growing in the faith, in grace and in knowledge? We need him. I hope he is yours. If he is not yours, and you're convinced that you wanna be his, you'll come as we stand to sing our Hymn of Invitation, 240. Let us stand as we sing.

[Congregation sings first three verses of Hymn Number 240, "Just as I Am." No one responded to the altar call.]

We'll sing the last stanza, and if there's a need for you to come publicly for any reason, we'll be here to try to help you. You come. Let's sing the last stanza.

[Congregation sings last verse of hymn 240. No one responded to the altar call.]

[Benediction] Now let us pray. We thank You, Father, for this time, for (the) the view of what a Christian really is. And for us to seek out your way for us in the word, and finding there your direction, help us to follow it. Dear Lord, thank you for your presence tonight. We pray that you will be with us as we walk among our fellows this week. Grant to us a double portion of the spirit, so that good things may come to our lives, and not bad. We pray it in Christ's name, amen.

Notes

I assured my informants that I would conceal their community and their personal identities by using pseudonyms. In order to conform to this ethical consideration, I must also conceal the identity of some of my published sources. Though others have written about this community, this is the first scholarly treatment of this community and topic. Those references given pseudonyms are as follows:

> *Cypress Pond Baptist Church History,* 1974.
> *Salkehatchie Baptist Association History,* 1867.
> *Salkehatchie Baptist Association Report,* 1985.
> Salkehatchie County Library Pamphlet File.
> *Salkehatchie County Newspaper.*

Introduction

1. The term *evangelical* is discussed in detail in chapter 1. I use the term here to denote Protestant churches which stress the importance of personal salvation through belief in Jesus Christ.
2. The Southern Baptist Convention (SBC) is the largest Protestant denomination in the United States (*Yearbook of American and Canadian Churches* 1990). According to Ammerman, small rural churches similar to Cypress Pond make up about half the denomination's churches (1990:53). See chapter 1 for a lengthier discussion of the SBC and its place in American society.
3. For the biblical account, see Acts 9:1–19.
4. In this work I use the term *Southern Baptists* to refer to members of the Southern Baptist Convention. The members of Cypress Pond, an SBC church, are Southern Baptists. However, there are other types of Baptist churches in the South which do not belong to the SBC.

5. In chapter 1, I argue extensively that it is possible to make inferences about the status of belief. However, I do not believe it is possible accurately to "measure" the "truth" of professed states of belief. Much research in the social sciences, of course, has attempted to do just that. From the early work of James (1902) and Starbuck (1911) on conversion experiences, to Galanter (1989), Lofland and Stark (1973), Snow and Machalek (1984), and Stark (1965)—to cite just a few—many scholars have tried to make such assessments. In chapter 7, I discuss salvation as a form of conversion, in terms of criteria used by these Southern Baptists themselves to make such judgments, and not as a religious experience that can be measured by the outside observer (except insofar as believers themselves make such judgments).

6. I was continuously in the field from May 1985 through June 1986. All the ethnographic material about Cypress Pond Church members and the community surrounding the church is drawn from this period. While I frequently give specific dates for events in the text, general ethnographic patterns are not always specified by reference to the fourteen months of fieldwork.

7. Indeed, as this work repeatedly shows, many Cypress Pond members use similar strategies to demonstrate their status as saved.

1. The Cultural Theme of Salvation

1. All belief systems contain certain blocks to falsifiability, or cultural assumptions that make questioning the "truth" of "beliefs" difficult. Evans-Pritchard's (1976; original 1937) study of Azande witchcraft is a famous anthropological account of how religious belief systems operate so that basic tenets never are questioned. Reynolds (1991) has given a similar account of Western science.

2. According to Hill, "Calvin was willing to posit three tests for helping one discern his destiny: a correct profession of faith, an upright life, and participation in the sacraments. The later Puritans continued the use of Calvin's first two tests, but substituted personal experience for participation in the sacraments" (1966:85). Hill says that the Baptist tradition came to posit that the knowledge of one's salvation came from the conversion experience itself (1966:85).

3. On the sociological dimensions of the SBC, see Ellen Rosenberg (1989); on SBC politics, see Ammerman (1990; 1993).

4. Hill notes that these three verses are not designated by this label in all Chris-

tian contexts. According to Hill, the southern church rather uncritically took the "Great Commission" as a summary of the gospel and hence as their directive for living (1966:80–81).

5. On the debates between rationalism and relativism in anthropology and philosophy, see Geertz (1984); Hollis and Lukes (1982); Skorupski (1976); Sperber (1982); and Wilson (1970). Today these debates usually are formulated under a postmodern rubric, with postmodernists in anthropology claiming to have formulated a "new relativism" (Marcus and Fischer 1986:33). For postmodernist theoretical perspectives, see Clifford (1988); Clifford and Marcus (1986); Marcus and Fisher (1986); and Rosaldo (1989). For postmodernist ethnographic approaches to religion, see, e.g., Mumford (1989), Peacock and Tyson (1989), and Wafer (1991).

6. Brown (1977) terms this perspective on science the "new philosophy of science." Its origin usually is attributed to Kuhn (1970), though he apparently drew heavily on Fleck (1979; original 1935). For radical philosophical critiques of science, see Feyerabend (1975 and 1988). For radical social science critiques of science, see Barnes (1974); Barnes and Bloor (1982); Bloor (1976); Morkzycki (1983); and Reynolds (1991). For a laudatory defense of science, see Krathwohl (1985).

7. See n. 6 for references concerning this ongoing debate. One recent "relativist" claim illustrates the type of rhetoric being used to argue that science is "untenable":

> Yet within the philosophy of science most would agree that empiricist foundationalism is untenable. The prospects of positivistic philosophers of the 1930s, along with empiricists and critical rationalists of later vintage, are no longer compelling. Within the human sciences, cultural anthropologists have been in the vanguard of those discerning flaws in traditional empiricist assumptions. (Gergen 1990)

8. In Redfield's original formulation, world views are constructed from the point of view of individuals within a given society. He conceived of world view in these terms:

> Every worldview is a stage set. On that stage myself is an important character; in every worldview there is an "I" from which the view is taken. On the stage are other people, toward whom the view is directed. And man [humans], as a collective character is upon the stage; he [and she] may speak his [and her] lines very loudly or he [and she] may be seen as having but a minor part among other parts. (Redfield 1953:86, cited in Ginsburg 1989)

The term *world view* has been used in many different ways in the anthropological literature (Kearney 1984). Here I use the term primarily with reference to the religious belief system, including how individuals conceive of themselves in relation to southern Protestantism.

9.   For Needham's criteria, see his *Belief, Language and Experience* (1972:64–108).

10.   An emic term is specific to the group in question, in this case speakers of the English language. I use the term *emic* to highlight the contrast with other languages, which may or may not have a comparable term for *belief.*

2. Place, Church, and Family

1.   Hymns cited are from the *Baptist Hymnal* in use at Cypress Pond during the fieldwork period (Sims 1956). "Blest Be the Tie," written by Fawcett and Nageli, arranged by Mason. "Faith of Our Fathers," written by Faber and Hemy, arranged by Walton. "Just As I Am," written by Elliott and Bradbury.

2.   I am playing on the title of Foster's recent work on cultural memory, *The Past Is Another Country* (1988). Focusing on change in the Blue Ridge Mountains of North Carolina, this book explores how people use the past in coping with the present. Many other social scientists are concerned with how members of a culture represent the past in their narratives of the present. Bauman (1986) argues that people create the narrated event in the process of narration itself (which he calls the "narrative event"). In saying that the "past is not another country," I mean simply that, whenever the "past"—however defined—is invoked as a justification of the present, it becomes part of current discourse.

3.   An extensive literature deals with how the brain works in "remembering." Ashcroft (1989) presents a good summary of recent research. This chapter deals with the ways in which Cypress Pond members speak of their memories of the historical past. I compare the remembered accounts with historical records, which in themselves represent a selective documentation of the past. Neither source ever can be taken to represent a "true" past, though both provide glimpses into the past.

4.   Dialect differences reflect ethnic, class, and even sex differences. Sociolinguistic studies of class differences reveal systematic linguistic differences in dialects among classes, though these differences vary from place to place. While it is difficult to pinpoint specific differences,

linguists classify the differences into three types: social indicators, social markers, and stereotypes (Labov 1964). Stereotypes are widespread differences recognized consciously and commented upon as indicators of social status. The examples cited in the text are grammatical "stereotypes" which carry social stigma (Wolfram 1981). In America, working-class dialects are identified, in part, by such nonstandard grammatical usages (see also Heath 1983; Trudgill 1983).

5.   Recall that Cypress Pond, Southville, and Salkehatchie all are pseudonyms. To protect the anonymity of my informants, the demographic information presented is only approximate. Local sources of information also have been disguised with pseudonyms.

6.   For further information on ethnic distributions in South Carolina, see Kovacik and Winberry (1987). They state: "The virtual absence of European immigrants [after the Civil War] left South Carolina and most other Southern States outside of what traditionally is known as the 'melting pot.' . . . Ethnicity in South Carolina usually means blacks and whites, and the white population is relatively homogeneous" (1987:126).

7.   The brief sketch given here does not take into account the views of African Americans on the question of continued segregation in the local churches. While many Cypress Pond members seemed to think that the African Americans in their community were ready to cross these ethnic boundaries, in fact the situation was much more complex. For perspectives on the black church in America, see Lincoln and Mamiya (1990) and Dvorak (1991). For a contemporary assessment of racism within the SBC, see Knight (1993).

8.   Salkehatchie County had a Ministerial Association which included both African-American and white pastors. During my fieldwork, one week-long, countywide revival was sponsored jointly by African-American and white churches. I attended one of the meetings and saw approximately 20 African Americans (out of several hundred people) in the audience. The president of the Salkehatchie Ministerial Association was the only African-American speaker. He spoke briefly on the need to praise God, before the guest evangelist gave the principal message. Very few persons from Cypress Pond were present at the revival, and the church itself had not sponsored the event. Other SBC churches were much more active, including Salkehatchie First Baptist Church, which opened its buildings for the revival meetings after a rented tent collapsed earlier in the week (due to rain; no one was hurt).

9. In conversation, Cypress Pond members told me that the Ku Klux Klan
    had burned crosses in the area during the fieldwork period. I could not
    verify this from other sources. The march around Southville's town
    circle was reported in the *Salkehatchie County Newspaper*:

    > The Ku Klux Klan kept its parade dates Saturday in three Salkehatchie
    > County towns without incidents. Southville police report that the marches
    > by approximately 20 Klansmen and children were orderly and drew only
    > small crowds along the parade routes. In white robes, the marchers cov-
    > ered the designated parade routes in less than 30 minutes while state,
    > county, and city law officers looked on. (Mar. 27, 1986)

10. I used several sources in determining the number of churches in the
    county. Quinn's 1980 survey included information on the white church
    congregations in the community, the Salkehatchie Baptist Association
    listed its member churches, and local Chamber of Commerce references
    and maps indicated additional church locations. I physically located 77
    church buildings in the county, took photographs of all churches in the
    town of Southville and in the Jingletown region, and interviewed pas-
    tors of 15 of the local Protestant congregations.

11. From building exteriors and surrounding grounds, one could judge
    whether a church was prosperous. However, usually it was not possible
    to tell from the exterior alone just what type of Baptist church a specific
    church was. SBC churches in the South usually do not display associa-
    tional affiliation on signs. Since many independent Baptist churches, as
    well as those belonging to such Baptist groups as the American Baptist
    Association, fail to advertise their affiliations, interested parties have to
    ask local residents.

12. In household interviews, Cypress Pond members classified themselves
    as belonging to either the working class or the middle class. Using in-
    come and educational levels reported in these interviews, I classified
    most members as belonging to either the middle working class or the
    upper working class.

13. Since the settlement patterns differed for whites and for African Ameri-
    cans (who at that time were slaves), and since the members of Cypress
    Pond were white, I focused on white settlement patterns.

14. On Homecoming, see the last section of this chapter; on revivals, see
    "Activities" in chapter 3.

15. As noted above, the initial settlers appear to have come primarily from England, with some settlers arriving from other colonies (primarily Virginia). Presumably, most of these settlers had some connection with the Church of England. I have been unable to determine to what extent the Scotch-Irish settled in this area. This question is of interest, as the Scotch-Irish were Presbyterians. Salkehatchie is located on the inner coastal plain, south of the Piedmont region settled by the Scotch-Irish when they poured into South Carolina in the 1760s after the Cherokee Indian Wars. The Scotch-Irish primarily came overland along land routes from Pennsylvania, Maryland, and Virginia (Leyburn 1962:213). Even if a significant contingent of the Scotch-Irish did settle in Salkehatchie, they became Baptist shortly after settling. Neville discusses this process in her *Kinship and Pilgrimage* (1987).

16. Since the 1980 report on church membership states that most African Americans were excluded (Quinn 1982), I took the figures for the number of SBC adherents and divided them into the total white population reported in the 1980 Census Bureau data. This yielded a rough estimate of the percentage of SBC members in the white population.

17. The questions about genealogy formed part of the household census interviews I conducted in 31 households of attending church members.

18. Only by reference to fixed points in time could a researcher (or church member, for that matter) trace kin ties within the church. While members often spoke as if these ties were immutably fixed, probing readily elicited indications of change. One fascinating example illustrates these points. Dick Nichols had become very angry at the Reverend Ted Squires at some point prior to the fieldwork. He stopped attending church and justified his action with criticisms of Squires. When Squires left, Nichols not only began suddenly to attend church but also tried to wrest leadership away from his brother, who had been an outspoken supporter of Squires. Dick Nichols failed in that effort, but the possibility had existed that he might gain ascendancy. His brother then might have continued their open rivalry, might have stopped coming himself, might have switched churches, or might peacefully have retired from the field. Such scenarios preoccupied church gossips.

19. Those "in the know" understand the potential for disruption inherent in these unwritten seating patterns. One Presbyterian minister's wife told me that she elects to sing in the choir, in part because doing so solves the seating dilemma she faces in each new church.

3. Cypress Pond Demographics,
Activities, and Social Structure

1. The origins and history of the current SBC organizational structure are not discussed in this work. For histories, see Brackney (1988) and Yance (1978). For a sociological assessment of the SBC organization as a whole, see Ammerman (1990). See also Hill (1993).

2. While I was at Cypress Pond, the Visitation Committee met only once. I attended and paired with a member of the committee, Deborah Griffin, in visiting several homes. She merely asked the people we visited to come to Cypress Pond for services. I heard about visits in which other members of this committee or the pastor explicitly censured behavior. Manning once mentioned in a sermon that a person with whom he had visited the previous week was going to hell if he did not change. In the past, Cypress Pond's Visitation Committee had met regularly, and toward the end of my fieldwork, there were efforts to revive its activities.

3. Household census interviews were conducted in 31 households, a subset of all households of attending church members. Interviews usually lasted between two and three hours per household. The structured interview schedule used is available upon request.

4. From the household surveys and from interviews with key informants, complete demographic data were gathered on 138 of the 262 Cypress Pond attenders (those in core, regular, and occasional attendance categories). The discussion is based on a spreadsheet analysis of the demographic data on these 138 attenders. Partial demographic information was collected on an additional 104 attenders; it indicated that the pattern described here presents an accurate picture of those who attended.

5. Several holidays from the traditional church calendar, such as Advent, Epiphany, Lent, and Pentecost (Cowie and Gummer 1974), were not marked by pastors in their sermons or by the congregation. That is, no reference was made to these church events, and no special dress or rituals were employed. I believe that these religious calendar dates were ignored in part because the congregation and its pastors chose to stress the theme of salvation. As we shall see in chs. 4–6, the focus of most services was the altar call for salvation. The lack of attention to these church holidays also may reflect Protestant critiques of Catholic liturgical forms (Maltz 1985).

6. At Cypress Pond, the congregation assumed that the roles of pastors and deacons were gender-based. Only males were thought qualified for

these roles. In the SBC as a whole, women occasionally have been ordained as pastors and as deacons, but these ordinations frequently are
disputed. With fundamentalists currently in control of the SBC, the
ordination of women is even more problematic (Anders and Metcalf-
Whittaker 1993).

7.   In southern Protestant churches, this office usually is called the "super-
intendent" of Sunday school. However, at Cypress Pond, official church
documents referred to the "director" of Sunday school.

4. Preaching Salvation

1.   Mojtabai discusses the incongruities between Christian principles and
warfare in *Blessed Assurance: Living with the Bomb in Amarillo* (1986). I
once inadvertently made a comment in a Women's Missionary Meeting
one night about the fact that "we could blow ourselves up." When everyone present turned to look at me as if I were crazy, to conform to the
belief system, I hastily added that this would be Armageddon.

2.   In linguistics, the strong version of the Sapir-Whorf hypothesis holds
that language actually determines cultural reality (*linguistic determin-
ism*). Today most anthropologists reject this hypothesis, but a weaker
version, holding that "one's language determines how one segments the
world," usually is upheld (Eastman 1990:103). This version claims that
language influences both the perception and the thought of members of
a culture, and to some extent creates "social reality" (see Sapir 1931;
Whorf 1956). The evangelical view that the power of the "word" has the
ability to reconstitute the individual's whole being and his perception of
the social world is akin to the notion that language determines reality.
Evangelicals too see the fallacy in that proposition, however, because
they hold that the words—the profession of belief—are not enough. One
also must act.

3.   Determining the ends or goals of speakers is an extremely difficult task.
Sherzer (1983) attempts to give the goals for formal speech genres among
the Kuna, as I attempt to do so here for the sermon speech genre. However, speakers and participants certainly had other motivations and
goals of which I was unaware.

4.   See table 1 for a summary of the services in which invitational calls were
omitted. In none of these services was the omission of the invitational
call a necessity; similar services observed on other occasions included
invitations.

5. In his sermons, Squires occasionally read from a version of the Bible
    called "The New King James Version." The only differences between
    the new and the old versions are minor changes in the archaic language,
    such as changing "thee" to "you." Squires justified his choice by saying
    that this translation did not "really" differ in meaning from the original
    King James Version. Since the sentence structures and many of the
    archaic forms remain, his argument was persuasive.

6. Unless otherwise noted, each sermon quotation has been transcribed
    from audiotapes. Ochs (1979) has discussed in depth the impact of vari-
    ous choices made by the researcher in transcribing a text. In the tran-
    scriptions included in this book, a speaker's false starts are enclosed in
    parentheses; observer's additions are in brackets. All nonstandard verb
    forms and colloquial expressions have been recorded as uttered by the
    pastors. In general, I have avoided the use of "eye dialect" transcrip-
    tions, since readers tend to equate "eye dialects" with stereotypes
    (Bauman 1984:209).

7. The transcription used here is based on guidelines given by Moerman
    (1988). According to his transcription notations:

    > #   Bounds passages said very quickly.
    >
    > TEXT Upper-case letters indicate noticeably loud volume. . . .
    >
    > °   Indicates noticeably low volume.
    >
    > <u>text</u>   Underlining indicates emphatic delivery.
    >
    > :   [Colon] Indicates that the sound that precedes it is prolonged
    > (STRETCHED).
    >
    > ,   The comma is intonational, not a syntactic punctuation mark. It
    > indicates a slight intonational rise of the sort that English speakers typi-
    > cally take to indicate that the speaker plans to continue his utterance.
    >
    > ?   The question mark, like the comma, is intonational, not a syntactic
    > punctuation mark. It indicates a sharp intonational rise, of the sort used by
    > some English questions. (1988:122–23)

    Moerman includes other notations which I have not used here. In the
    future, I plan a full analysis of the prosody in Southern Baptist sermons.

8. One of the debates raging in the SBC while I did fieldwork at Cypress
    Pond (1985–86) concerned how to interpret the Bible. Squires was a Fun-
    damentalist who believed that the Bible contained the inerrant word of
    God—that it was true literally and without error. Manning was a Moder-
    ate who argued that different interpretations of the Bible should be stud-

ied, and that God would lead the believer to the correct interpretation. See Heriot (1993) on this controversy at Cypress Pond, and Ammerman (1990 and 1993) on the SBC debate.

9. Borker notes that evangelicals conceive of the Holy Spirit as present in three different ways when any person, including these preachers, delivers the gospel's message of salvation. Most important, the Holy Spirit speaks through the Bible's words, which continue to carry their undiluted power because they are God's words. The Holy Spirit also acts on the speaker, speaking through him the words the hearer needs to hear. The hearer, in turn, if attuned to the voice of the Holy Spirit within himself, responds to this message as "moved" by the Holy Spirit (1974:31–32).

10. Lawless argues that both men and women pastors must acknowledge God's authority in guiding their sermons, but that women Pentecostal preachers must "pay a deeper kind of reverence" by asserting that they really are "nothing" (1988:93). From her data, it appears that women do make such pronouncements more often than the male SBC preachers analyzed here. This deference is a matter of degree, however, for these SBC pastors always must acknowledge that their sermons are not really their own.

11. See Samarin (1973) on the difference between preaching as a vocation, or being "called by God," and preaching as inspiration.

12. Nine different visiting pastors had occasion to preach the main message. Seven such pastors were recorded on audiotape. These guest preachers came because a pastor was on vacation, was attending a conference, or was giving a special message in another church. There were more guest speakers than usual at Cypress Pond during the fieldwork period, because Squires left in October 1985 and Manning was not engaged as an interim pastor until mid-November; moreover, even then, Manning had prior commitments elsewhere that caused him to be away more than was usual.

13. For a comparable list from women Pentecostal preachers, see Lawless (1988). She claims that women's sermons are gender-specific in their reliance on the two major themes of "sacrifice and salvation" (1988:113). Her basic comparison is with African-American sermons, since she notes that most published linguistic analyses of the sermons of male preachers come from this tradition (though she says that she has heard hundreds of white males preach sermons). My data indicate that the emphasis on salvation is as important to white male Southern Baptist

preachers as it apparently was to her female Pentecostal Holiness preachers. This suggests that the themes may not be as gender-specific as Lawless believes, though in emphasis and in style there are many differences between the two groups. The theme of sacrifice does appear to be either gender-specific or group-specific, as the male Southern Baptist preachers I studied emphasized "commitment" rather than sacrifice.

14. In technique, this story is remarkably similar to that used by Cantrell and reported in Harding (1987:177–78). Wayne's story is less shocking, but the style of the account is the same.

15. In 1986, during the time of my fieldwork, the SBC sponsored a nation-wide period of revival worship meetings entitled "Good News America, God Loves You." As part of this effort, New Testaments emblazoned with the revival's title were purchased and distributed by SBC churches, with the intention of saving individuals. These New Testaments had passages marked to emphasize messages about salvation. The marked scripture references in part overlapped those listed above: John 1:12 and 3:16; and Rom. 3:23, 5:8–10, 5:23, 6:23, 10:9–10, and 10:13.

16. Weber discussed the contemplative path to salvation in *The Sociology of Religion* (1963).

17. There is much debate over the existence of so-called altered states of consciousness, of which spirit possession is one type. Social scientists often try to determine the extent to which any given possession was "real" or "faked," in order to separate "conscious" manipulation of the phenomenon from a presumed altered state. I prefer the complementary approaches of Wafer (1991) and Frigerio (1989), since they attempt to place the phenomenon of spirit possession in social context, examining how individuals describe their own possession experiences and how these experiences are socially constructed. From their reports on Candomblé in Brazil (Wafer 1991) and on Afro-Brazilian religion in Argentina (Frigerio 1989), it appears that an elaborate social epistemology exists for determining which spirit is in possession of the individual at any given time. The reality of the possession state, while sometimes questioned, is *not* the subject of much epistemological speculation.

5. Preaching Commitment

1. This view of blessings contrasts with those given by many television evangelicals, who promise earthly rewards for Christian service. See, e.g., Harris (1981:141–65) and Harris (1991:390–95).

2. Explanations of the existence of evil and suffering offered at Cypress
    Pond bring to mind descriptions of various blocks to falsifiability found
    within religious belief systems (see Evans-Pritchard 1976). Chapter 7
    considers the problem of explaining suffering from the perspective of
    the individual who strives to live as saved. Erwin evaluates the evan-
    gelical approach to suffering, death, and problematic social issues as
    follows:

    > In my judgment, Evangelicalism is committed to a view of God whose
    > fundamental purpose is to give gifts to people and to keep their life happy.
    > Evangelicalism, therefore, has a difficult time admitting the presence of
    > death-inducing tragedy. When conflict, differences, and evil arise within
    > its purview, it is usually reduced to withdrawal, denial, and escapist
    > prayer. (Erwin 1985:56)

    I do not agree completely with Ervin's evaluation, but, as we shall see,
    there are elements of truth in his characterization. See also Greenhouse
    (1986).

6. The Altar Call

1. SBC churches do not have "altars," though pastors and members some-
    times refer to "the altar." Pastors usually label the request to "come
    forward" an invitational call rather than an "altar call." Most social
    scientists label this linguistic and ritual performance the "altar call." For
    variety I use both terms, but the reader should remember that, during
    the "invitation," the pastor stands in the center of the church on the
    same level as his congregation. No physical mark designates this space
    as special. Behind the pastor is a raised platform on which stand the
    pulpit and several chairs. Behind that platform is a raised "box" in
    which the choir sits, and behind that is a curtained area that is revealed
    only during the rite of baptism. To restate: there is no altar as such.
2. The altar calls discussed in this chapter were issued in the following
    contexts. The transcribed data come from 53 audiotaped services, re-
    gardless of whether or not I attended the services. The analysis of re-
    sponders is based only on services that I attended. During the fieldwork,
    121 services took place in which pastors had the option of giving altar
    calls. I attended 111 of the 121. Of the 10 I missed, 7 were taped. The 121
    services were of the following types: 57 Sunday morning worship ser-

vices, 51 evening worship services, and 13 revival services. I attended all revival services, but missed 5 morning and 5 evening services during the 14 months.

3.   The number of altar calls on tape is less than the number of guest speakers, for the following reason. If a pastor was a guest speaker and the regular pastor was present, the guest speaker usually turned the invitation over to the church's ongoing pastor.

4.   As the references above to Borker (1974) and Baumer (1985) indicate, altar calls traditionally have been associated with evangelical preaching. Both Borker and Baumer note that altar calls can ask members to indicate both salvation and commitment. Mathews (1977), in his discussion of the evangelical religion of the Old South, also indicates that those who heard altar calls were asked to respond to both salvation and commitment. I was not able to document that the changes in the altar call genre reported by Cypress Pond members also had occurred in churches outside the Southville area; however, from my observations in the South, I suspect that these changes reflect a much larger trend.

5.   This form was called "Personal Commitment Information." The address for return was "Vocational Guidance, 127 Ninth Avenue, North, Nashville, Tennessee 37234."

6.   Sixty-five people responded only once. Of the 65, 46 were known to the observer by name, while 19 were not. Forty-six persons responded two or more times; all these were known by name.

7.   Frankly, I was surprised that any individual could for so long avoid making "the decision for Christ" and remain within the community. That she did so for many years indicates that conformity to the evangelical tradition was, of course, not uniform.

7. Conversion, Self-Transformation, and Conflict

1.   Underhill (1955; original 1911) opens her work on mysticism with a good critique of the various philosophical and scientific approaches to the study of religion. She takes the perspective of a religious believer; however, in my opinion, her critiques are valid even if the reader is not a "believer."

2.   I was familiar with this religious belief system at the time I began the fieldwork and already had encountered a number of problems with its tenets. Thus, limits on my openness existed at the outset. Nevertheless, I was intensely interested in the subject matter and was more than will-

ing to listen to those who approached me to discuss the nature of their beliefs, even if the discussions sometimes made me uncomfortable.

3. We can see this trend beginning in James's work. He classifies individuals into two types: the healthy-minded and those with "sick souls" (1902:112–13). He views conversion as "the process, gradual or sudden, by which a self hitherto divided and consciously wrong[,] inferior and unhappy [a sick soul], becomes unified and consciously right[,] superior and happy, in consequence of its firmer hold upon religious realities" (1902:157). He considers sudden conversions the most interesting (1902:170) and analytically distinguishes conversion experiences *per se* from their "duration" (1902:205).

4. See Eighmy (1972); Greenhouse (1986 and 1992).

5. Lawless is building on cross-cultural research on gender roles, especially Ortner's (1974) much-cited and much-disputed formulation.

6. I came perilously close to letting my own anger at the blatantly authoritarian male role override my anthropological training and mission during this particular service. I wondered (and was almost mad enough to discover) what would have happened if *I* had stood up and declared that I was a *woman* and "living for the devil."

7. While I have similar data on older women and on men at Cypress Pond, here I present the conversion stories of three women from the same age group. This comparison allows the reader to see differences in approaches to conversion *within* a socially marked category, rather than differences *across* categories (as in male versus female; older versus younger; single versus married).

8. Goffman discusses, under the term "career contingencies," the impact of life events on decisions about hospitalizing mental patients (1961:134–35). He notes that similar kinds of life events do not always result in similar decisions. That is, the effects of life events on the individuals in his study depended on the conjunction of a set of factors which might or might not lead to institutionalization. So, too, among these church members, similar kinds of life events did not necessarily lead to similar decisions. Their decisions depended both on the individuals' reactions and on the contingencies affecting them.

9. Though no one ever asked members to construct such a "graph" at Cypress Pond, I once attended a United Methodist Church Sunday school class in Los Angeles, California, in which members were asked to take a piece of paper and graph the high and low points in their Christian life.

10. I never learned the full details of the controversy. According to some accounts, the individuals involved were Bruce and Samantha. Others claimed that the incident involved another couple, friends and relatives of Bruce and Samantha. In a sense, the absolute "truth" did not really matter; they were criticized on the basis of the community rumors.

11. These rules certainly applied to me as a single woman in the church. For example, when I went with a deacon to visit an aged local celebrity, the deacon insisted that his wife accompany us.

12. The story of Job is told in the Old Testament's Book of Job. Job was tested by God, who destroyed his home and wealth, killed his children, and afflicted him with disease. Job passed the test by continuing to believe in God despite these horrors and was rewarded by God with increased wealth and more children. This surface plot line was the one to which Leslie Harris referred in likening her life to Job's. The questions that Job asked God about the nature of suffering, which God did *not* answer, were not addressed by Leslie.

13. These are societal forces which have an impact well beyond this local community and may be contributing to changes in the definitions of gender roles in American society. Though I have noted here these causal forces, my focus was not on these, but rather on how these women interpreted their lives. See Ammerman (1987); Anders and Metcalf-Whittaker (1993); Greenhouse (1986); Lawless (1988); and Ellen Rosenberg (1989) for analyses of the roles women play in fundamentalist and evangelical religious traditions. See Ginsburg (1989), esp. chapter 12, for a useful treatment of American women's conflicting gender roles.

8. Belief and Action

1. My data could be used to argue that such changes already are on the way, especially given the tension concerning gender roles noted in chapter 7. However, during the fieldwork, I did not perceive levels of stress sufficient for the group to begin to reformulate the belief system—as, for instance, in some form of revitalization movement (Wallace 1956). This observation, of course, does not preclude the church from beginning such a process later.

2. The recent Public Broadcasting System series on fundamentalism in Christianity, Islam, and Judaism certainly made the case that believers are redefining the secular in terms of the sacred ("The Glory and the Power: Fundamentalists Observed," aired on June 15, 22, and 29, 1992).

Companion volume to the series by Marty and Appleby (1992). See also Marty and Appleby (1991).

3. Such answers would run the gamut of the major social science theories of religion. Among them would be, of course, functionalist formulations such as those of Durkheim or Radcliffe-Brown; Marxist formulations; structuralist arguments; postmodern formulations; and any number of psychological arguments about the needs religion fills in the individual.

4. If one takes language itself as one of the primary frameworks for transmitting meaning, then no individual who has mastered a language lives without meaning. But one may live with more or less inadequate answers to the issues of bafflement, suffering, and ethical paradox so eloquently examined by Geertz (1973).

References

Agar, Michael H.
1980   *The Professional Stranger.* New York: Academic Press.
1986   *Speaking of Ethnography.* Qualitative Research Methods, vol. 2. Beverly Hills,
        Calif.: Sage Publications.

Altheide, David L., and John M. Johnson
1977   Counting Souls: A Study of Counseling at Evangelical Crusades. *Pacific Socio-
        logical Review* 20:323–48.

Ammerman, Nancy Tatom
1987   *Bible Believers: Fundamentalists in the Modern World.* New Brunswick, N.J.: Rutgers
        Univ. Press.
1990   *Baptist Battles: Social Change and Religious Conflict in the Southern Baptist Conven-
        tion.* New Brunswick, N.J.: Rutgers Univ. Press.

Ammerman, Nancy Tatom, ed.
1993   *Southern Baptists Observed: Multiple Perspectives on a Changing Denomination.*
        Knoxville: Univ. of Tennessee Press.

Anders, Sarah Frances, and Marilyn Metcalf-Whittaker
1993   Women as Lay Leaders and Clergy: A Critical Issue. In *Southern Baptists
        Observed: Multiple Perspectives on a Changing Denomination,* ed. Nancy T.
        Ammerman. Knoxville: Univ. of Tennessee Press.

Ashcroft, Mark H.
1989   *Human Meaning and Cognition.* Boston: Scott, Foresman.

Baptist Courier
1987   "Simultaneous Revivals for 1990 Set." 119 (Apr. 23):5.

Barnes, Barry
1974   *Scientific Knowledge and Sociological Theory.* London: Routledge and Kegan Paul.

Barnes, Barry, and David Bloor
1982   Relativism and Rationalism. In *Rationality and Relativism,* ed. Martin Hollis and
        Steven Lukes. Oxford: Basil Blackwell.

Bauman, Richard
1974   Speaking in the Light: The Role of the Quaker Minister. In *Explorations in the
        Ethnography of Speaking,* ed. Richard Bauman and Joel Sherzer. London: Cam-
        bridge Univ. Press.
1977   *Verbal Art as Performance.* Rowley, Mass.: Newbury House.
1984   "Any Man Who Keeps More'n One Hound'll Lie to You": Dog Trading and
        Storytelling in Canton, Texas. In *Language in Use,* ed. John Baugh and Joel
        Sherzer. Englewood Cliffs, N.J.: Prentice-Hall.
1986   *Story, Performance, and Event.* Cambridge, England: Cambridge Univ. Press.

Baumer, Fred A.
1985   Toward the Development of Homiletic as Rhetorical Genre: A Critical Study of
        Roman Catholic Preaching in the United States Since Vatican Council II. Ph.D.
        diss. Northwestern Univ.

Beckford, James A.
1979   *The Trumpet of Prophecy: A Sociological Study of Jehovah's Witnesses.* Oxford: Basil
        Blackwell.

Bellah, Robert N.
1972   Religious Evolution. In *Reader in Comparative Religion,* ed. William Lessa and
        Evon Vogt. 3d ed. New York: Harper and Row.

Berger, Peter L.
1969   *A Rumor of Angels: Modern Society and the Rediscovery of the Supernatural.* New
        York: Doubleday.

Berger, Peter L., and Thomas Luckmann
1966   *The Social Construction of Reality.* Garden City, N.Y.: Doubleday.

Black, Larry
1987   A Price Tag on Salvation. *Macleans* 100 (Mar. 2): 43.

Black, Mary
1974   Belief Systems. In *Handbook of Social and Cultural Anthropology,* ed. John J.
        Honigmann. Chicago: Rand McNally.

Bloor, David
1976   *Knowledge and Social Imagery.* Boston: Routledge and Kegan Paul.

Borker, Ruth Ann

1974 Presenting the Gospel: Religious Communication and Expressive Strategies in Three Evangelical Churches in Edinburgh, Scotland. Ph.D. diss. Univ. of California at Berkeley.

Bourguignon, Erika

1968 World Distribution and Patterns of Possession States. In *Trance and Possession States*, ed. Raymond Prince. Proceedings of the Second Annual Conference, R. M. Burke Memorial Society. Mar. 4–6, 1966. Montreal.

1991 *Possession*. 2d ed. Prospect Heights, Ill.: Waveland Press.

Brackney, William Henry

1988 *The Baptists*. New York: Greenwood Press.

Brown, Harold I.

1977 *Perception, Theory, and Commitment*. Chicago: Univ. of Chicago Press.

Bryant, F. Carlene

1981 *We're All Kin: A Cultural Study of a Mountain Neighborhood*. Knoxville: Univ. of Tennessee Press.

Caplow, Theodore, et al.

1983 *All Faithful People*. Minneapolis: Univ. of Minnesota Press.

Carroll, Jackson W., et al.

1979 *Religion in America: 1950 to the Present*. San Francisco: Harper and Row.

Clifford, James

1988 *The Predicament of Culture*. Cambridge, Mass.: Harvard Univ. Press.

Clifford, James, and George E. Marcus, eds.

1986 *Writing Culture: The Poetics and Politics of Ethnography*. Berkeley: Univ. of California Press.

Conrad, Charles

1988 Communicative Action in Church Decision-Making. *Journal for the Scientific Study of Religion* 27:345–61.

Cowie, L. W., and John Selwyn Gummer

1974 *The Christian Calendar*. Springfield, Mass.: G & C Merria Co.

Crystal, David

1976 Non-Segmental Phonology in Religious Modalities. In *Language in Religious Practice*, ed. William J. Samarin. Rowley, Mass.: Newbury Publishing House.

Davis, Gerald

1985   *I Got the Word in Me and I Can Sing It, You Know.* Philadelphia: Univ. of Pennsylvania Press.

Dorgan, Howard

1987   *Giving Glory to God in Appalachia.* Knoxville: Univ. of Tennessee Press.

Duranti, Alessandro

1983   Samoan Speechmaking across Social Events: One Genre in and out of a Fono. *Language in Society* 12:1–22.

1988   Ethnography of Speaking: Toward a Linguistics of the Praxis. In *Linguistics: The Cambridge Study.* Vol. 4: *Language: The Socio-cultural Context,* ed. Frederick J. Newmeyer. Cambridge, England: Cambridge Univ. Press.

Dvorak, Katharine L.

1991   *An African-American Exodus: The Segregation of the Southern Churches.* Chicago Studies in the History of American Religion, vol. 4. Brooklyn, N.Y.: Carlson Publishing.

Eastman, Carol M.

1990   *Aspects of Language and Culture.* 2d ed. Novato, Calif.: Chandler and Sharp.

Eighmy, John Lee

1972   *Churches in Cultural Captivity: A History of the Social Attitudes of Southern Baptists.* Knoxville: Univ. of Tennessee Press.

Erwin, Dan Roland

1985   A Study in the Preaching of John Claypool: The Rhetorical Function of Narrative. Ph.D. diss. Univ. of Texas at Austin.

Evans-Pritchard, E. E.

1956   *Nuer Religion.* New York: Oxford Univ. Press.

1976   *Witchcraft, Oracles, and Magic among the Azande.* Abridged by Eva Gillies. Oxford: Clarendon Press. Original version published in 1937.

Farnsley, Arthur E.

1993   "Judicious Concentration": Decision Making in the Southern Baptist Convention. In *Southern Baptists Observed: Multiple Perspectives on a Changing Denomination,* ed. Nancy T. Ammerman. Knoxville: Univ. of Tennessee Press.

Festinger, Leon

1957   *A Theory of Cognitive Dissonance.* Palo Alto, Calif.: Stanford Univ. Press.

Feyerabend, Paul

1975   *Against Method.* London: Verso.

1988   Knowledge and the Role of Theories. *Philosophy of Social Science* 18:157–78.

Fleck, Ludwig
1979   *Genesis and Development of a Scientific Fact.* Translated by Fred Bradley and
        Thaddeus J. Trenn. Chicago: Univ. of Chicago Press. Original published in 1935.

Foster, Stephen William
1988   *The Past Is Another Country.* Berkeley: Univ. of California Press.

Frazer, Sir James George
1956   *The New Golden Bough,* ed. Theodore H. Gaster. New York: Criterion Books.
        Originally published in 1922.

Frigerio, Alejandro
1989   Levels of Possession Awareness in Afro-Brazilian Religions. *Association for the
        Anthropological Study of Consciousness Quarterly* 5:5–11.

Galanter, Marc
1989   *Cults: Faith, Healing, and Coercion.* New York: Oxford Univ. Press.

Garrett, James Leo, Jr.
1983   Evangelicals and Baptists—Is There a Difference? In *Are Southern Baptists
        "Evangelicals"?* Edited by James Leo Garrett, Jr.; E. Glenn Hinson; and James E.
        Tull. Macon, Ga.: Mercer Univ. Press.

Geertz, Clifford
1973   *The Interpretation of Cultures.* New York: Basic Books.
1983   *Local Knowledge.* New York: Basic Books.
1984   Distinguished Lecture: Anti Anti-Relativism. *American Anthropologist* 86:263–78.

Gergen, Kenneth J.
1990   Social Understanding and the Inscription of Self. In *Cultural Psychology,* ed.
        James W. Stigler, Richard A. Shweder, and Gilbert Herdt. Cambridge, England:
        Cambridge Univ. Press.

Gerlach, Luther P., and Virginia M. Hine
1970   *People, Power, and Change.* Indianapolis, Ind.: Bobbs-Merrill.

Ginsburg, Faye D.
1989   *Contested Lives.* Berkeley: Univ. of California Press.

Goffman, Erving
1961   *Asylums.* New York: Doubleday.

Golding, Gordon
1981   "That Old Time Religion:" Portrait de la religion traditionnaliste des blancs du
        sud, 1950–1970. In *Revue Française d'Études Américaines.* Vol. 12: *La Religion aux
        États-Unis.* Paris: L'Association Française d'Études Américaines.

Goodenough, Ward H.
1981   *Culture, Language, and Society.* 2d ed. Menlo Park, Calif.: Benjamin/Cummings Publishing Co.

Gordon, D. F.
1974   The Jesus People: An Identity Synthesis. *Urban Life and Culture* 3: 159–78.

Gossen, Gary
1976   Language as a Ritual Substance. In *Language in Religious Practice,* ed. William J. Samarin. Rowley, Mass.: Newbury Publishing House.

Greenhouse, Carol
1986   *Praying for Justice: Faith, Order, and Community in an American Town.* Ithaca, N.Y.: Cornell Univ. Press.
1992   Signs of Quality: Individualism and American Culture. *American Ethnologist* 19:233–54.

Gumperz, John J.
1982   *Discourse Strategies.* London: Cambridge Univ. Press.

Hallen, B., and J. O. Sodipo
1986   *Knowledge, Belief, and Witchcraft: Analytical Experiments in African Philosophy.* London: Ethnographica.

Harding, Susan F.
1987   Convicted by the Holy Spirit: The Rhetoric of Fundamental Baptist Conversion. *American Ethnologist* 14:167–81.
1993   Epilogue: Observing the Observers. In *Southern Baptists Observed: Multiple Perspectives on a Changing Denomination,* ed. Nancy T. Ammerman. Knoxville: Univ. of Tennessee Press.

Harris, Marvin
1981   *America Now: The Anthropology of a Changing Culture.* New York: Simon and Schuster.
1991   *Cultural Anthropology.* 3d ed. New York: Harper Collins.

Hays, Brooks, and John E. Steely
1963   *The Baptist Way of Life.* Englewood Cliffs, N.J.: Prentice-Hall.

Heath, Shirley Brice
1983   *Ways with Words.* Cambridge, England: Cambridge Univ. Press.

Heirich, Max
1977   Change of Heart: A Test of Some Widely Held Theories about Religious Conversion. *American Journal of Sociology* 83:653–80.

Heriot, M. Jean

1982   The Implications of an Emic Model: Conversion as Process in the Mormon Church. Master's thesis, Univ. of California, Los Angeles.

1993   Rural Interpretations of Conflict. In *Southern Baptists Observed: Multiple Perspectives on a Changing Denomination,* ed. Nancy T. Ammerman. Knoxville: Univ. of Tennessee Press.

Hill, Samuel, Jr.

1966   *Southern Churches in Crisis.* New York: Holt, Rinehart and Winston.

1981   The Shape and Shapes of Popular Southern Piety. In *Varieties of Southern Evangelicalism,* ed. David Edwin Harrell, Jr. Macon, Ga.: Mercer Univ. Press.

1993   The Story before the Story: Southern Baptists since World War II. In *Southern Baptists Observed: Multiple Perspectives on a Changing Denomination,* ed. Nancy T. Ammerman. Knoxville: Univ. of Tennessee Press.

Hollis, Martin, and Steven Lukes, eds.

1982   *Rationality and Relativism.* Oxford: Basil Blackwell.

Holy, Ladislav, and Milan Stuchlik

1983   *Actions, Norms and Representation: Foundations of Anthropological Inquiry.* Cambridge, England: Cambridge Univ. Press.

Hudson, Charles

1972   The Structure of a Fundamentalist Christian Belief System. In *Religion and the Solid South,* ed. Samuel S. Hill, Jr. Nashville: Abingdon Press.

Hunter, James Davison

1982   Operationalizing Evangelicalism: A Review, Critique, and Proposal. *Sociological Analysis* 42:363–72.

Hymes, Dell

1964   Introduction: Toward Ethnographies of Communication. Special Publication: *The Ethnography of Communication,* ed. John Crumperz and Dell Hymes. *American Anthropologist* 66:1–34.

1972   Models of the Interaction of Language and Social Life. In *Directions in Sociolinguistics: The Ethnography of Communication,* ed. John J. Gumperz and Dell Hymes. New York: Holt.

James, William

1958   *The Varieties of Religious Experience.* New York: New American Library. First published 1902.

Jones, Ilion T.

1954   *A Historical Approach to Evangelical Worship.* New York: Abingdon Press.

Katz, Jonathan
1989   Rational Common Ground in the Sociology of Knowledge. *Philosophy of the Social Sciences* 19:257–71.

Kearney, Michael
1984   *World View.* Novato, Calif.: Chandler and Sharp.

Keesing, Roger M.
1975   *Kin Groups and Social Structure.* New York: Holt, Rinehart, and Winston.

Kilbourne, Brock, and James T. Richardson
1989   Conversion and Conversion Theories. *Sociological Analysis* 50:1–21.

Knight, Walker L.
1993   Race Relations: Changing Patterns and Practices. In *Southern Baptists Observed: Multiple Perspectives on a Changing Denomination,* ed. Nancy T. Ammerman. Knoxville: Univ. of Tennessee Press.

Kovacik, Charles F., and John J. Winberry
1987   *South Carolina: A Geography.* Boulder: Westview Press.

Krathwohl, David R.
1985   *Social and Behavioral Science Research.* San Francisco: Jossey Bass.

Kuhn, Thomas S.
1970   *The Structure of Scientific Revolutions.* 2d ed. Chicago: Univ. of Chicago Press.

Labov, William
1964   Stages in the Acquisition of Standard English. In *Social Dialects and Language Learning,* ed. R. W. Shuy. Champaign, Ill.: National Council of Teachers of English.

Lang, Kurt, and Gladys Engel Lang
1960   Decisions for Christ: Billy Graham in New York City. In *Identity and Anxiety,* ed. Maurice R. Stein, Arthur J. Vidich, and David Manning White. New York: Free Press.

Lawless, Elaine J.
1980   Make a Joyful Noise: An Ethnography of Communication in the Pentecostal Religious Service. *Southern Folklore Quarterly* 44:1–32.
1988   *Handmaidens of the Lord: Pentecostal Women Preachers and Traditional Religion.* Philadelphia: Univ. of Pennsylvania Press.

Lett, James
1987   *The Human Enterprise.* Boulder: Westview Press.

Leyburn, James G.
1962   *The Scotch-Irish: A Social History.* Chapel Hill: Univ. of North Carolina Press.

Lincoln, Eric C., and Lawrence H. Mamiya
1990   *The Black Church in the African-American Experience.* Durham, N.C.: Duke Univ. Press.

Lofland, John, and N. Skonovd
1981   Conversion Motifs. *Journal for the Scientific Study of Religion* 20:373–85.

Lofland, John, and Rodney Stark
1973   Becoming a World Saver: A Theory of Conversion to a Deviant Perspective. In *Religion in Sociological Perspective,* ed. Charley Y. Glock. Belmont, Calif.: Wadsworth.

McMillan, Jill J.
1988   Institutional Plausibility Alignment as Rhetorical Exercise. *Journal for the Scientific Study of Religion* 27:326–44.

Maltz, Daniel N.
1985   Joyful Noise and Reverent Silence: The Significance of Noise in Pentecostal Worship. In *Perspectives on Silence,* ed. Deborah Tannen and Muries Saville-Troike. Norwood, N.J.: Ablex Publishing.

Marcus, George E., and Michael M. J. Fischer
1986   *Anthropology as Cultural Critique: An Experimental Moment in the Human Sciences.* Chicago: Univ. of Chicago Press.

Marty, Martin E.
1983   Religion in America Since Mid-Century. In *Religion and America,* ed. Mary Douglas and Steven M. Tipton. Boston: Beacon Press.

Marty, Martin E., and R. Scott Appleby
1992   *The Power and the Glory: The Rapid Rise of Fundamentalism in the 1990s.* Boston: Beacon Press.

Marty, Martin E., and R. Scott Appleby, eds.
1991   *Fundamentalisms Observed.* Chicago: Univ. of Chicago Press.

Mathews, Donald G.
1977   *Religion in the Old South.* Chicago: Univ. of Chicago Press.

Meriwether, Robert Lee
1940   *The Expansion of South Carolina, 1729–1765.* Kingsport, Tenn.: Southern Publishers.

Moerman, Michael
1988   *Talking Culture: Ethnography and Conversational Analysis.* Philadelphia: Univ. of Pennsylvania Press.

Mojtabai, A. G.
1986   *Blessed Assurance: At Home with the Bomb in Amarillo, Texas.* Boston: Houghton Mifflin.

Morkzycki, Edward
1983   *Philosophy of Science and Sociology.* London: Routledge and Kegan Paul.

Morland, John Kenneth
1958   *Millways of Kent.* Chapel Hill: Univ. of North Carolina Press.

Mumford, Stan Royal
1989   *Himalayan Dialogue.* Madison: Univ. of Wisconsin Press.

Needham, Rodney
1972   *Belief, Language, and Experience.* Oxford: Basil Blackwell.

Neville, Gwen Kennedy
1987   *Kinship and Pilgrimage: Rituals of Reunion in American Protestant Culture.* New York: Oxford Univ. Press.

Ochs, Elinor
1979   Transcription as Theory. In *Developmental Pragmatics,* ed. Elinor Ochs and Bambi B. Schiefflen. New York: Academic Press.

Ortner, Sherry B.
1974   Is Female to Male as Nature Is to Culture? In *Woman, Culture, and Society,* ed. Michelle Rosaldo and Louise Lamphere. Stanford, Calif.: Stanford Univ. Press.

Peacock, James L.
1975   Weberian, Southern Baptist, and Indonesian Muslim Conceptions of Belief and Action. In *Symbols and Society: Essays on Belief Systems in Action,* ed. Carol E. Hill. Southern Anthropological Society Proceedings, No. 9. Athens: Univ. of Georgia Press.
1988   A Pentecostal Account of Spiritual Quest. In *Diversities of Gifts,* ed. Ruel Tyson, Jr.; James L. Peacock; and Daniel W. Patterson. Chicago: Univ. of Chicago Press.

Peacock, James L., and Ruel W. Tyson, Jr.
1989   *Pilgrims of Paradox: Calvinism and Experience Among the Primitive Baptists of the Blue Ridge.* Washington, D.C.: Smithsonian Institution Press.

Pelto, Pertti J., and Gretel H. Pelto
1978   *Anthropological Research: The Structure of Inquiry.* 2d ed. Cambridge, England: Cambridge Univ. Press.

Prus, Robert C.
1976   Religious Recruitment and the Management of Dissonance. *Sociological Inquiry* 46:127–34.

Quinn, Bernard, et al.
1982   *Churches and Church Membership in the United States in 1980.* Atlanta, Ga.: Glenmary Research Center.

Reynolds, Peter C.
1991   *Stealing Fire: The Atomic Bomb as Symbolic Body.* Palo Alto, Calif.: Iconic Anthropology Press.

Richardson, James T.
1985   The Active vs. Passive Convert: Paradigm Conflict in Conversion/Recruitment Research. *Journal for the Scientific Study of Religion* 24:163–79.

Roof, Wade Clark, and William McKinney
1987   *American Mainline Religion: Its Changing Shape and Future.* New Brunswick, N.J.: Rutgers Univ. Press.

Rosaldo, Renata
1989   *Culture and Truth.* Boston: Beacon Press.

Rosenberg, Bruce A.
1970   The Formulaic Quality of Spontaneous Sermons. *Journal of American Folklore* 83:3–20.

Rosenberg, Ellen M.
1989   *The Southern Baptists: A Subculture in Transition.* Knoxville: Univ. of Tennessee Press.

Samarin, William J.
1973   Protestant Preachers in the Prophetic Line. In *Sociological Theories of Religion: Religion and Language.* International Yearbook for the Sociology of Religion, vol. 8, ed. Gunter Dux, Thomas Luckmann, and Joachim Matthes. Opladen, Germany: Westdeutscher Verlag.

Sapir, Edward
1931   Conceptual Categories in Primitive Languages. *Science* 74:578.

Schneider, David M.
1980   *American Kinship: A Cultural Account.* 2d ed. Chicago: Univ. of Chicago Press.

Scobie, Geoffrey
1973   Types of Christian Conversion. *Journal of the Behavioral Sciences* 1:265–71.

Sherzer, Joel
1983   *Kuna Ways of Speaking: An Ethnographic Perspective.* Austin: Univ. of Texas Press.

Sims, Walter Hines, ed.
1956   *Baptist Hymnal.* Nashville, Tenn.: Convention Press.

Skorupski, John
1976   *Symbol and Theory: A Philosophical Study of Theories of Religion in Social Anthropology.* Cambridge, England: Cambridge Univ. Press.

Snow, David, and Richard Machalek
1984   The Sociology of Conversion. *Annual Review of Sociology* 10:167–90.

Sollod, Robert N.
1992   The Hollow Curriculum. *Chronicle of Higher Education* (Mar. 18): A60.

Southern Baptist Convention
1980   *Annual of the Southern Baptist Convention.* Nashville, Tenn.: Executive Committee, Southern Baptist Convention.

Sperber, Dan
1982   *On Anthropological Knowledge.* Cambridge, England: Cambridge Univ. Press.

Staples, Clifford L., and Armand L. Mauss
1987   Conversion or Commitment? A Reassessment of the Snow and Machalek Approach to the Study of Conversion. *Journal for the Scientific Study of Religion* 26:133–47.

Starbuck, Edwin D.
1911   *The Psychology of Religion.* New York: Charles Scribner's Sons.

Stark, Rodney
1965   Social Contexts and Religious Experience. *Review of Religious Research* 7:17–28.

Straus, Roger
1979   Religious Conversion as a Personal and Collective Accomplishment. *Sociological Analysis* 40:158–65.
1981   The Social Psychology of Religious Experience: A Naturalistic Approach. *Sociological Analysis* 42:57–67.

Taylor, Brian
1976   Conversion and Cognition: An Area for Empirical Study in the Microsociology of Religious Knowledge. *Social Compass* 23:5–22.
1978   Recollection and Membership: Convert's Talk and the Ratiocination of Commonalty. *Sociology* 12:316–24.

Titon, Jeff Todd
1988   *Powerhouse for God.* Austin: Univ. of Texas Press.

Townsend, Leah

1935   *South Carolina Baptists, 1670–1805.* Florence, S.C.: Florence Printing Co.

Travisano, R. V.

1970   Alternation and Conversion as Qualitatively Different Transformations. In *Social Psychology through Symbolic Interaction,* ed. G. P. Stone and H. A. Farberman. Waltham, Mass.: Ginn-Blaisdell.

Trudgill, Peter

1983   *Sociolinguistics.* 2d ed. London: Penguin.

Turner, Ralph

1976   The Real Self: From Institution to Impulse. *American Journal of Sociology* 81:989–1016.

Underhill, Evelyn

1955   *Mysticism.* New York: New American Library. First published 1911.

U.S. Department of Commerce. Bureau of the Census

1930   *Fifteenth Census of the United States.* Population.

1980   *United States Census of the Population.* Vol. 1: Characteristics of the Population, pt. 42, South Carolina.

Wafer, Jim

1991   *The Taste of Blood: Spirit Possession in Brazilian Candomblé.* Philadelphia: Univ. of Pennsylvania Press.

Wallace, Anthony F. C.

1956   Revitalization Movements. *American Anthropologist* 58:264–81.

Weber, Max

1958   *The Protestant Ethic and the Spirit of Capitalism.* Translated by Talcott Parsons. New York: Charles Scribner's Sons.

1963   *The Sociology of Religion.* Translated by Ephraim Fiscoff. Boston: Beacon Press.

Whorf, Benjamin

1956   A Linguistic Consideration of Thinking in Primitive Communities. In *Language, Thought, and Reality,* ed. John Carroll. Cambridge, Mass.: MIT Press.

Wilson, Bryan, ed.

1970   *Rationality.* Oxford: Basil Blackwell.

Wimberly, Ronald C., et al.

1975   Conversion in a Billy Graham Crusade: Spontaneous Event or Ritual Performance? *Sociological Quarterly* 16:162–70.

Wolfram, Walt

1981   Varieties of American English. In *Language in the USA,* ed. Charles A. Ferguson and Shirley Brice Heath. Cambridge, England: Cambridge Univ. Press.

Yance, Norman Alexander

1978   *Religion Southern Style: Southern Baptists and Society in Historical Perspective.* Danville, Va.: Association of Baptist Professors of Religion.

Yearbook of American and Canadian Churches

1990   *Yearbook of American and Canadian Churches.* Nashville, Abingdon Press.

Index